David Ruggles

The

JOHN HOPE FRANKLIN SERIES *in*

AFRICAN AMERICAN HISTORY *and* CULTURE

Waldo E. Martin and Patricia Sullivan,

EDITORS

David Ruggles

A RADICAL BLACK ABOLITIONIST

AND THE UNDERGROUND RAILROAD

IN NEW YORK CITY

GRAHAM RUSSELL GAO HODGES

The University of North Carolina Press CHAPEL HILL

Designed by Courtney Leigh Baker. Set in Dante and Chateau by Tseng Information Systems, Inc. Manufactured in the United States of America. The paper in this book meets the guidelines for permanence and durability of the Committee on Production Guidelines for Book Longevity of the Council on Library Resources. The University of North Carolina Press has been a member of the Green Press Initiative since 2003.

Library of Congress Cataloging-in-Publication Data
Hodges, Graham Russell, 1946–
David Ruggles : a radical black abolitionist and the Underground Railroad in New York City /
Graham Russell Gao Hodges.
p. cm. — (The John Hope Franklin series in African American history and culture)
Includes bibliographical references and index.
ISBN 978-0-8078-3326-1 (cloth : alk. paper)
1. Ruggles, David, 1810–1849. 2. Abolitionists—New York (State)—New York—Biography.
3. Abolitionists—Massachusetts—Biography. 4. African American abolitionists—New York
(State)—New York—Biography. 5. African American abolitionists—Massachusetts—Biography.
6. Underground Railroad—New York (State)—New York. 7. Underground Railroad—Massachusetts.
8. Antislavery movements—New York (State)—New York—History. 9. Antislavery movements—
Massachusetts—History. 1. Title.
E449.R94H63 2010   326'.8092—dc22   [B]   2009031106

Frontispiece:
David Ruggles. This undated charcoal print ably captures Ruggles's features and his penchant for stylish clothing. Courtesy Negro Almanac Collection, Amistad Research Center at Tulane University.

14 13 12 11 10   5 4 3 2 1

With love and devotion to my wife,

GAO YUNXIANG (高云翔), who has made my future,

and to my sons, GRAHAM ZHEN GAO-HODGES

(Gao Ranmo 高然墨) and RUSSELL DU GAO-HODGES

(Gao Ranshi 高然诗), who are my future

CONTENTS

ILLUSTRATIONS

David Ruggles

INTRODUCTION

The euphoria that Frederick Augustus Bailey felt after escaping from slavery on September 3, 1838, evaporated soon after his coming to New York City. At two o'clock in the morning on the night of his arrival, Bailey was stranded on the docks. He worried about slave catchers and saw in "every white man an enemy and in every colored man cause for distrust." Broke, lonely, and homeless, Bailey spent the night sleeping among the wharf barrels. He had planned to find a black man named David Ruggles, who headed the New York Committee of Vigilance, an organization famous among enslaved people fleeing from their bondage. Before going to Ruggles's home, however, Bailey met a friend from home, "Allender's Jake," now calling himself William Dixon. Dixon warned him against trusting anyone. Deep in distress, Bailey anxiously pondered his future. Luckily, Ruggles searched for the forlorn fugitive and took him home, where Bailey joined several other fugitives from slavery. At Ruggles's house at 36 Lispenard Street, Bailey had long talks into the night with Ruggles about abolitionism. Ruggles advised Bailey that New York was unsafe. The fugitive from bondage indicated a desire to go to Canada, but Ruggles favored New England, where a fugitive could find work as a caulker or go seafaring.

In addition to advice on work and safety, Ruggles helped Bailey forge a new identity. To celebrate his freedom and to throw off potential slave catchers (and possibly inspired by Allender's Jake), Bailey adopted the name of

Frederick Johnson. Feeling more secure, Johnson, with Ruggles's help, informed his fiancée, Anna Murray, that it was safe for her to join him. When she arrived safely on September 15, the Reverend James W. C. Pennington, a former escaped slave from Maryland and now a Presbyterian minister in Hartford, Connecticut, married the couple in a ceremony at Ruggles's home. Bailey cherished the marriage certificate that was witnessed by Ruggles and a Mrs. Michaels, who owned a boardinghouse nearby. Soon after, the newlyweds left, armed with a five-dollar bill and a letter of introduction that Ruggles addressed to another black abolitionist, Nathan Johnson, who lived in New Bedford, Massachusetts, the seaport known as the "Fugitives' Gibraltar." Soon after their arrival there, Frederick Johnson found work as a caulker. His hosts suggested that he change his name to one less common. Frederick borrowed a heroic family name from Sir Walter Scott's poem "Lady of the Lake" and thereby became Frederick Douglass. Nurtured in New Bedford's antislavery community, within a few years Douglass soared into prominence as the most famous black abolitionist of his time. In his 1845 autobiography, Douglass recalled Ruggles's "vigilance, kindness, and perseverance." He had learned that Ruggles was a man of action as well as words and feeling. During the days that Ruggles sheltered Douglass, Ruggles was beaten and thrown into jail for his part in the Darg case, a highly complex slave rescue. Upon his release, Ruggles quickly resumed his antislavery activism. Douglass observed that, "though watched and hemmed in on every side, [Ruggles] seemed to be more than a match for his enemies." Ruggles was the kind of black man that Douglass wanted to emulate.[1]

Douglass wrote three autobiographies during his lifetime. Since Benjamin Quarles revived popular interest in Douglass in 1960, numerous biographers have retold his story. Other black abolitionists have attracted attention. As historian Manisha Sinha has pointed out, renewed interest in social histories of northern black communities has led to a proliferation of biographies of prominent black abolitionists such as Douglass, Martin Delany, Sojourner Truth, Alexander Crummell, and Henry Highland Garnet and of lesser-known but important figures including Richard Allen, Paul Cuffe, Jermaine Loguen, and Pennington. Harriet Tubman is the focus of numerous recent biographies. This biographical outpouring has led to clearer understanding of how blacks created a new style of antislavery activity based on militant conduct and community mobilizing.[2]

One key figure has remained in shadow. David Ruggles's life story needs retelling. His significance is larger than his role in perhaps the most symbolically important slave escape in American history. In addition to his service as the key conductor of the Underground Railroad in New York City in the 1830s, Ruggles was a tireless, fiery, pioneering journalist, penning hundreds of letters to abolitionist newspapers, authoring and publishing five pamphlets, and editing the first African American magazine, the *Mirror of Liberty*. He opened the first black bookstore and reading room in New York City and published his own pamphlet in 1834, the first time a black New Yorker had his own imprint—all achievements that illuminate the autonomy blacks found in the world of print. Ruggles built upon these firsts with a burst of antislavery activism that captured the enthusiasm of his peers. He was among the first black antislavery agents. Ruggles operated at a time when his words sparked angry and dangerous reactions in a society still devoted to slavery. He gave his health, indeed his very life to the movement, dying at age thirty-nine. The weight of his battle for black freedom likely hastened his physical demise. Ruggles held uncompromising ideals and commitment in the struggle against the deviltry of slavery. Known as a "whole-souled man," or someone thoroughly imbued with a right spirit, noble-minded, and devoted, Ruggles gained respect throughout the abolitionist community. By recounting Ruggles's extraordinary narrative, I work unabashedly in the "contributionist" tradition that establishes African American heroics within American culture and society. As Ruggles worked equally well with white and black abolitionists, he exemplifies the cooperative tradition of antislavery described by Benjamin Quarles in his book *Black Abolitionists*.[3]

His activism alone is reason to recapture Ruggles's life. But there are many other reasons. His biography helps recenter the history of abolitionism in the antebellum period. Until recently, historians of the abolitionist movement have overemphasized the efforts and achievements of white activists. This slanted historiography has resulted in a partial historical amnesia about the contributions of African American antislavery. As Michel-Rolph Trouillot has demonstrated in another context, power produces history, and, again, until now, antebellum activists of color had few supporters. Renewed investigation of black abolitionism has properly corrected this neglect. At the same time, study of abolitionism still has a "separate but equal" character to it. As Timothy Patrick McCarthy and John Stauffer have observed, there is a one narrative for wealthy, educated white males, another for black males, and a third for white women and a few African American females. These historians call for a new synthesis that will twine these strands together. A biography of one man cannot tell all about such a significant movement, but Ruggles's life story shows how he worked equally and frequently among male and female abolitionists of both races. His story is an important building block of a new understanding of abolitionism, a movement that shook nineteenth-century America to its core.[4]

Ruggles matured within a shifting understanding of the philosophy and tactics of the abolitionist movement. While Ruggles and myriad other blacks admired the powerful energy and message of William Lloyd Garrison and others who demanded an immediate end to American slavery, Ruggles was uncertain about moral suasion, the nonviolent method intended to persuade slaveholders to free their bond people. Black New Yorkers, as Leslie Harris has shown, were fervent supporters of the American Anti-Slavery Society, formed in Philadelphia in December 1833. It, like Garrison's movement in Boston, endorsed the immediate end of slavery across the nation. This radical notion jolted many whites. Radical abolitionism acknowledged that racial discrimination involved moral suasion and the reeducation of whites. It also sought the uplift of blacks in order to deserve equality.[5]

While accepting the tenets of radical abolitionism, Ruggles pushed it further. He used a "practical abolitionism" that embraced civil disobedience and self-defense for black families battling slave catchers and kidnappers of free blacks. Circumstances in New York City required that Ruggles use a directly confrontational approach and view slave masters and their agents as morally evil and incapable of positive change. This hard-won perception stemmed from racial discrimination and violence in the city, kidnapping of free blacks, the recapture of enslaved fugitives through legally questionable means, and the resurgence of the slave trade in New York City's port. Ruggles and his co-workers rallied local blacks against such practices; in addition, he created contacts with whites throughout the Northeast that could help fund his movement and offer protection to self-emancipated blacks. Ruggles thereby connected the battles in New York City with the nascent Underground Railroad.[6]

Ruggles played a major role in creating a connection between abolitionism and the Underground Railroad, a link historians have overlooked. Fergus Bordewich's thorough survey of the Underground Railroad, *Bound for Canaan*, includes a fine chapter on Ruggles and the events of 1835–38 and makes African American involvement much more central. Yet more needs to be done. Most studies of the Underground Railroad follow the lead of William M. Mitchell, William Still, Wilbur Siebert, and other nineteenth-century writers in emphasizing the loosely organized, volunteer methods used in the Ohio River Valley and Midwest of the 1850s. Beyond this geographical slant, vaunted but unsubstantiated claims, the paucity of hard data showing its effectiveness, and the loose connection with the abolitionist movement have given historians pause about crediting the Underground Railroad with much importance. Ruggles's life, however, not only illuminates his lifelong commitment to helping enslaved freedom seekers but also broadens our understanding of what William M. Mitchell, the first historian of the Underground Railroad, called the abolition community. In addition, close examination of Ruggles's writings gives good estimates of the numbers of self-emancipated people he helped.[7]

During the 1830s, David Ruggles was a linchpin figure between the inchoate patterns of the early Underground Railroad and the systematic network of conductors, safe houses, and freedom destinations that expanded dramatically in the 1840s and 1850s. Specifically, Ruggles was the key connector between rural, upstate collaborators and their New York City counterparts, both male and female, in the Underground Railroad. Since the 1670s, African Americans had been emancipating themselves by following the North Star to freedom among native peoples or in New France and, later, to northern colonies and British Canada. After the American Revolution, nearly ten thousand enslaved peoples gained freedom by going into exile in Nova Scotia and the West Indies as part of the largest escape before the Civil War. As northern states ended bondage, the question of whether their lands should become freedom soil had vexed lawmakers since passage of the Fugitive Slave Act of 1793. Increasingly, northern citizens refused southern demands to return self-emancipated bond peoples, an issue that threatened to dissolve comity between the states. During his most intensive period of activism in the 1830s, Ruggles created sinewy knots of collaborators who built the Underground Railroad. Milton Sernett, among others, has detailed the saga of the Underground Railroad in upstate New York. Ruggles's contacts made as an agent for the *Liberator* and *Emancipator* and as a participant in conventions strengthened the ties between the city and the upstate region.[8]

Ruggles became a national figure. As his reputation grew and his actions gained more notice, newspapers around the country commented with favor or with hostility. He was quick to use print media to further his message. He also viewed slavery and discrimination as national problems and did not limit his attacks on slavery's defenders to southerners. As a resident of a state barely removed from legal slavery, Ruggles knew many New Yorkers who had suffered from slavery and racism. He was acutely aware of slavery's bleak shadow in the city. Ruggles, as secretary of the New York Committee of Vigilance, wrote in 1837 "It is a very prevalent error that there are no slaves in this state," for there are "persons having estates in the South, who reside here, and keep slaves in defiance of the laws of the states. In the city of New York alone, these slaves must be very numerous." Slavery was therefore a *national problem* and it was the duty of Ruggles and other practical abolitionists to organize a self-defense committee to battle it everywhere. They would seek help from any sympathetic person, white or black, and he worked exhaustively to spread the word across the nation.[9]

Explaining Ruggles's profound impact on his generation of black activists is a another purpose of this book. One contemporary editor called Ruggles "a General Marion sort of man . . . for sleepless activity, sagacity, and talent." Frederick Douglass was among the young blacks who revered Ruggles; his influence in evident in the former's famous autobiography and in his choices of journalism and confrontational issues as means to battle racism and the slavocracy. Douglass was not alone in his admiration for Ruggles. As a sponsor of talent or a motivator, Ruggles became the central figure in the lives of a number of young black activists. James W. C. Pennington, James McCune Smith, Samuel Ringgold Ward, William Cooper Nell, and William Wells Brown all credited Ruggles with assistance or inspiration for their careers.[10]

Ruggles magnified his impact on an emerging abolitionist movement by pushing a radical abolitionist agenda further than the founding fathers of the movement. His relationship with the more conservative black Presbyterian minister and journalist Samuel Eli Cornish is one of the undercurrents of this narrative. Cornish mentored Ruggles early in his career; later the two split sharply over tactics. Navigating the often-rocky relationships of black and white abolitionists has been the focus of much scholarship, notably by Lawrence Friedman. Other historians are critical of black activist philosophies, regarding them as primarily responsive to white attitudes and immersed in internecine fights that debilitated the movement. Any of these perceptions may have held truth at times, but they slight the achievements of black activism under arduous conditions. The combined efforts of the black and white activism strived to convince America of its culpability about slavery. Telling the story of Ruggles's life uncovers how black activists learned to negotiate their paths with white reformers and to carve out independent ideas and actions.[11]

Recovering Ruggles's life allows for greater nuance in understanding the development of radical abolitionism. For much of his career, Ruggles was primarily focused on improving the fortunes of self-emancipated slaves and the besieged free blacks of New York City. His writings and activities illuminated their struggles. Ruggles had no doubts that he was a black man striving to improve and protect urban black residents. In so doing, he fits well into the black nationalist ideology that Craig Wilder, Leslie Harris, and Leslie Alexander, among others, have ably documented. At the same time, Ruggles did not act in a hermetically sealed world and eagerly sought the assistance of sympathetic whites. Ruggles partnered with the venerable white activist Isaac T. Hopper and the radical Episcopalian Barney Corse. Ruggles also worked extensively with Lewis Tappan and William Lloyd Garrison. This insight is hardly new. What is special about Ruggles is how independently and confidently he conducted his affairs with all comers. His achievements were a big step forward in black assertiveness and white acceptance of African American agency.[12]

The rise of radical abolitionism produced innumerable societies and talented young leaders. Inevitably, such rapid development led to conflicts over tactics and personalities. Ruggles was often a focus of these skirmishes and suffered grievously from them. His appeal was broader than most. Ruggles galvanized the black laborers and *Lumpenproletariat* into action against slavery and white racism. Whether working with rough protégés such as Douglass, Samuel Ringgold Ward, and other self-emancipated slaves, Ruggles built upon earlier anger and protest to sustain a new black radical abolitionism in the 1830s. His leadership of black activists in New York City extends far beyond the fratricidal battles he had with Cornish. Ruggles often spoke directly to and for the ordinary black New Yorker and impressed young African Americans, white farmers, housewives, and small business people far from the city.

Ruggles's radical abolitionism mixed reform streams such as evangelical religion, temperance, education, black migration to Canada, opposition to the American Colonization Society, antislavery legislation, and advocacy for improved black civil rights with a more confrontational defense of fugitive slaves and opposition to slave traders. Ruggles joined white and black reformers who preferred the church, convention hall, and private discussions to battle slavery and racism. But his milieus were also street rallies, church meetings, and personal confrontations of slaveholders and kidnappers. While most black reformers of the 1830s generally eschewed violence, Ruggles refused to rule it out.

Ruggles extended his influence far beyond a small group of white and black activists by reaching out to the community of ordinary black men and women struggling for survival and dignity in an often-hostile, dangerous city. As an educated, committed activist, Ruggles qualified to be among the black elite. Still, he came from very modest circumstances in Connecticut. In New

York City, he was by occupation briefly a mariner, then a grocer, a book-store proprietor, an editor, and a printer. None of these jobs propelled him into prosperity. At times he was impoverished. His ordinary status did not differentiate him from other black activists, who were primarily ministers, petty proprietors, and a very few editors and professionals, whose jobs did not place them far above the most ordinary black laborers. Samuel Eli Cornish, one of the most prominent clerics, opened a shoemaker's shop in 1836 to bolster his income; other educated black elites held similar positions. Their property ownership was minuscule compared to whites'.[13]

Ruggles's story demonstrates that a more nuanced approach is necessary in discussing how class divided the black community. Scholars have emphasized how education and social uplift ambitions of the black elite created a class divide among people of color in New York City.[14] A class analysis based on wealth is apt for African Americans in Charleston (South Carolina), New Orleans, St. Louis, and possibly for Philadelphia, but not for New York City. There was, save for the Downing family, no black economic elite in New York City. Most black New Yorkers struggled to survive. Elite status, such as it was in New York, derived from education, family association, and, for a very few, occupations. Dr. James McCune Smith, for example, was elite in education and work, but not in finances. The most common occupation of the black elite was the ministry. Preachers might hector their congregations about immoral behavior, but they could hardly hold themselves above their parishioners, especially the female majority. Ruggles, a printer and bookseller, had far less income than any of his often-wealthy white counterparts did. He, as noted, appealed directly to the black rank and file, male and female, and strived to bring them into the abolitionist community.[15]

Ruggles's story also belies conventional wisdom on gender divides within the abolitionist movement. As white and black female activists pushed for gender as well as racial equality, otherwise enlightened leadership opposed their demands. Not so with Ruggles, the son of a strong woman. He appealed directly to females, supported their entrance into the movement, and worked equally with them. While the majority of runaways he assisted were self-emancipated men, Ruggles did what he could for black females in pursuit of freedom. Still, masculinity played a crucial role in Ruggles's identity and in the force of his example. As he inspired young black activists with his words and actions, so did Ruggles epitomize for them a masculine resistance to the big problems of the day: white denial of civil rights and the slavocracy. As James and Lois Horton have suggested, such heroic battles became the benchmarks for black male manhood in the 1830s.[16]

Battles over slavery and civil rights often originated or were resolved within the context of religion. In their otherwise comprehensive studies of abolitionism, Richard Newman and Patrick Rael, for example, have lately downplayed religion as a factor, either limiting discussion or avoiding it entirely. As a young man, Ruggles engaged with Congregationalists, Unitarians, Methodists, Baptists, the Society of Friends, Presbyterians, Episcopalians, and at least two black congregations. His contacts and alliances often happened through church membership. As James Brewer Stewart has reminded us, we live in a profoundly religious age and would be remiss to ignore the powerful impact of faith among abolitionists.[17]

Richard Newman has demonstrated how Philadelphia and Boston black activists pushed for equality in the abolitionist movement.[18] David Ruggles took matters further by battling for the personal freedoms of blacks in the streets of New York, insisting upon carving out a public space for blacks in the abolitionist movement and using direct confrontation to ensure the liberty of fugitive slaves and kidnapped free blacks. Ruggles took the literary defiance of David Walker and married it to quotidian confrontations.

Although Ruggles was but one man, I have placed the burdens of many interpretations on his shoulders. Taken together, these variances on older and contemporary themes about abolitionism and radical change in antebellum New York City shed light on America's rapidly changing society. Historians have explained the rush of the new in this period using manifest destiny, the market revolution, the opening of the political order, and the communications revolution. Recounting Ruggles's life reaffirms how the decades of conflict over slavery and civil rights led to the Civil War. Unlike other explanations, within this biography, ordinary black and white men and women take active roles. Their participation is not implicit, but real.

In the pages that follow, I chart Ruggles's brave writings and deeds and indicate the paramount place he occupied in the creation of a black radical intellectual tradition. His radical ideals, commitments, and achievements are best understood by chronicling his life. The first chapter details Ruggles's early life and influences, many of them based on the lingering effects of the American Revolution. I then follow him to New York City, where he set up a grocery shop at the age of seventeen and became immersed in antislavery politics. Chapter 3 discusses Ruggles as a journeyman abolitionist, who learned the trade by working along its circuits of conventions, meetings, and rallies. After serving as an agent for the *Liberator* and the *Emancipator*, he began expressing his own views in letters to the editor and in pamphlets. Chapters 4 and 5 delineate Ruggles's rise and fall as champion of the oppressed in New York

City and beyond. An epilogue discusses Ruggles's legacy on the antislavery movement and the Underground Railroad.

At this juncture, I should indicate who David Ruggles was not. At least two contemporaries shared his name and were occasionally mistaken for him. David Ruggles of Poughkeepsie, New York, was a white man and a land speculator. Descended from the Ruggles family of New Milford and Bridge-water, Connecticut, towns near the New York border and distant from the seaport home of the African American David Ruggles, the Poughkeepsie resident was a brother of Charles H. Ruggles, the lawyer who served in the Twelfth U.S. Congress and was elected to be chief justice of the State of New York in the 1840s. This David Ruggles once offered to organize a settlement of farmers in West Florida for the Marquis de Lafayette, a proposal accorded by mistake to our David Ruggles. David Ruggles of Poughkeepsie was litigious and his name appears frequently in New York City court records. But he had no known abolitionist sympathies. Another David Ruggles, with the middle initial *W*, was African American and was actively antislavery. He lived in New Bedford, Massachusetts, and was an ally of our subject. Occasionally I indicate in notes when confusion occurred in the historical records.[19]

❄ ❄ ❄

CHAPTER ONE

A Revolutionary Childhood

David Ruggles was born free in Connecticut, a state with a rich revolutionary heritage. Those facts affected his later life immensely. Born on March 15,
1810, in Lyme, a small fishing village near Norwich, Connecticut, Ruggles was
the first of eight children of free blacks David and Nancy Ruggles. David Sr.
was born in Norwich in 1775; his wife was born in 1785 in either Norwich or
nearby Lyme. Sylvia, the only one of Nancy's sisters who is known, was baptized in the First Congregational Church of Norwich in 1773. The origins and
extended family remain obscure.[1]

Sometime after David's birth, the Ruggles family moved from Lyme to
nearby Norwich, Connecticut, a secondary seaport roughly halfway along
the Atlantic Coast between Boston and New York City. Situated at the junc-
tion of the Thames River tributary, Norwich is fourteen miles from the Long
Island Sound and accessible to oceanic shipping, making the city a conduit
for goods coming in and out of eastern Connecticut. First established in the
1660s by New England Congregationalists, the city by 1810 was home to 3,525
people, of whom 152 were free blacks and 12 were enslaved blacks. Substantially dependent on sea trade, the city suffered badly during the Embargo
of 1807 and the War of 1812. After the war, coastal shipping reached earlier
heights, but long-distance seafaring took many years to recover. Norwich
did boast some industry. It was one of the first towns in colonial Connecticut
to manufacture paper money and prided itself for its numerous daily and

weekly newspapers. Its foundries cast cannons and mortars for the Patriot side during the Revolution, bringing ample work for blacksmiths.[2]

The demand for blacksmiths continued after the Revolution and may have enticed the Ruggles family to leave Lyme for the larger coastal city. During the younger David's childhood, David Sr. and Nancy and their children lived in an old tenement located on a tiny triangular plot on Sylvia's Lane just off the main road in the Bean Hill section of Norwich. They received this slender plot from Sylvia and her husband, who was known as Negro Cuff. This couple lived on Bean Hill after gaining their freedom from their owners, the Cleveland family, who were also residents of the neighborhood. Even after Sylvia's departure, the alley retained her name. Neither black family actually owned the land.

The man who freed Sylvia and Cuff and perhaps David's parents, Aaron Cleveland, great-grandfather of President Grover Cleveland, was a man of versatile talents. A hatter by trade, Cleveland was also a poet, songwriter, essayist, lecturer, and sermonizer who made public and private pronouncements about religious truth and individual freedom. Among the first writers in Connecticut to question the morality of slavery, Cleveland published a number of antislavery articles and poems in the *Norwich Packet* in the 1770s. While representing Norwich in the state legislature during the American Revolution, he introduced a bill calling for the abolition of slavery. He later became a Congregational minister. Although Cleveland died when Ruggles was but five years old, doubtless his parents taught their eldest son and his siblings to revere the man and his beliefs. Ruggles learned that some white men were worthy of trust and kept their promises.[3]

The Ruggles family was of sturdy artisan stock. Though Ruggles Sr. worked in a blacksmith's shop owned by someone else, his occupation had special status. Blacksmiths were respected figures in early black American societies, were noted for their important parts in slave rebellions in the southern states, and played significant roles as go-betweens for white and black Americans. Whites also revered the blacksmith. John Neagle's famous portrait, *Pat Lyon at His Forge*, commissioned by the white industrialist himself, presented the blacksmith as the embodiment of power, individualism, and a testament to an open, democratic society. Although blacks were rarely portrayed in such exalted fashion, the blacksmith's daily life demanded respect. No matter how grand was Bean Hill society, an eminent personage could be quickly brought low by a broken wheel or axle on the family carriage or a damaged shoe on the horse. As with all artisans who closely served the public, blacksmiths held power far beyond social rank. In any emergency, customers had to placate

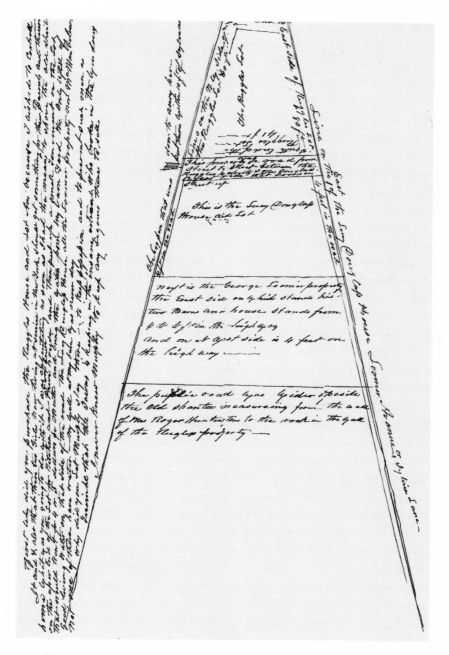

Map of the Ruggles Family Plot, Bean Hill, Norwich, Connecticut. The Ruggles family lived in a cramped tenement located on this tiny triangular plot in Bean Hill. Courtesy of the City of Norwich.

busy forge men to get their attention. The brawny bodies of blacksmiths and their work twisting molten steel into usable objects gave them greater prestige than financial worth might warrant.[4]

Undoubtedly, David Ruggles must have thrilled at the sight of his father at the forge. He could watch and, as he grew, help as his father worked his lusty bellows to roil the immense fire, delight as the sparks danced from the hammers on the anvil, and be enthralled as the red-hot gems flowed from the molten iron. The glow that illuminated his father's powerful body would have spellbound his son and other onlookers. From his father, Ruggles learned about the dignity of labor and, according to occasional descriptions, inherited his powerful physique.[5]

Similarly, Nancy Ruggles held a valued position in local society. A celebrated cook who toiled in the nearby tavern of Count Henry Felix, she was widely known for her skills as a caterer. A. B. Sherman, a contemporary resident of Beantown, recalled that for fifty years for any "wedding party, funeral, or a childbirth or a tea party Nancy must come and make the cake and pass it around."[6] His recollections indicate the impact Nancy had on local ritual events. One can easily imagine her eldest son accompanying her as she delivered and served cakes at festive occasions in which, however briefly, the presence of a bright young man of color was acceptable. In sum, Ruggles inherited from his parents a strong sense of family pride and respect.

The family seems to have prospered in its neighborhood and grew rapidly after David's birth. A sister, Livinia, was born in 1814, and a brother, Felix, arrived in 1817. Arriving later were four other brothers: Thomas (b. 1819); George (b. 1821); Henry (b. 1825); and Richard Baxter (b. 1827). One last child, Frances Jane, was born in 1832.[7] That all lived to maturity is testament to the strength and fortune of the family. Strong nuclear families were common among abolitionists, who testified to the power of their parents' intense religious fervor. Home was where, as James Brewer Stewart noted, displays of conscience and upright behavior brought the rewards of parental love and approval. Self-control was mixed with a strong sense of individuality, utter seriousness about moral issues, and a confidence to meet the world head-on to improve it, all of which produced people who expected to become leaders.[8]

Ruggles thrived in his cozy neighborhood. Bean Hill was a tiny outgrowth just to the north of Norwich. According to folk recollections, it was so named after the baked beans that its residents ate every Saturday. Located at the northern limit of the town plot of Norwich, Bean Hill possessed institutions and residents who surely influenced David Ruggles. Life in Bean Hill softened class and racial barriers. Many of the prominent families of Norwich lived there. Families such as the Hydes, Backuses, Clevelands, Blisses, and Huntingtons moved there to escape the crowded downtown. Norwich, and Bean Hill in particular, produced numerous state governors, congressmen, and senators. Within this tightly knit, elite society, the Ruggles family, though black and poor, was a regular, accepted presence. This familiarity between the races fostered a confidence in the young Ruggles, which would later enable him to move comfortably among New York City's elite. The few other blacks in the village were servants. One named Caesar Reynolds lived in an adjacent house.[9]

Churches were the center of Bean Hill life, as was true in any New England village. Central to Ruggles's youth was the Bean Hill location of the first Norwich Methodist Episcopal Church, of which Nancy was a member. The congregation met in a multipurpose building that also served as a classical academy and a free school. Although the church had lay preachers, it was a regular stop for itinerant evangelists. Major Methodist figures including the Reverend Jesse Lee and Bishop Francis Asbury, and the Pentecostal preacher Lorenzo Dow spoke before the congregation. Even though the ardor of Methodists had cooled a bit from the colonial days, the church's evangelical message still informed its congregants that personal perfection was possible and to strive for it was mandatory and that each individual was responsible for his or her own salvation. Avoiding damnation required steering away from dependence on alcohol and tobacco. Linked to these sins was slavery. Methodism initially barred membership to slaveholders. Gradually the church accepted slave masters nationally, but in the northeast strong antislavery beliefs still held sway.

Black families such as the Ruggleses found acceptance in the church. There is no record indicating that they had to worship apart from the rest of the congregation, in the hated "Negro pew," by which blacks in other churches were often segregated to rear galleries, distant from the pulpit. And there were other reasons for belonging to the church. Among its activities was protection for freedom-seeking slaves from the South. There were already fugitive slaves hidden in Norwich, which had its notable black residents. One who lived with the family of Dina Manning was Jean Pierre Boyer, who later became president of the Republic of Haiti. Although he left Norwich before David Ruggles's birth, memory of Boyer surely lasted among its black inhabitants. Another local black was Primus, an enslaved African, who memorized whole tracts of the Bible and told stories to the local black children. In his published works, Ruggles demonstrated remarkable biblical knowledge, some of which may have come from Primus.[10]

Bean Hill was about a mile from the center of Norwich and its main road wound down into the town. This street had many figures sure to have fascinated young Ruggles. The local wood carter was a Revolutionary War veteran who never tired of telling children of his military exploits. A missionary who had served in Ceylon and India had a small shop on the village green. All the local excitement from Cleveland's antislavery harangues to anniversaries, balls, and dinners, at which Nancy Ruggles's confections were required, were held on the village green.[11]

Small shops in the area filled young Ruggles with possibilities and aspirations. More than twenty retail tradesmen operated along this road or nearby. The small community boasted dry goods and grocery stores, gristmills and sawmills, and two taverns. There were numerous bookstores and a circulating library, and two printing offices, each with a bookshop and bindery. Both published a weekly newspaper. There were a watchmaker's shop, a cotton jenny, and hotels, including one where President John Adams had dined on his journey to and from Boston and Philadelphia. There were horse traders, mule teamsters, and frequent drovers of cattle. In short, any walk David Ruggles took around his neighborhood and into town was filled with potential fascination for a bright, lively child who could gain reverence for the American Revolution from the humble but successful entrepreneurs. These small independent businesses created in his mind the pleasures of owning one's shop. The mix of artisan and intellectual endeavors instilled in the young Ruggles a conviction that there was no boundary between work and the mind.[12]

Education was central to the youth of any Connecticut resident. There is evidence that David Ruggles gained some literacy at home. The Bible was, of course, an important resource and, for any devout American family, both the final answer to any question or dispute and a source of deep inspiration. At home and school, children were expected to learn vast numbers of Bible verses. In addition, both David Sr. and Nancy received letters. Although their correspondents are unknown, the expectation was that both could read the communications or had access to someone who could help.[13] Ruggles gained a more formal education in the town. He received his earliest education at the Sabbath School for the Poor in Norwich, which first admitted blacks in 1815. Connecticut's Manumission Society in association with Congregational and Episcopal societies founded the school. Ruggles may have gained admission to the school through the intercession of William Cleveland, son of Aaron, and a deacon of the church. This Sabbath School was the first in that part of

Connecticut. Beginning with a "class of five African boys, who were collected and taught by Charles T. Harrington, at his house in Franklin Street, and by him induced to attend church," the school quickly increased in numbers and success. Within three years, at least seven male and female teachers instructed forty-one young and old people of color. After an organizational change, the Second Congregational Church continued the school through the antebellum period. In the absence of regular public schools for blacks, this Congregational school provided Ruggles's formal education, mixing piety with individual initiative and firm knowledge of the Bible among other books. One instructor, Harriet Wadsworth Winslow, recalled teaching black children at the school around the time Ruggles was there. Her method, doubtless copied by others, was to instill religion in her pupils through memorization of the Bible. Each day she would read twelve verses of the New Testament to them over and over again until her charges could read and write the scripture. The extraordinary erudition Ruggles demonstrated in his publications years later stood as testament to his successful education, indicating a powerful family and institutional investment in him.[14]

Association with the Congregational church helped instill in Ruggles a commitment to systematic labor in pursuit of radical social reform. Although scholars have given much attention to African American Methodist and Baptist ministers and their congregations, much of the leadership in northern cities came from black Congregational and Presbyterian clergy. As black clerical activists in key states, they, as David E. Swift has pointed out, could foster the social and political goals of the black freedom movement at large. Ruggles may not have encountered such black Congregationalists in Norwich, but his exposure to the church's racially egalitarian politics prepared him for later involvement.[15]

School was not all hard work. In a pamphlet published in 1834, David Ruggles recalled his "by-gone days in New England, the land of steady habits where my happiest hours were spent with my playmates in her schools and in her churches." Ruggles remembered ice-skating and playing with balls and hoops in Connecticut. He happily spoke of how he and his friends "walked and swam her beautiful streams—when we climbed her tall pines and elms and oaks—when we rambled thro' all her fine orchards." Ruggles clearly remembered his early upbringing with happiness and was quick to point out that his childhood days were racially integrated. Unlike virtually every other African American memoirist, Ruggles did not recall a terrible day when racial prejudice intruded on childhood friendship. Rather, the lessons he learned in

Connecticut were about racial equality. Ruggles quoted from English poet William Cowper's widely circulated poem, "The Negroe's Complaint" to affirm this egalitarian message:

Fleecy locks and black complexion
Did not forfeit nature's claim,
Skins did not differ, but affection
Dwelt "in black and white the same."[16]

School presented a mixed message. His later erudition indicates good pedagogy with sound preparation in logic, literature, and debate. But his teachers may not have envisioned an activist life for him in America. One of his teachers was Lydia Huntley Sigourney, the daughter of a prosperous shipping family who later became a famed essayist and poet. Sigourney recalled her black pupils as obviously grateful for common attention, as being most of them quite young, and intellectually untrained. School anniversary celebrations earned money for a library in Liberia, which according to Sigourney "was just lifting its head above the surrounding darkness." This was an early reference to the plans of the American Colonization Society's efforts to convince free blacks to abandon life in America and migrate to Africa. In his youth, Ruggles came into contact with white paternalism. However disquieting it may have been to hear his beloved teacher recommend that he find a future in Africa, Ruggles otherwise benefited from the school. As his career indicates, he came out of the Norwich schools highly literate and versed in classical and sacred literature. He was at home with the sayings of great writers and had a penchant for logic and ethics.[17] Ruggles believed his school days taught him morals and virtue, elements that enabled him to stand up to the debilitating racism he would later face.[18]

His schooling did not inure Ruggles from the misadventures of youth, and he went through a wild period in his early teenage years. He experienced the near miss or fateful collision with the law that have too often imprisoned or doomed young black men throughout American history. Ruggles and his neighborhood chum, Caesar Reynolds, were caught stealing watermelons from "Mr. Hyde's garden." Reynolds was originally from Wickford, Rhode Island. After his father left his mother when Reynolds was an infant, she placed him as a servant with a wealthy man named Carter Hazard of Newport, Rhode Island. Reynolds was seven years older than Ruggles and had already been flogged for stealing a pen.

Having discovered the theft by the two boys, Hyde agreed to say nothing provided that Reynolds paid him five dollars, which the youth obtained from

Lydia Huntley Sigourney. One of
Ruggles's first teachers, Sigourney
went on to become a well-known
writer of belles lettres. From Francis
Manwaring Caulkins, *History of Norwich,*
Connecticut: From Its Possession by the Indians to the
Year 1866. Norwich: Published by the Author, 1866.

his guardian, "under some pretense." Reynolds related that he did not know
how young Ruggles settled the problem. Sometime afterward, the pair went
to the General Training Day between Colchester and New London, Connecticut. General Training Days were annual militia musters. In addition to
the parading of the troops, there was also substantial drinking, gambling,
and other frolicking. Reynolds recalled that Ruggles and he fully understood
what they planned. Toward nighttime, they found a trooper's horse, "fully
equipped with saddle, bridle, martingale, pistols, hostelers, and other gear,"
tied to a fence. Pretending to be servants, they led the horse off for some distance, and then rode it back to Bean Hill. The trooper found it there the next
day and demanded ten dollars to satisfy the incident. Shortly afterward, Hazard fired young Reynolds for disobedience. The lad then drifted into a life of
robbery and burglary. He received a seven-year sentence for theft in 1820 and
then was sent away again in 1830. During his second term in prison, Reynolds
and another inmate, William Teller, killed a guard. After their conviction, the
two were hanged in 1833.

A Revolutionary Childhood

Reynolds's childhood confederate, David Ruggles, escaped this fate because of the strength of his family's local connections, which helped young David avoid harsher punishment. These petty violations today may not seem indicators of a life of crime, and certainly watermelon stealing would now be considered a youthful prank, but Connecticut's early nineteenth-century magistrates were known to give sizable prison terms for minor thefts. Horse stealing was a more serious misdeed. Other blacks received whippings for first offenses of this felony, and prison terms of many years were common. Had he followed his playmate into a life of crime, Ruggles may have had his own date with the gallows.[19]

Young African Americans like Ruggles faced other hazards besides the criminalization of petty offenses in early nineteenth-century Connecticut. The state was moving through the final stages of gradual emancipation. This method of freeing enslaved black Americans was less violent than its later southern counterpart, but it had its own limitations. The lunar shadow of slavery over the Northeast gave rise to a virulent white racism and fostered discrimination in all walks of life. At the same time, antislavery talk and attitudes at home and at the church enabled Ruggles to focus his energies and intelligence to battle against the lingering aspects of servitude in the North.[20]

As in other northern states, revolutionary egalitarianism and religious abhorrence meant that the institution of slavery was slated for extinction. Nonetheless, slavery's shadow loomed long over the lives of Connecticut blacks. Once considered by historians to be an unimportant aspect of New England's social and economic makeup, slavery is now understood to have played an integral part of the economy of northern port cities such as Norwich. Nowhere was it more important than in Connecticut where, at the end of the colonial period, more slaves lived than in any other province of New England. Although the colony's merchants were not involved in the slave trade as extensively as those in Massachusetts or Rhode Island, by 1774 there was a ready market for bonded labor. By that year, more than 6,500 enslaved blacks lived and worked in Connecticut. Many of them were concentrated in the port cities laboring in the fishing, whaling, and slave trades. The colony also had important copper, iron, shipbuilding, and rum industries, which employed slave labor. Black farm hands labored on small farms and on large plantations such as Godfrey Malbone's in Brooklyn, Connecticut, north of Norwich, which employed 50 to 60 slaves in the mid-eighteenth century. In 1774, 295 slaves made up about 4 percent of Norwich's population of 7,032. The largest slaveholder in Norwich was Samuel Huntington, who lived in

Bean Hill. Even as late as 1800, more than 200 blacks remained in bondage in New London County and 11 sufferers were still enslaved in 1820. Ruggles, therefore, grew up in a society where slavery was on the decline, but its influence remained strong.[21]

By the time of Ruggles's birth, the battle to end slavery stretched back over thirty years. The efforts of blacks had contributed to the demise of servitude. The revolutionary service of Connecticut's black population enhanced the confidence that Ruggles felt about his place in the American republic. In the aftermath of the American Revolution, the number of free blacks increased sharply by their enrollments in the Connecticut militia and Continental army. Spurred by an offer of freedom in exchange for military service, several hundred Connecticut blacks volunteered for service in the army. Black revolutionaries had to secure a sum equal to their sale value, and masters had to forgo all future claims on their bondage. Blacks had to demonstrate that they could sustain themselves after discharge.[22] They had constituted a significant percentage of Connecticut's military forces during the American Revolution. Blacks served in both the infantry and the navy.

The exchange of freedom for service proved highly successful in retaining the loyalty of the state's black population. There were blacks in Connecticut who served the king, but generally the state's people of color were Patriots. Their choice was testament to a positive perception of their future chances in the state. Consider that in New York and New Jersey few blacks were enrolled in the American forces and virtually no effort was made to negotiate with them about military service. Not surprisingly, blacks in those states tilted decidedly to the British, who regularly published broadsides promising freedom to enslaved people who joined the king's army.

In Connecticut, as black soldiers gained freedom, they were quick to point out contradictions in Patriot ideologies. Several blacks petitioned the Connecticut legislature in 1779 for general emancipation, noting, "We are endowed with the same faculties with our masters and the more we consider the matter, the more we are convinced of our right to be free." Another black, enslaved by a Tory, argued that Patriots, who were engaged in a war against tyranny, should not sell them, because they as "honest Whigs . . . ought to be free, and the Tories ought to be sold." Blacks in Connecticut plainly believed that patriotic service mandated civil rights, even if their white counterparts did not agree. Lemuel Haynes personified Connecticut's black revolutionary heritage. The black minister combined revolutionary egalitarianism and antislavery to infuse his clerical career. Haynes's calling provided a model for ambitious, bright young blacks such as Ruggles.[23]

A Revolutionary Childhood

Black wartime appeals did not impress Connecticut's lawmakers, and the legislature routinely rejected emancipation bills during the conflict. Connecticut's African Americans learned that persistent efforts were needed to end slavery. Not until 1784 did Connecticut's assembly adopt an emancipation law, which provided for freedom for black and mulatto children born after March 1 of that year, and only after they had served their masters for twenty-five years. The law was tacked onto a statute reorganizing the colonial laws governing slavery. Although Connecticut's lawmakers reaffirmed the enslavement of contemporary blacks, they held out the promise of eventual freedom for black infants. However, the law did condemn future generations of blacks to more than two decades of servitude, a period that included most of their productive work lives. Living under the terms of gradual emancipation left blacks frustrated and yearning for freedom. It could also create a distrust of political solutions that left true freedom dangling long into the future.[24]

The enactment of gradual emancipation did not end the struggle to abolish slavery. Both blacks and helpful whites worked to hasten its demise. By 1794 fewer than 2,500 people remained enslaved in Connecticut, and there was legal help for them. Organized in 1790, the Connecticut Society for the Promotion of Freedom and the Relief of Persons Unlawfully Holden in Bondage litigated in defense of aggrieved free blacks and promoted the cause of antislavery and black uplift. Political efforts were underway to extirpate servitude. In 1795 Connecticut became the only northern state to debate and nearly pass a bill that would immediately end slavery and free those still held in bondage. As Peter Hinks has ably demonstrated, the ideas and strategies of the supporters of the immediate emancipation bill anticipated those used by William Lloyd Garrison and his supporters in 1831. Behind the earlier drive, which was approved by the General Assembly but finally failed before the Governor's Council, were the leaders of a hyper-Calvinist New Divinity movement that swept the state's Congregational churches in the late eighteenth century. Fundamental to the tenets of this theological movement was the belief that slavery and the slave trade were sinful and un-Christian, that the Bible in no way justified slavery, and that no white person was excused from responsibility for the sin of slavery. Inattention and indifference were as malignant as actual ownership. Leaders of the New Divinity movement Jonathan Edwards Jr. and Timothy Dwight taught that the crime of "man-stealing" was the slave owner's and trader's fundamental violation of the inalienability of human liberty.[25] Although the bill failed, leaving gradual emancipation intact by the time of David Ruggles's birth in 1810, its tenets were common in the churches he and his family attended. New Divinity teachings anticipated Garrison's ideas and forecast the emerging sectional divide in American religion, society, and politics that culminated in the Civil War.

Religious condemnation of slavery did not translate into a drive for black political equality. Connecticut's political leaders, moreover, did not foresee a prominent role in the state's future for free blacks. Having barred the importation of slaves in 1774, Connecticut's political leaders hoped that its black population would dwindle, as had its Native Americans. Convinced by leading clergymen including Jonathan Edwards Jr. and the Reverend Levi Hart that slavery was sinful, Connecticut's white population made a critical correlation that free blacks, having been degraded by slavery, would naturally be improvident and vicious. Undergirding these racist attitudes was a belief, taking shape in the late colonial period, that blacks would be better off somewhere else, preferably in Africa. Ruggles would face similar attitudes later in New York and found them wholly unacceptable. He was not the only black to voice such views, but he was among the loudest and most articulate.[26]

The pessimistic attitudes lawmakers held about blacks affected Connecticut's negotiation positions at the Constitutional Convention in Philadelphia in 1787. During the debate over apportionment, Connecticut's delegates contended that with the abolition of slavery in the United States — which they saw as positive — economic and population changes would "render slaves useless. . . . Slavery in time will not be a speck in our country." Clearly, Connecticut's leaders did not foresee a role for African Americans in the nation's future development.[27] In part, such opinions matched perceptions that poorer whites had few political rights. Connecticut was barely more liberal with its white citizens. Even after the American Revolution, the original royalist charter of 1662 remained the governing force. A Federalist oligarchy of wealthy merchants and the Congregational Church, still supported by tax dollars into the 1820s, ran the state with little opposition. In the 1790s, only about 5 percent of the white population of the state could actually vote in gubernatorial elections, although Jeffersonian reforms boosted that total in the early nineteenth century. What this meant for Ruggles was that, unlike citizens in other states (New Jersey and South Carolina are good examples), ordinary whites could not lord over blacks through extensive political power.[28]

Black residents of Connecticut did not accept their oppression easily. The colony and the state experienced high rates of illegal behavior by enslaved people. Most crimes involved petty theft, although there were also incidents of significant violence. Meanwhile, the ports in New London County, which included Norwich, offered better opportunities for enslaved people to "steal themselves" and run away. In the closing years of the gradual emancipation process, around the time of Ruggles's birth, the county's newspapers provided frequent advertisements of runaway blacks who fled their masters. Although the numbers decreased as slavery in Connecticut expired, Ruggles doubtless saw rootless young black men in flight who passed down Bean Hill toward the docks, where sea captains rarely asked for personal references. In a family as militant as his, these searchers for freedom were more admired than feared.[29]

Self-emancipated blacks from the South could expect aid from Connecticut citizens. One freedom seeker escaped from South Carolina in 1788 and made his way to Hebron, a town not far from Norwich. When a slave catcher arrived to seize him, residents of the region rescued and set free the former bondman. In 1798, in a sensational moment, a mixed-race mob protected the eight-year-old James Mars from a Virginia slave catcher. Such incidents became part of the lore of Connecticut blacks and were surely told to the young Ruggles. Voluntary assistance to self-emancipated slaves was integral in community actions about slavery, instilling in Ruggles the view that such behavior was honorable, courageous, and moral.[30]

Connecticut's black population had a long-standing history of criticizing slavery in print. As early as 1754, an enslaved man named Greenwich spoke before a "strict Congregationalist" audience and offered a critique of slavery based upon biblical justification. Greenwich showed broad understanding of scriptural exegesis, disputing, for example, the popular theory that Africans were condemned to enslavement as descendants of Noah's disrespectful son, Ham. He also addressed theories that supported servitude as spoils of war, showing a sophisticated, literary power that presaged further black thinking in the postwar gradual emancipation period.[31]

A decade before David Ruggles's birth, Venture Smith, who lived in New London, a port town adjacent to Norwich, published a narrative about his rise from slavery into economic independence. Through his own exertions, Smith bought himself and his family members from slave masters, demonstrating to young men such as Ruggles how hard work and determination could enable enslaved people to free themselves.[32]

During the late colonial period, Connecticut's newspapers conducted an active debate over the merits of slavery. Antislavery attitudes were common among blacks and whites. Leading ministers campaigned against servitude. Blacks made their own public statements against enslavement. A slave named Grinning, who lived in Canterbury, a short distance from Norwich, vowed that slavery lacked biblical justification and that baptized blacks should be freed immediately. The examples of Greenwich and Grinning indicate how openly Connecticut's black population spoke against slavery. Ruggles grew up in an environment where such sentiments were standard, whether made by white or black citizens. He knew that blacks could publicize their views in print.[33]

The lowly place that most Connecticut blacks held in the economy did not always indicate their social importance. Whether slave or free, black women commonly served as domestics in the homes of prosperous whites. Nancy Ruggles, famed for her cooking, probably earned cash as a domestic between catering jobs. Domestic labor could entail innumerable tasks and a faithful, long-term servant literally became part of the family. Lydia Sigourney wrote that "our faithful Amy" helped shape her childhood personality. To be served by such a faithful servant, recalled Sigourney, was "a luxury, a privilege for whose continuance we should give thanks to God." Amy taught Sigourney dairying, butter churning, and spinning. Despite the writer's fond memories, New Englanders used their paternalist recollections to sublimate the harsher history of enslavement. Because the value of housework was never quantified, this historic amnesia also enabled white northerners (and scholars) to dismiss the valuable contributions of enslaved Africans to the region's evolution.[34]

For many years, the lines between free and enslaved domestics were not always clear. As it was not uncommon for free women to marry enslaved men, legal status was often confused, especially in the years after gradual emancipation commenced. Their presence in white families meant that black women, whether enslaved or free, were part of two families. Enslaved people wishing to marry had to gain permission of their masters and mistresses, a power that extended to the free person. White New Englanders perceived black unions with much more gravity than in other regions. In New York, for example, the Anglican and Lutheran churches were the sole denominations to consecrate black marriages in the colonial period. In New England, Congregational clerics regularly performed marital rites for blacks, enslaved or not. Marriages across racial lines also occurred with some frequency. Reverend Lemuel Haynes was the son of a white woman and an African man; he, too, married a white woman. Casual sex between black and white, while punishable by law under strict Puritan codes, occurred often enough, but only Massachusetts passed any laws forbidding interracial lovemaking, however futile such prohibitions were. In the aftermath of the American Revolution, blacks, whites, and Native Americans intermarried. It is significant that Ruggles was born into a society in which interracial sex was generally tolerated and certainly not condemned with ferocious punishments. This could

A Revolutionary Childhood

be the case even in nearby New York, where couples desiring to marry across racial lines had to pay financial penalties and suffer social ridicule well into the nineteenth century.[35]

The work life of Norwich's black men fostered independent sensibilities. Norwich's male slaves worked largely in seafaring occupations. Although many farms employed blacks, it was on the docks and vessels where most earned a living. Ruggles may have worked on one of the coastal vessels that plied goods to merchants from Maine to New York City. He had to be aware of such work, and had he served this way, he would make the connections between antislavery-minded black sailors and wharfingers and sympathetic whites. Such contacts were essential in his adult life in his activities against illicit slave trading and in finding secure spots for southern runaways arriving in northeastern ports.

Norwich and Connecticut blacks in general lived in a society with divided positions on race. The racial attitudes of white Connecticut residents did not mean that they favored southern solutions. Quite the opposite was the case. Connecticut's leaders balked at what they considered the excessive demands of the southern slave owners. They offered radical changes to the U.S. Constitution to curtail the growing power of slavery in national government. In the early nineteenth century, anxiety over the balance of power between free and slave states caused Connecticut's Federalist senator, James Hillhouse, to try unsuccessfully to add antislavery amendments to proposals that would make territories eligible for statehood in the newly acquired Louisiana Purchase. Connecticut's leaders endorsed both Federalist plans to limit the constitutional power of the slavocracy by eliminating the three-fifths rule and the Great Compromise clause that allotted equal numbers of senatorial seats to each state, controversies that survived the War of 1812 and into the era of the Missouri Compromise. Equally annoying to northerners was the Fugitive Slave Act of 1793, which mandated that white citizens of the northern states arrest and return self-emancipated slaves. Southern proslavery sympathizers in Congress had put further strength in the 1793 legislation by detailing how easily a slave master could seize runaway chattel by sending agents north with certificates that granted immunity from any prosecution for crimes stemming from the capture of a runaway. Taken together, such northern anxieties coalesced into fears of the Slave Power.

Northern worries over excessive and growing power for the southern states were part of the political discussions of Ruggles's youth and had to inform his early understanding of national politics. The Federalist positions were undoubtedly discussed in the Congregational and Methodist Churches where he spent his youth. In public, he could overhear local white leaders fulminate against southern tyranny.[36]

Lacking any legal means to join the new republican state government, Connecticut's African American population used rituals to emulate free politics and, in so doing, created a shadow government. Throughout the colonial period, enslaved Africans in New England regularly elected "governors" and "kings." Held in late May or early June, these informal ballots included expansive frolics with parades, feasts, drinking, fiddling, and dancing. Similar to Pinkster festivals in New York and New Jersey, Jon Cannoe festivals in the Carolinas, and Mardi Gras in Louisiana, election days became customary holidays in the mid-eighteenth century. Masters regularly allowed a week off to their celebrating bond peoples. After viva voce or public elections were held around ten o'clock in the morning, the loser toasted the winning candidate at the inauguration. The day continued with dancing, games of quoits, and other merriment. Norwich blacks practiced election day during the colonial period. Boston Trowtrow was governor until his death in 1772. Following him, Sam Hun'ton, the enslaved man of Governor Samuel Huntington, a Bean Hill resident, became governor of Connecticut blacks in his own right. After his election, he rode through town "on one of his master's horses, with plaited gear, his aides by his side, *a la militaire.*"[37] The governors exerted extensive control over fellow blacks. Although they lacked any legal powers, secret slave governments included judges, sheriffs, magistrates, and courts that tried other blacks for minor crimes and even administered such punishments as whippings.

While clearly important in the communal lives of Connecticut blacks, the election day custom does not yield a generally accepted historical interpretation. Joseph Reidy has interpreted election days as white-sponsored safety valves to release the daily pressures of servitude. There is also a fierce debate regarding whether election days were examples of African cultural survivals, as Sterling Stuckey and William Pierson contend, or indications of the assimilation of blacks into European mores, as Lorenzo Greene and Shane White propose. White suggests that election days enabled blacks to maintain some control over their lives. Eventually, he points out, such festivals transitioned into political processions. Joanne Melish has advanced a fourth and very useful interpretation, that the customs allowed blacks to institutionalize a shadow political identity parallel to formal, white political formations. Such an "imagined community," to borrow Benedict Anderson's well-known phrase, was a necessary precondition to black campaigns for actual civil rights in the nineteenth century. As the powerful egalitarianism of the

A Revolutionary Childhood

American Revolution sank roots deeper in society, second-generation free blacks such as Ruggles regarded all men and, at times, women as equals. There was never a doubt in their minds that blacks deserved the fruits of the revolutionary struggle. Infused with such republican ideals, they set forth to right the wrongs of society.[38]

Northern blacks after the Revolution strived to create institutions that would promote community and self-improvement. An additional step toward the reification of African concepts of government came from the formation of the Prince Hall Masons in Boston in 1775. Stymied from admission into the St. Andrew Lodge of white Masons, Hall and fourteen other blacks joined a British army lodge station near Boston that year. After the close of the Revolution, Hall and his cohorts applied to the Grand Lodge of England for permission to set up an independent black lodge. Although they did not receive permission until 1787, the Prince Hall Masons became leaders in the New England black community and, again, prepared blacks in the region for a form of self-governance and helped create a black social elite that was ready for a political fight for general rights and against slavery.[39]

Other political inspirations came directly from mainstream white politics. One of the major events in Norwich during David Ruggles's youth was the visit by the Marquis de Lafayette. Lafayette was a guest of James Monroe, who was president of the United States during the Revolutionary War hero's American tour in 1824–25. Lafayette, who had passed through Norwich several times during the American Revolution, stopped in the town again on August 21, 1824. He visited old friends there in town who embraced him and wept. It is impossible to know if Ruggles met Lafayette on this occasion (as indicated in the introduction, they were never correspondents), but certainly Lafayette made himself available to blacks. The teenage Ruggles may have been near when the Frenchman met Norwich's black leaders during his visit to the city. During the 1824 tour, he went to the homes of blacks in the South and publicly criticized the survival of slavery in the young republic. In Brooklyn, New York, he met with newly emancipated free blacks and greeted black children warmly.

There were ideological reasons for Lafayette's popularity among American blacks. He had always been antislavery and his friendship with the openly abolitionist lecturer Frances Wright brought the hero to a stronger position against human servitude. During his tour, he openly talked about the valor of black soldiers, to the consternation of his hosts. Even more threatening to whites in the United States, who were becoming more racist, was the encouragement and support he sought for Mrs. Wright's project for the settlement

Lithograph of Marquis de Lafayette by Maurin, ca. 1832. Lafayette's famous return tour of the United States in 1824–25 thrilled American blacks because he acknowledged their significant role in the American Revolution and denounced slavery. Ruggles may have been in the crowd when Lafayette passed through Norwich, Connecticut. Courtesy of the Division of Rare and Manuscript Collections, Cornell University Library.

of free blacks in what would become Tennessee. As a recent biographer concluded, the crowds that greeted the aging soldier were mixed with blacks and workers, pointing to the diversity of his fame.[40]

Lafayette's visit to Norwich perhaps opened David Ruggles's mind and eyes to the outside world. A year after Lafayette's visit, David Ruggles, now fifteen, departed from home, bound for New York City. There were practical reasons for leaving. The birth of his brother Henry meant that eight people now filled the tiny house on Sylvia's Lane. Ruggles had reached an age when further education was unlikely, and it was time for him to support himself. Perhaps still a turbulent young man at the age of fifteen, he went to sea, taking the trade of a mariner.

Why did he not stay to work with his father at blacksmithing? In a family of the size of David Ruggles Sr.'s, his eldest son had become redundant and even a burden. One can only speculate about tensions in the family, although either parent might have tired of the young David's misadventures. It is notable that David Jr. was the only child of the Ruggles family to leave Norwich.

If the tiny house on Sylvia's Lane had become confining and perhaps unwelcoming, the sea promised adventure and employment. Records for the percentages of blacks among Norwich's maritime workers are not available, but contemporary black proportions of crews in nearby Providence, Rhode

Island, and in New York City were between a fifth and a quarter of the whole. Ruggles's age, and perhaps the fears of his parents, probably restricted him to the relative familiarity of coastal work rather than the dangers of overseas travel. Moreover, there was far more work in the booming steamship business than in oceanic travel. Ruggles stationed himself in New York City, where he was first listed in the city directory as a mariner, living at 15 Chapel Street.[41]

Seafaring exposed Ruggles to militant black abolitionism. While his name does not appear on surviving crew lists from Norwich and nearby ports, it is highly likely that Ruggles worked at first from home. This would mean that he sailed in and out of New Bedford, Massachusetts, an important seaport close to Norwich. New Bedford's population included antislavery members of the Society of Friends (Quakers) who gave the town an abolitionist reputation. Female Quakers in New Bedford were unusually assertive and well organized, so that any contact Ruggles may have had with them would have reaffirmed the vision of women given him by his mother. The town was also home to sizable numbers of blacks working as sailors, boardinghouse keepers, and artisans. By the 1820s black residents in New Bedford had achieved sufficient militancy to combat any slave catchers who came to town seeking fugitives from bondage. New Bedford was not large and the physical distance between its respectable and rowdy worlds was but a block or so. A young seaman such as Ruggles could move easily from one to the other.[42]

In New Bedford, Ruggles met Nathan Johnson, a local black abolitionist leader. Johnson had become part of the antislavery movement in 1822, had participated in several legal actions to prevent the return of self-emancipated black people, and did not hesitate to join riots against perceived injustices. At one point, he asked to join the local Quaker meeting and received careful consideration, but his street rowdiness surely disqualified him. Given his later associations with Johnson, it is likely that Ruggles learned much from the New Bedford militant. Johnson would become one of Ruggles's most valuable and used contacts for safe placement of runaways. Johnson's methods combined legal actions and armed struggles to combat slave catchers, qualities that impressed Ruggles deeply.[43]

Life in New York as a coastal seafarer brought Ruggles into contact with a variety of sailors. Many were tough, rowdy proletarians. Peter Wheeler, for one, expressed his own vision of freedom through drinking and claimed that ownership of a pocket watch was his greatest pride. Approximately three-quarters of the free blacks in New York were such workers. Ruggles would encounter enslaved sailors, brought along by their masters and or hired out by landed masters. There were also intelligent, politically committed young men like himself among New York's mariner class. Even though racist exclusion was beginning to seep into saltwater work, going to sea remained one of the few occupations open to blacks in New York City and graduates of the elite African Free School learned navigational skills as part of the curriculum.[44]

Ruggles likely encountered free black sailors from the southern states who were veterans of the saltwater routes to freedom. The Atlantic Coast was the workplace for many free blacks from North Carolina, the Chesapeake, and northwards who had sheltered freedom-seeking bond people. Throughout the colonial period and into the early nineteenth century, ship captains rarely insisted on work references, and fugitive slaves were often able to make permanent the distance between themselves and their masters by shipping out on a coastal or international vessel. As David S. Cecelski has demonstrated, sailors provided runaways with a complex web of informants, messengers, go-betweens, and potential collaborators. From such men, Ruggles learned the mechanics, dangers, and successes of ocean-borne fugitives.[45]

Unlike the many fugitives he would later assist, Ruggles emerged from adolescence armed with a solid education, powerful self-esteem instilled by his strong and proud parents, and an ideology that encompassed evangelical perfectionism, antislavery resistance, and the legacies of the American Revolution. Ruggles combined his education, the political memories of the American Revolution, and Connecticut's antislavery legacy with the lived realities of his family and neighbors, particularly Aaron Cleveland. Ruggles learned ecumenism from Methodists, Baptists, and especially Congregationalists, members of denominations that fostered biblical knowledge and powerful self-will mixed with a sense of social responsibility. He imbibed the New Divinity movement at the Congregational Church with its inherent antislavery doctrines. At home, Ruggles became a hard worker, taking lessons from his father and mother and the local artisans. The valuable patronage of prosperous whites, abetted by his personal qualities, poised him for success in New York City.

✽ ✾ ✽

CHAPTER TWO

An Apprentice Abolitionist in
Post-Emancipation New York City

David Ruggles's seafaring brought him to New York City as early as 1825. He probably shuttled back and forth between New York and Norwich, as he had no recorded address in the big city. By 1827 he was listed in the city directory as a mariner. Unless he was on a voyage, Ruggles was in New York for the celebrations marking the extinction of slavery on July 4 and 5, 1827. *Freedom's Journal*, the nation's first black American newspaper, which began publication on March 16, 1827, heralded the festivities for months in advance. On July 4, New York City blacks held separate dinners to avoid confrontations with whites unwilling to yoke together the national holiday with the closure of slavery. Samuel Eli Cornish and John Russwurm, editors of *Freedom's Journal*, and other black leaders were anxious to avoid rowdy behavior that would undercut their efforts at self-uplift. They need not have worried. On July 5, two thousand blacks, including members of the New York African Society for Mutual Relief, the Wilberforce Benevolent Society, and the Clarkson Benevolent Society marched from St. John's Park to the Zion Church and then heard orations marking abolition day. Despite insulting behavior by white cartmen who interrupted the march by weaving their wagons among the celebrants, the parade announced that all blacks in New York State were legally free. Divisions among New York City blacks over proper public behavior and the participation of the masses were temporarily shelved, although they would reappear in the coming years. Whether or not he was present at the celebrations marking slavery's end in the state, the seventeen-year-old Ruggles now became part of New York City's freedom generation.[1]

New York City, David Ruggles's new home, was a dynamic city whose population had doubled every ten years since 1790. In 1830 census takers enumerated more than 200,000 New Yorkers. Blacks accounted for nearly 14,000 of that total. Their percentage of the total had dropped sharply since the initiation of gradual emancipation in New York in 1799, largely because of declining economic opportunity, worsening racism, illegal sales out of state, and unhealthy conditions stymieing natural population increase. Blacks had been a significant part of New York City's populace since the origins of settlement in 1613. Characteristically, colonial black New Yorkers were enslaved. Still, the city's black population had a rich heritage of cultural accomplishments. One area of achievement was education. The famed Trinity Church School, later labeled by W. E. B. Du Bois as the origin of black America's talented tenth, transformed after the American Revolution into the African Free School. Led by paternalist whites who were members of the New York Manumission Society or the Society of Friends, the school produced innumerable members of the local black elite, including the bulk of its ministry. Since 1795, black New York had had its own churches, including charter parishes of the African Methodist Episcopal and Zion churches, and St. Philip's Episcopal Church, ministered by the saintly Peter Williams Jr. Ancillary to these churches were the male African Society of Mutual Relief and the female Dorcas Society, both self-help organizations.[2]

Self-help and community organizations were mandatory in a charged racial environment. New York State had legally ended slavery, but in the aftermath of chattel bondage, the city's white residents were generally hostile toward the newly freed black population. Blacks had little political power. New York State had effectively disenfranchised them in the revised constitution of 1821 by requiring a heavy bond of $250 in property values for potential black voters. Even political reformers rejected blacks. In 1829 blacks attempted to join the Workingmen's Movement drive to end the city licensing of semiskilled jobs, including carting, meat cutting, and tavern keeping, but were firmly rebuffed. Job discrimination was rampant, from skilled work in the new industries to semiskilled labor in the carting business. There was an antislavery constituency among artisans, as many signed petitions against human bondage or joined the Manumission Society, but most city tradesmen opposed the hiring of black workers. Social ostracism of blacks was painful and annoying. Blacks were not allowed to ride on the city's ubiquitous horse-drawn omnibuses, forcing them to walk everywhere. There was no sanctuary in church, where Protestant denominations routinely restricted blacks to "Negro pews" far from the pulpit.[3]

Generally, New York City was unsafe for blacks. Much of this had to do with their miserable economic status. Blacks lived in the poorest neighborhoods, suffered most from epidemic diseases, and had shorter life expectancies. Public discrimination and insulting behavior toward blacks were rampant. New York's watchmen routinely harassed blacks and arrested them on the slightest pretext. Popular culture forms including plays, jokes, broadsides, and cartoons portrayed free blacks as vulgar, pretentious frauds, especially by lampooning their dress and language. To add insult to injury, New York's journalists regularly derided the presence of free blacks in the city and urged their expulsion.[4]

Making matters worse, New York City was highly receptive to southern slaveholders who enjoyed visiting the new metropolis and expected to be allowed to bring their chattel with them to provide the amenities of home. New York's shops, hotels, and restaurants catered to wealthy male and female southerners. Its streets and stores dazzled, frightened, and provoked envy among southerners on the Grand Tour. Doctors provided cures for illnesses untreatable in the South. Southern college students enjoyed the city during semester breaks from Princeton and other northern schools that welcomed their tuition fees and promised not to admit blacks. Southern businessmen and writers preferred the expertise of New York's printers. The sizable southern presence in the city meant that a fugitive slave's chance encounter with his former master was not slight.[5]

When masters were not able to come to New York, many hired slave catchers, widely labeled in the abolitionist community as kidnappers. The 1793 Fugitive Slave Act had several pernicious effects on black people's feelings of security and freedom. The law allowed state governments and military officers a pretext for invading territories of other nations, as shown in Andrew Jackson's Florida campaign against the Creek Indians in 1819. Despite the ban on the Atlantic slave trade enacted in 1808, the Fugitive Slave Law gave cover to illicit slave trading by Americans contracting with Portuguese sea captains. Finally, it practically invited southern masters to hire ruthless men to scour northern cities in search of runaway chattel or to prey upon free blacks. Enabled by sympathetic judges in New York, kidnappers regularly came to the city and grabbed any black whose appearance resembled their quarry.[6]

John Russwurm, the second editor of *Freedom's Journal*, warned fugitives not to settle in New York City or other northern ports. Rather, he advised, self-emancipated blacks should find "some sequestered country village where they might be out of danger." In New York City, fugitives could not trust "even their most intimate friends." He thundered that New York had many "vile traitors," who would quickly turn in their brethren. Elsewhere, Russwurm described blacks who turned in runaways as "snakes in the grass, charming unwary birds." Russwurm's angry words must have inspired the youthful Ruggles, who would use similar language in the future.[7]

Save for traitors to the race, New York's blacks did not passively accept the depredations of kidnappers. Black mobs openly battled the illegal seizure of free blacks and opposed the return of runaway slaves to the South. On several occasions in the early nineteenth century, blacks working with the New York Manumission Society rescued free blacks ensnared by kidnappers who were about to transport them for sale in the South. Riots against slave catchers first happened after the American Revolution and continued regularly during the early national period and then into the 1820s. In 1826, as David Ruggles was settling into the city, a large mob of blacks attended a judicial hearing designed to return a family of slaves to their Virginia masters. The crowd jostled the witnesses and complainants as they entered the court building. When the police came to break up the crowd, its members showered the constables with bricks and stones. These street-level actions showed the outrage of the black community toward official sanction of slave catchers. Ruggles thus found himself in a city where nameless, ordinary blacks did not hesitate to pick up a club or rock or use their fists to help ensure the freedom of their fellows. Anonymous crowds of blacks formed a major public opposition to slavery that inspired Ruggles.[8]

Ruggles was an educated man, so the vigorous number of books and pamphlets created by black New Yorkers surely exhilarated him. New York City's black community possessed a lengthy history of antislavery publishing. Beginning in the first years after the American Revolution, and picking up momentum after the end of the American involvement in the Atlantic Ocean slave trade in 1808, black pamphleteers commemorated distinguished blacks, annually lauded the closure of the Middle Passage, and proclaimed great moments in black history. In their writings, black writers challenged the nationalist deceptions of white political leaders and of historian George Bancroft, who proclaimed liberty and equality while sanctioning slavery and denying northern blacks basic civil rights. Black pamphleteers created a public intellectual tradition with their proud recounting of racial achievements and critiques of northern society and southern slavery.[9]

In 1828 David Ruggles, having abandoned seafaring, opened a small grocery shop at 1 Cortlandt Street at the corner of Broadway, just south of the city hall. He apparently lived in the shop, which was listed as his residence in the city directory. Unlike most young black migrants to the city, who often arrived penniless whether free or self-emancipated, Ruggles was armed with sufficient cash and credit to open a small shop. That he did so at the age of eighteen is even more remarkable and strongly indicates that he had sponsors other than his parents. He probably did not have to apply for a license. Grocers, chimney sweeps, porters, and livery drivers were the few city-licensed jobs blacks could undertake. Unlike bread baking, meat cutting, and carting, which were strictly controlled and almost entirely reserved for whites, regulation of grocers had loosened sufficiently enough that licenses were no longer necessary to open a shop. The trade had expanded to include innumerable unlicensed shops, many of which primarily sold alcohol. He was also fortunate that his store was located right in the city's central business district in a building that also housed a stagecoach company, a painter of miniature portraits, and a hairdresser. Although the neighborhood lacked the density of black population in the wards further north, Ruggles appealed to the black community for customers by placing store advertisements in *Freedom's Journal*.[10]

The editor of this pioneering newspaper was Samuel Eli Cornish, who would have an important impact on Ruggles. Born in a free black family in Delaware in 1795, Cornish moved to Philadelphia in 1815. There, after some schooling, he announced that he wanted to become a Presbyterian minister. At the time, there was but one black Presbyterian cleric, John Gloucester, a former slave from Tennessee. Gloucester was the founding minister of the nation's only black Presbyterian church, established in Philadelphia in 1807. From Gloucester, Cornish learned the value of effective leadership and organization as well as the need to master street-corner preaching. After eighteen months of arduous study, writing, and practice preaching, Cornish earned a probationary license from the Philadelphia Presbytery. When Gloucester fell ill, Cornish took partial ministerial responsibility at the First African Presbyterian Church. There he learned the difficult task of fundraising. Later the Presbyterian hierarchy recruited Cornish to minister to the impoverished New York City black population. Cornish's goals included battling poverty, prostitution, gambling, and drinking among the impoverished people of color. Cornish found a mentor in Reverend Ezra Stiles Ely, who pastored at the New York City Alms House, where he became committed to missions to the impoverished, lonely, and suffering. Cornish succeeded in establishing the

Samuel Eli Cornish. One of the first important black Presbyterian ministers, Cornish mentored Ruggles in journalism and antislavery. Courtesy of the Presbyterian Historical Society, Presbyterian Church (U.S.A.), Philadelphia.

First Colored Presbyterian Church in New York in 1824, although the costs of construction proved to be a financial millstone for the congregation. He was able to turn the church over to a younger man, Theodore S. Wright, who helped the congregation gain prominence in the next decade. Freed from the burdens of begging from white Presbyterians, Cornish turned his energies to combating the hostile prejudices of white New Yorkers.

The First Colored Presbyterian Church became a home base for Ruggles, a move that required a denominational change. In Norwich, Ruggles was raised in the Methodist and Congregational traditions. In New York City, black and white Presbyterians were more prominent in urban ministry and in the antislavery movement. The theological distance from Congregation-alism to Presbyterianism was not large. Membership there provided closer access to educated blacks such as Cornish and Wright and to fellow New Englander Charles Ray, Henry Highland Garnet, and self-emancipated slaves James W. C. Pennington and Samuel Ringgold Ward, all of whom would work closely with him in the near future. Ruggles may have been a member of more than one church. There is evidence that Ruggles later affiliated with the African Methodist Episcopal Church, the parish of New York's black working class. In the congregation around the same time as Ruggles was a recently freed woman named Isabella Van Wagenen, later to be known as Sojourner Truth.[11]

When Ruggles met him in 1828, Cornish had enlarged his goals of black uplift to combat an additional foe: the American Colonization Society (ACS). Supported by presidents, social leaders, and border-state southerners, the ACS proposed to sponsor the emigration of free blacks "back" to Africa where they could help Christianize the continent. The ACS's plan to cleanse the United States of free blacks appealed to few of them. In fact, the ACS was unable to convince many northern blacks to emigrate. Between 1834 and 1847, it convinced only fifty-six black northerners to go to Liberia. If its bite was ineffective, its bark was annoying. Its monthly magazine, the *African Repository*, routinely described free blacks as degraded and useless, characteristics that proud, educated blacks such as Cornish found false and insulting. For most of his career, Cornish, in his sermons at the First Colored Presbyterian Church, in his speeches, and as a newspaper editor fiercely attacked the colonization society. Ruggles, who had already experienced the condescending racism of the ACS in Connecticut, became an enthusiastic adherent of such messages.[12]

Cornish's other major achievement at this time was the creation of *Freedom's Journal*. Under Cornish's editorship, the newspaper was essential for blacks intent on learning about meetings of mutual relief, temperance, and literary and fraternal organizations; for information on births, marriages, and deaths; for advertisements for black-friendly businesses; and for historical articles aimed at bolstering black pride. Its editorials promoted black improvement and castigated perceived enemies of the black community. *Freedom's Journal* kept alive the memory of significant blacks with series on Paul Cuffe and Toussaint Louverture. Cornish spent ample time and space on efforts to improve black morality and education and used black heroes as examples to affirm self-discipline and achievement. By challenging racism, and emphasizing education and intellectual improvement, writers in *Freedom's Journal* heightened black consciousness, inspired racial egalitarianism, and created a culture of dissent. For the youthful Ruggles, all this was heady stuff that informed much of his thought and writing for years to come.[13]

Freedom's Journal was a good example of how black abolitionism worked and was financed. For gathering subscriptions, it relied substantially on its agents, who included the Boston radical David Walker, brothers Nathaniel and Thomas Paul, and Theodore S. Wright, all of whom were well connected in black communities in Boston, Albany, and New York City. They could tap benevolent whites such as Isaac Barton of Philadelphia, who knew Cornish through the esteemed black cleric Peter Williams Jr. Upstate New York abolitionist Gerrit Smith may have been another contributor. Other revenue came from advertisements and from subscriptions, though Cornish often complained about a lack of support from the black community.[14]

Within the pages of *Freedom's Journal*, Ruggles could read about current fugitive slave cases and illegal trafficking in slaves. The newspaper also printed contemporary words of revolution. In the winter of 1828, David Walker gave a fiery speech that was quickly reprinted in the black weekly. A year later, Walker expanded the jeremiad into a pamphlet titled *An Appeal to the Colored Citizens of the World*. Walker's slim pamphlet hit American society like a bomb. In it he condemned slavery and Thomas Jefferson's racial beliefs, blasted general racial prejudice, and denounced any black person who refused to fight for the citizenship rights of the race. Walker asserted the rights of black people to American citizenship, arguing that they had earned it with their labor and sacrifices. While he conceded that many white Americans, including Benjamin Rush, Benjamin Franklin, and Alexander Hamilton, had disputed Jefferson's smug, pretentious racism, Walker demanded that blacks must battle for their rights and must halt slavery and kidnapping. In a ringing affirmation of black manhood, Walker beseeched fathers to teach their sons to confront slave masters. In the most incendiary words, Walker counseled that if confrontation leads to violence, "kill or be killed . . . had you not rather be killed than to be a slave to a tyrant, who takes the life of your mother, wife, and dear little children?" Walker's words so aggravated white southerners that they administered severe punishments to blacks found with the pamphlet. Northern blacks received Walker's words proudly. As James and Lois Horton have observed, only through this primal assertion of masculinity could blacks ascend to the more humane and socially acceptable manhood associated with republican citizenship. Black writers had decried the evils of slavery for decades. Walker's message was that slavery had to end immediately. Two years before William Lloyd Garrison coined the term "immediatism," Walker announced the concept in his pamphlet.[15]

Walker's fusion of political sarcasm and biblical allusions caught fire with northern blacks. Imagine the impact the pamphlet must have had on the nineteen-year-old Ruggles. Already imbued with abolitionist sentiments, Ruggles could see that the time to battle slavery and prejudice with one's life was now. Walker's demands upon his fellow blacks mandated activism and wholehearted confrontation with the forces of slavery and northern discrimination. As Walker dismantled Jefferson's hypocrisy (at the very time when Jefferson's collected works were selling widely among white readers), young blacks such as Ruggles no longer had to settle for the patronizing words of colonizationists or northern apologists for slavery. Rather, Walker made anger into a driving force for change and the immediate emancipation of all slaves into a rallying cry. Although Walker died suddenly in 1830, his words lived on. Many black New Yorkers and more than a few white southerners believed erroneously but tellingly that Walker's *Appeal* directly encouraged Nat Turner's Revolt in Virginia in 1831, an action that indicated to black activists that the time for militant action toward slavery was nigh.[16]

There is little doubt that Ruggles read Walker's *Appeal*. Yet, should he or any other young black New Yorker have missed it, there was an equally messianic jeremiad available in the city. Robert Alexander Young's *Ethiopian Manifesto* told of a coming race war led by a man who appeared to be white but was born of a black woman. Once he appeared, this leader would teach slaveholders that their hour was coming "when poverty would be a blessing." Even more than Walker's *Appeal*, Young's *Manifesto* was radically divorced from political solutions and spoke to the messianic hopes of the disenfranchised black population in New York City. While Young was vague about a specific course of action, he was adamant about racial pride in blackness, in a membership of a people who would emerge triumphant in a day of reckoning. Young gave voice to the apocalyptic rage felt by a postslavery generation angry about the loss of civil rights in New York City.[17]

After Walker's death and the closing of *Freedom's Journal* in 1829, northern blacks lacked a print outlet for radical expression. David Ruggles and other black New Yorkers coalesced to support William Lloyd Garrison and his newspaper, the *Liberator*, founded on January 1, 1831. Within a month after the weekly's first appearance, "young men of color" in New York City met at the Boyer Lodge to rally for the newspaper. The group first resolved to condemn the American Colonization Society. Then a committee of nine formed to build support for the Boston abolitionist's newspaper. Ruggles joined with members of the New York African Society for Mutual Relief as agents for the newspaper and was soon canvassing young city blacks to help increase readership of the *Liberator* and of Benjamin Lundy's *Genius of Universal Emancipation*. Black subscribers to his weekly, acknowledged Garrison, outnumbered whites and were more prompt in paying their bills. Garrison cemented his friendship with New York's black abolitionists when he condemned the ACS

William Lloyd Garrison.
Garrison's newspaper, the *Liberator*,
and his uncompromising antislavery ideology and actions lifted the hearts of free blacks
around the country. Collection of the author.

in his publication, *Thoughts on African Colonization*, in 1832. New York black leaders Peter Williams, William Hamilton, Thomas Sipkins, and Thomas L. Jennings gave financial assistance to Garrison to publish his book and joined many other black abolitionists with testimonials in a lengthy appendix. Garrison returned their support by making the newspaper a forum for articles by blacks about black issues.[18]

The arrival of radical black and abolitionist publishing between 1827 and 1832, in addition to the revolutionary example of Nat Turner in Virginia, excited and inspired Ruggles and his contemporaries, who constituted a new wave of committed, demanding activists in 1830s New York City. To be sure, there were admired elders such as Peter Williams Jr., William Hamilton, and Christopher Rush, all born before 1783 and slightly younger men such as Samuel Eli Cornish, born in 1795, and Theodore S. Wright, born in 1797, but the bulk of New York's black leadership was Ruggles's age or even younger. This youthful cohort of frustrated, intelligent, ambitious, well-educated activists butted against the prejudices of white New Yorkers and gave the new black radicalism a harder, more militant style. David Ruggles later summed up this new attitude well by noting, "The pleas of crying soft and sparing never answered the purpose of a reform, and never will."[19]

Ruggles's comment nailed the dilemma that would inspire and plague abolitionism over the next decade. In William Lloyd Garrison's embrace of moral suasion, there was no room for physical resistance. Garrison himself had been mobbed and tossed in jail and would be again. Still, white abolitionists eschewed the subject of resistance and argued that violence lowered them to the level of slaveholders. This abstract argument went to the heart of the differences between white and black immediatists. Although white abolitionists suffered mobbing and, on rare occasions, martyrdom, few experienced the frequent pangs of anguish when kidnappers and slave traders tore families apart or stood humiliated as slave catchers paraded their young blacks in chains through the streets en route to the docks, where vessels would speed their prey southward for sale. Both were common hazards for blacks, whether activists or ordinary citizens. This is not to downplay the suffering that white abolitionists experienced, but the damage to free blacks was more widespread and occurred outside of any ideological stance. This meant that the tension over resistance, posed clearly by Walker, remained taut.[20]

Writing and public talks were in the future. For now, Ruggles had to attend to the business of making a living. His first contributions to *Freedom's Journal* were advertisements. Promoting his new store, Ruggles emphasized the quality and quantity of his supply of butter. A notice, dated April 8, 1828, suggests that Ruggles had recently opened the shop, located in the "large Cellar under Mr. Whitefield's Stage Office" at 1 Cortlandt Street at the corner of Broadway. Ruggles primarily sold butter and sugar in wholesale or small quantities. He also publicized abolitionist sentiments in the advertisements, proclaiming that the "Sugars above mentioned are free sugars—they are manufactured by free people, not by slaves." Ruggles's alliance with the Free Produce movement had several effects. For one thing, it brought him into contact with white and black women who were against slavery and for whom purchasing Free Produce goods was a conscious moral choice, especially in a city with abundant food for sale. Ruggles and his female customers were able to make political decisions out of mundane daily purchases. Female advocates of Free Produce spread the word about his sin-free staples and thereby helped business. At the same time, getting the food was inconvenient; its purchase required special orders from sympathetic farmers and merchants.[21] Ruggles now accentuated his supplies of Goshen butter. He probably obtained the

An Apprentice Abolitionist

butter from Goshen, New York, up the Hudson River, and easily accessible to the city.[22] By the following spring, the grocer's notices changed substantially.

Ruggles had embraced a second reform movement. When he first opened his store, Ruggles advertised the sales of "Rum, Gin, Brandy, Wine, Cordials, Porter and Cider, etc. as well as "superior Canton Tea and Sugars . . . Coffee, Tea, Flour, Goshen Butter, Cheese, etc." Ruggles stopped vending alcohol when *Freedom's Journal* underwent an editorial change. On September 14, 1827, Samuel Eli Cornish, pressured by his Presbyterian superiors who were upset at the anticolonization line taken in the newspaper, stepped down as editor. Cornish's decision indicates that he valued his ties to the Presbyterian Church more than to the newspaper. John Russwurm replaced Cornish as editor for two years, and then shocked the black community in 1829 by embracing the cause of colonization and, embittered by racism in American society, taking a job as minister of education in Liberia. He closed down the newspaper. In March 1829 Cornish, presumably with the permission of Presbyterian officials, started a new black weekly, the *Rights of All*. Ruggles advertised his grocery shop in Cornish's newspaper but no longer mentioned sales of alcohol. Cornish clarified this change in a brief notice published in the fall of 1829, which commended Ruggles for his patriotic use of American groceries and because he no longer sold liquors, which "should recommend him to our patronage." Cornish had espoused temperance in *Freedom's Journal* in 1827, and his approval of Ruggles's conversion was among the first of their many collaborations. Ruggles may have been impressed as well by the links reformer Heman Humphrey made in his widely distributed 1828 tract, *A Parallel Between Intemperance and the Slave Trade*.[23]

Ruggles's brief dalliance with alcohol sales indicates another aspect of his young personality. Trumpeting sales of spirits was hardly surprising, as many groceries in New York were little more than grog shops, where on Saturday nights laborers spent their weekly earnings. Ruggles doubtless enjoyed the vibrant social world of the young in New York City. He lived a short walk from the Five Points, a neighborhood where grocery stores selling cheap alcohol competed for attention with basement groggeries and every night music, dancing, and prostitutes were readily available. One possible insight into his mentality at this time may be found in his ownership of a small pamphlet now housed at the American Antiquarian Society. Titled *The Humorist*, this compendium included "Entertaining Tales, Anecdotes, Epigrams, Bon Mots filled with stories of bacchanalias, witchcraft and the virtues of strong alcohol." The American Antiquarian Society copy bears Ruggles's autograph. Had he desired sexual companionship, the streets were filled with prostitutes who sold sex to the city's significant bachelor population. Some catered to the black citizens of the city.[24]

Black New York had a sizable picaresque population. At the top were young black swells and their ladies. Apolitical in attitude, made blasé by the repressive racism and lack of civil rights, these young blacks preferred fun to activism. Of the first generation of New Yorkers who could afford ready-made clothing attainable through the city's factories and sweat shops, black dandies spent ample cash on expensive clothing. Their lives focused around pleasurable activities, including evenings strolling in their finery at Castle Garden or on Broadway, at dress balls, enjoying ice cream, and attending dramas at the African Grove Theatre. The theatrical fare at the Grove included Shakespeare's plays, with lines adapted especially for the black audience. An equally popular presentation was *Life in London*, derived from Pierce Egan's popular novel of college students and youthful gentry slumming at cockfights, boxing matches, and hired amours in Regency London. Just as Londoners did, black New Yorkers preferred partying to battling the harsh limitations on their lives. If Englishmen lived under the tyranny of a monarch, black New Yorkers chafed under the rule of a *Herrenvolk* democracy that offered freedom of opportunity to whites and barred blacks from economic success. Despairing of any progress, many in this first generation of black New Yorkers coming of age after the abolition of slavery preferred dancing, blood sports, and the bottle to the battle against discrimination. Described by Shane White as exemplars of cultural freedom in the aftermath of slavery, such laborers, domestics, artists, and small tradesmen were petty urbanites. They lacked the wealth and social status of their counterparts in New Orleans, St. Louis, or Charleston, South Carolina. Contemporary white artists lampooned this new generation in racist cartoons, which are now studied by scholars in search of the roots of racism; black urbanites anticipated and influenced the styles of the later Bowery B'hoys and G'hals. Still, just as the sports of Regency England performed for nobility, the black entertainers of New York did their best before crowds of butchers. Overcoming their cynicism and convincing petty urbanites of the utility of activism for civil rights and against slavery would not be easy. Ruggles would have more success with the black middle class and aroused members of the black working class.[25]

Ruggles faced personal struggles. In October 1829 he moved his business down the street to 36 Cortlandt Street. He advertised his groceries for sale at the store or "delivered to any part of the city." He obtained this store through Norwich connections. The previous proprietor was Elizabeth Bliss, widow of David Bliss, a bookseller, a native of Bean Hill, and next-door neighbor to the Ruggles family. When Ruggles moved into the shop, it undoubtedly still had shelves with room for butter and books. The *New York Spectator* reported on December 18, 1829, that someone using a stolen key entered Ruggles's store late on Sunday night and, "after taking $280, various articles, and destroying others, attempted to set the place on fire." Between three and four o'clock in the morning, a watchman discovered the blaze and was able to extinguish it; however, the fire destroyed most of the store. The newspaper noted that Ruggles "was an industrious man" who, despite prejudice against his skin color, had "by his conciliating manners, laid the foundation of a desirable little business, in the butter and grocery trade." Unluckily, the writer continued, "his prospects have been totally blighted."[26]

Ruggles went out of business after the fire, but when he returned to the public record, he had joined the abolitionist movement. By 1831 he reopened a store at 3 Cortlandt Street where he remained until 1832, then moved up the block to 15 Cortlandt Street until late in 1833. He combined the grocery business with antislavery activity in this store. Upon the recommendation of Thomas L. Jennings, a leader of the black middle class and a staunch advocate for black civil rights, Ruggles hired escaped slaves Samuel Ringgold Ward and his brother Isaiah Harper Ward. Samuel Ringgold Ward subsequently taught at a church school before becoming a distinguished Congregational minister and proponent of expanded black civil rights.[27]

The early 1830s were transitional times for the abolitionist movement in New York City. Calls for the immediate end of slavery in the United States, a cause that blacks had desired for years, now found adherents among whites. Many white abolitionists were formerly adherents of the colonization movement. Now they moved to the belief known as immediatism, which generally held that slavery was a sin and that slaves should be freed unconditionally, immediately, and without any compensation to their former masters. Among immediatists, the followers of William Lloyd Garrison were the most radical. Garrisonians believed that American society, North and South, was fundamentally immoral. Slavery was but the worst of American faults, and only a complete change in institutional structure and ideology could cure its evil. Gradualist reformers, in contrast, upheld the essential goodness of northern society and believed that elimination of slavery would solve a vexing but marginal problem. Such differences were deeply ideological and fueled growing divisions within the overall antislavery movement.[28]

In theory, immediatists subscribed to a doctrine of racial equality. But beyond those general tenets, agreement faltered. What immediatism meant and how it would be conducted differed sharply among its supporters. While the colonization movement accused its former allies of wanting instant freedom for all slaves, most immediatists had a conservative view by which freed people would be under the constraint of the law, rather than outside it, as they now were as slaves. Immediatism in the early 1830s was a halfway step between the cold, legalistic formulas of gradual emancipation in the era following the Revolutionary War and the freedoms enjoyed by blacks following President Abraham Lincoln's Emancipation Proclamation in 1863. During the 1830s, white immediatists viewed their proposals for abolition as systems of restraint and protection, concepts that eventually were incorporated into the Fourteenth Amendment. They differentiated between civil rights and political rights, which, for example, meant that blacks would not have the power of the ballot.[29]

William Lloyd Garrison, in particular, was a lightning rod for the abolitionist debate. Garrison's messages and methods resonated powerfully, and within a few years, the number of organizations adhering to his principles multiplied. Shortly after the founding of the New England Anti-Slavery Society in Boston in January 1832, the movement blossomed into a national organization. The American Anti-Slavery Society, founded in Philadelphia in December 1833, held its first national convention in New York in May 1834. Its mission, articulated in its constitution, included the immediate abolition of slavery, an immediate end to the internal slave trade, and strong efforts toward the "elevation of the character and condition of the people of color." Garrison, whose activities largely centered on Boston, appealed to blacks through his platform of immediatism and equality.

Garrison forged a number of principles over the next decade. They included a staunch endorsement of moral perfectionism, by which he and his followers avoided contamination with involvement in politics, clericalism, and much of organized religion. Garrisonians advocated northern withdrawal from the American Union and regarded elections as shams that opened the true and pure citizen to compromise with devilish slaveholders. A significant tenet was firm adherence to pacifism and nonresistance. Garrison did more than avoid the impure life. For one, he advocated women's rights and quality. He also demanded civil rights for blacks and was way in advance of other white abolitionists in his social engagement with free people of color, two qualities that endeared Garrison to black Americans, who trusted him and offered powerful allegiance to his efforts. At the same time, as will be made plain, Ruggles and other black Americans did not follow in lock step with all of Garrison's beliefs. In so doing, they were akin to many white abolitionists who took some if not all of his teachings to heart.

Garrison's influence was wide. As Aileen Kraditor has explained, a Garrisonian was someone who, while not necessarily agreeing with Garrison's teachings on religion, politics, or the "woman" question, accepted that the movement incorporated many reforms, provided there was unity about abolitionist principles. An Anti-Garrisonian, whose beliefs coalesced later, sought to narrow activities and membership strictly to antislavery actions that would not alienate the general northern public. A radical Garrisonian, by opposition, believed that slavery had tainted northern as well as southern society and that a total overhaul was necessary.[30]

Garrison's widespread support among New York blacks led to their sponsorship of his 1833 publication of *An Address Delivered in Boston, New-York, and Philadelphia Before the Free People of Color in April, 1833*. In this publication Garrison used several themes that would percolate through radical abolitionism in the next few years. He applauded emancipation of the slaves in the British Empire and referred to Britain as a "repentant nation! . . . Her people are humbling themselves before God, and before those whom they have so long held in bondage." As appealing as this overture was to northern blacks, it infuriated southern slave owners, many of whom felt the abolitionist movement was treasonous. Garrison made no apologies for this. In the talk, he admitted his words were harsh, but noted that their "strength bears no proportion to the enormous guilt of the slave system. . . . I wish [the epithets of the English language] were heavier." Assuredly Ruggles was listening to or read these words of defiance, which gave him confidence that his vehement emotions and words had positive moral virtue. Garrison realized his effect on his black auditors: he admitted that his words were "calculated to make you bear all your trials and difficulties in the spirit of Christian resignation and induce you to return good for evil."[31]

Aligned to Garrison, yet separate in philosophy and approach were the Tappan brothers of New York City. Arthur and Lewis Tappan, originally from Northampton, Massachusetts, moved to New York City and became prosperous silk merchants. Initially Unitarian, the Tappans transferred to the evangelical Presbyterian Church in New York City. Both were staunch adherents of the peace movement and believed in "moral suasion" to end slavery. Because of their advocacy of pacifism, the Tappans did not yet endorse economic pressure or political action to bring about the extinction of slavery, but they moved inexorably toward those positions. Although they

Lewis Tappan, wealthy financier and bankroller of the black antislavery movement. Courtesy of the Library of Congress.

initially supported Garrison's New England Anti-Slavery Society, by 1833 they started publication of the *Emancipator*, a rival antislavery newspaper, and then formed the American Anti-Slavery Society in 1833 with Garrison. The new organization retained a limited version of immediatism, arguing that newly freed blacks should be placed under protection of the law and receive some education before full emancipation. Other statements in its constitution that Ruggles would find useful included assertions that black women had no protection against their masters and that slave ownership bred licentiousness. Arthur Tappan was especially generous with antislavery organizations and soon became one of the movement's most significant financial backers. Just as they pledged their cash to support Garrison, New York's black activists quickly subscribed to the *Emancipator*.[32]

A third arm of the white abolitionist community in New York City was the much older New York Manumission Society. Formed immediately after the American Revolution by a fusion of Quakers, Episcopalians, and some radical republicans, the New York Manumission Society was instrumental in pushing through the Gradual Emancipation Act of 1799; founded the African Free School, which educated local black leaders; and supported black refugees from slavery. By 1830 it had two main factions. One, led by William Jay, was primarily interested in a moderate approach to immediatism and the colonization society and to the continued efforts of the African Free School. A lesser-known but equally active wing led by Barney Corse, a wealthy Quaker tanner and leather dresser, and the venerable activist, Isaac T. Hopper, battled slave catchers who came into New York to kidnap free blacks. The committee, for example, had helped Isabella Van Wagenen (later Sojourner Truth) reclaim a son who had been kidnapped and taken to Alabama.

Agents of slave masters, abetted by local magistrates, were willing to grab any blacks who looked like escaped slaves, haul them onto boats, and take them south into servitude. A number of free blacks in New York had lost their liberty through this legally sanctioned method of slave trading. In 1828 the New York State legislature, following the lead of Pennsylvania, made writs of habeas corpus available to slave catchers, which allowed them to secure the arrest of an alleged fugitive. As conducted in New York courts, this was sometimes a pro forma matter, and the black person could be forced into transit to southern slavery in a matter of hours. A second component of the act was the writ of *homine replegiando*, which required a jury trial for accused fugitives, denied the masters the common-law right of recaption, and made the master liable for court costs and damages if his suit was rejected. It was the clearest attempt made by any state legislature to protect both the rights of master and of escaped slave in any New York judicial code. Barney Corse had used this writ effectively since the late 1820s. Blacks would push it further and further over the next decade.[33]

The Phoenix Society, a black self-improvement and abolitionist organization, dedicated itself to visiting the home of every black person in the city to convince him or her to subscribe to the *Emancipator*. The Phoenix Society was an expanded version of a reading-club concept initiated in 1825 in Philadelphia. The New York society included in its list of officers and members many notable local blacks, such as movement veterans Peter Williams Jr., Samuel Hardenburgh, Thomas Downing, Boston Crummell, and William Hamilton. Christopher Rush, the president, was among the few younger abolitionists. Ruggles would soon play an important role. The Phoenix Society was particularly concerned that cultural information be available to young black

New Yorkers, who were normally denied access even to such institutions as the Zoological Institute. The Phoenix Society members had ambitious plans, including raising cash for a building that would be used as a library, reading room, museum, or exhibition hall where young black New Yorkers could hear lectures and study classical and mechanical arts. Samuel Eli Cornish was a strong proponent of the library and sought donations for the building. The Phoenix Society was successful enough that it rented a building, offered lectures, and attracted crowds of more than five hundred people to them. Cornish was indicative of its members in that he put extraordinary energies into the society at the same time that he worked hard at antislavery efforts. For young blacks such as Ruggles, the Phoenix Society was a community commitment to emphasize reading and writing as expressions of freedom.[34]

New York City blacks created their own networks of antislavery activity. Key to their efforts was the black convention movement that began in Philadelphia in 1830 and met there until 1834, when it shifted to New York for a year, then returned to Philadelphia before lapsing until a meeting in Buffalo, New York, in 1843. Designed to build upon electoral conventions organized by the white political parties, the Philadelphia meetings first attracted significant members of the black leadership to debate emigration to Canada and then moved on to encouraging benevolent and temperance societies and educational institutions. As much as anything, they allowed black leaders to meet, form alliances, and prepare for the day when they would have real political power. New Yorkers were enthusiastic participants, and the first convention was nearly held there. To pursue their goals and to create local unanimity, blacks in New York City instituted their own antislavery society. Meeting on December 26, 1832, at the Abyssinian Baptist Church, the city's people of color elected Samuel Hardenburgh as chair and Henry Sipkins as secretary. The new organization first saluted European supporters of the black convention movement. Those whose support was widely reported included James Cropper and Thomas Cropper in England and Daniel O'Connell of Ireland, whom the group hailed as friends to black rights and religious freedom and saluted for their opposition to the American Colonization Society. Ruggles, not yet twenty-three years of age, surely watched eagerly in the audience while older men shaped this instrument of black abolitionism.[35]

As important as the antislavery institutions were, another force growing in importance was the legion of escaped slaves, who, undeterred by New York City's reputation as a slave catchers' paradise, filtered into the city alone or in groups. New York's black community was electrified in 1832 by the arrival of ten escaped slaves from Southampton County, Virginia. Angered, the governor of Virginia demanded their immediate return. The fugitives, the governor contended, had stolen a whaleboat in order to make their flight and were thereby guilty of a felony. Inherent in his demand was the belief that the slaves were also property and that failure to return them to Virginia was an attack on the fundamental premises of Virginia laws of property. The case would not be decided until 1837.[36]

As much as Ruggles and other black activists supported the actions of the antislavery societies and the New York Manumission Society, they found further unity in condemnation of the American Colonization Society (ACS). Founded in 1817 in Virginia and Washington City and quickly adopted by residents of northern states, especially New Jersey, the ACS offered bounties to free blacks willing to relocate to Liberia, an American-supported state on the West Coast of Africa. Blacks had previously supported a return to Africa. The revered Paul Cuffe sponsored an expedition by blacks during the second decade of the century. But northern blacks turned sharply against the ACS, deriding it as racist and caustically noting that it did nothing to end slavery. The ACS was, like the immediatist movement, a descendant of the post-Revolutionary evangelical desire to end racial antagonism. It was also descended from the gradualist, white-dominated abolition movements of the post-Revolutionary decades. To the members of the ACS, the immediatists were dangerous utopians willing to free slaves irresponsibly and wreak havoc on American society. If today the ACS's plan to convince free blacks to abandon America in favor of an insecure settlement in Africa seems hopelessly impossible, nonetheless the ACS enjoyed the greatest political and social support of white Americans of any scheme concerning black destiny before the Civil War. During its most popular period in the 1820s, ACS proponents tried to persuade masters to educate their bond people to seek new lives as Christian missionaries in Africa. Always attractive to the nation's elite, the ACS was dominated by Virginians, who denounced free blacks as ignorant, insane, hopeless, and "a vile excrescence upon society." They enthusiastically boasted of their respect for the legal rights of slave owners.[37]

The ACS had been active in New York since 1817 when prominent citizens, including Mayor Jacob Radcliffe, formed an auxiliary society to the national organization. The next year it sponsored a boatload of free blacks from the Middle Atlantic region who were willing to emigrate to Africa. The disastrous results—more than half of the migrants died within six months of landing in Liberia—curtailed the enthusiasm of the New York supporters of the ACS, and the auxiliary society soon withered. It was revived in 1823 by the Presbyterian cleric, Loring D. Dewey. Assisted by grants from Henry Rutgers and Dr. John Griscom, Dewey kept the colonization idea alive for several years without attracting many émigrés. In 1828 Dewey split the organization by pursuing free black migration to Haiti. In the late 1820s, newer leaders appeared. Lewis Tappan, later a key supporter of immediatism, pushed the formation of statewide societies. While this movement foundered, supporters of the ACS pursued the goal of a central society in New York City. Several attempts were made there in the late 1820s, and then a more formal society was founded in New York on January 11, 1831, in a public meeting held at the Middle Dutch Church. Numerous distinguished and notable New Yorkers attended. The new society declared itself a branch of the ACS and set a goal of instituting subsidiary societies around the city.

Despite the paucity of its record, the ACS was a potentially dangerous threat to black New Yorkers. In 1830 around fourteen thousand blacks lived in New York County (present-day Manhattan). A legislative decision akin to the federal government's expulsion of Cherokees from Georgia could reduce, if not eliminate, black life in New York City within a few years. Abolitionists were part of the campaign against Indian removal, using pamphlets and petitions to equate the tyranny against the Cherokee with slavery. There was but a small jump to link the ACS's intentions with that of the American governments actions toward native peoples of the Southeast, and some contended that the ACS "stands in the same attitude to our colored population, as Georgia does to the Cherokees." In a public meeting two weeks later on January 25, black activists Philip A. Bell and Samuel Ennals led a mass meeting to protest the organization, its methods, and its goals of forcing migration upon free blacks. Beginning now to speak more freely and openly in public, David Ruggles gave several words of encouragement at this meeting and at another one held a few weeks later in Battery Park.[38]

David Ruggles soon found an outlet to express his anger at the ACS. On June 26, 1833, the Tappans showed their confidence in Ruggles by making him the general agent of their fledgling newspaper, the *Emancipator*. In this role, he attended an informational meeting on July 10, 1833, in Philadelphia at which recently returned émigrés to Liberia told of their experiences. In his first published letter, Ruggles acted as a reporter for the *Emancipator*, though his aim was also to convince the *New York Observer* and the *Baptist Register* to publish his account. At the meeting, Joseph Washington, James Price, and a Reverend Gibbins gave reports on ACS activities in Africa and answered questions. Washington described Liberia as a death trap. He contended that the ACS deceived prospective migrants who, upon arriving, received tiny grants of five acres only after they had built a home. Widows and other single women, he declared, "are denied the right of holding property." According to Washington, coffee, rice, and sugar crops were insufficient for local use or export. James Price added that he left the United States because of oppressive laws but found only deception and corruption in Liberia. The only abundances were in rum and funerals. English lessons to the local inhabitants were given only to make them salable as slaves. Ruggles quoted the speakers carefully, then editorialized, "Comment on my part is useless. . . . Let those who profess to take the Bible for their guide, read these plain truths; mark, learn and inwardly digest them." Then they should decide for themselves if they should "support such unrighteous scheme which is now carrying devastation and death wherever its influence is felt." Ruggles was developing a theme he would pursue in larger form in the near future. The ACS acted in ways that violated its Christian duties. The Christian churches of the United States were culpable in the evil designs of the ACS; their lies led to the moral destruction, poverty, and death of any black naive enough to listen to them and leave for Liberia. The colony, as he described it in a May 1834 letter, was a "Sepulcher," where black Americans would find not prosperity but death. In Ruggles's mind, American Protestant churches were as culpable as the ACS and the slave masters.[39]

The animosities held by white and black antislavery activists against the ACS slowly moved into the general populace of New York State. One reason was the antislavery forces' effective mail campaign. Ralph Gurley, the secretary of the ACS, complained that every mailbox in upstate New York was filled with antislavery newspapers. Fundraising for the ACS declined in New York because of the attacks by abolitionist forces and because few local blacks showed any interest in migrating to Africa. Gurley wrote to his colleagues in Philadelphia in April 1834 about the low esteem the public felt toward the ACS. He wondered if the ACS had the means to get the commercial newspapers to print favorable stories about its programs. At the same time, the New York society had severe financial problems. By late 1833, it was nearly forty thousand dollars in debt.[40]

In 1833 Ruggles quit the grocery business and devoted himself full time to the abolitionist movement, first as general agent and then as general traveling agent for the *Emancipator*. It is unclear how much Ruggles was paid for his labors and traveling expenses because he is not listed in the American Anti-Slavery Society Agency Minutes. Most white agents were paid at the rate of five hundred dollars per year plus traveling expenses. Some were paid more.[41] Black agents were rarely listed or paid equal wages. Ruggles was one of the very few black agents for the *Emancipator*. Indeed, in 1833, he was one of the paper's only agents. The job paid little, required endless and difficult travel, and could be dangerous. Agents for antislavery newspapers were descendants of the religious missionaries who had worked the American countryside since the Great Awakening a century before. Traveling agents performed the critical work of convincing rural Americans of the evils of slavery. Beginning in 1832, the New England Anti-Slavery Society combined forces with the American Anti-Slavery Society to send emissaries on long trips into the countryside to rally people in the cause against slavery. Amos Phelps, Samuel J. May, and Charles Burleigh took yearlong missions by 1835.[42]

As did Phelps, May, Burleigh, and other agents, Ruggles traveled to spread the good word about abolitionism, making valuable contacts with local activists, booksellers, and publishers. He encountered local black activists, who, like their white counterparts, subscribed to the *Emancipator* and provided places for rest and refuge for the wandering agent. Black churches opened their doors to Ruggles and could be trusted to respond vociferously at rallies where Ruggles denounced slavery. Ruggles could, as Patrick Rael has pointed out, create a shared interest with other blacks through his powerful public speeches. He could also reach out to white men and women who were sympathetic or wanted to be.[43]

Ruggles was not listed in the New York City directory in 1833. It is possible that he was on the road almost continuously. His position, which involved much traveling, enabled Ruggles to become acquainted with fellow abolitionists throughout the Mid-Atlantic region. On April 18, 1833, he attended a public meeting in Newark, New Jersey, organized to support William Lloyd Garrison's trip to Europe. In addition, John A. King, the chair, announced that the meeting was intended to solicit subscriptions for the *Emancipator*. Ruggles spoke out against the American Colonization Society and "delivered an eloquent address" on the importance of education through the press. In July 1833 Ruggles attended a series of meetings in Philadelphia about the status of the colony of Liberia. Largely straight reporting, the articles were published in the *Emancipator*. The article quoted questions and answers that established that Liberia produced little coffee or rice, had few farms, and was a place where English was taught only to entice Africans into slavery; in addition, it sold much rum and was very hard place to leave. On August 19, 1833, he explained to an audience at a black church in Lewiston, Pennsylvania, the object of the First Convention of the Colored People that had been held recently in New York City. Back in New York City, on November, 13, 1833, he delivered another address on the purposes of the Ladies' Literary Society and the African Dorcas Society and the desired effects such organizations should have on black people. Ruggles then published accounts of his travels and activities in the *Emancipator*, thereby enlarging his reputation and contacts.[44]

How long Ruggles traveled throughout New Jersey and Pennsylvania is not known, but his efforts were among the earliest for any antislavery agent and among the most dangerous. Most agents traveled short distances near their hometowns. Ruggles went deep into Pennsylvania, going almost to the Ohio border. He mixed his antislavery talk with speeches designed to quiet fears over "amalgamation," the nineteenth-century term for mixed-race sex, probably debated colonizationists, and helped to form local antislavery societies. Although the work was hard, lonely, and sometimes dangerous, agents rarely regretted their tasks and finished their missions filled with inspiration. Ruggles became accustomed to working with and convincing large crowds of curious whites in settings far from New York City. Richard Newman has demonstrated the vast efforts and impact of white abolitionists in Massachusetts. Ruggles's impact on Pennsylvania and New Jersey must have been equally profound.[45]

An event during his tour of Anti-Slavery Societies in Pennsylvania in the autumn of 1833 alerted Ruggles to another theme in his message. Traveling from Pittsburgh after midnight, Ruggles described riding in a company in a coach composed of "two ladies, two gentlemen, a two-legged animal and myself." Because of the "Egyptian darkness," no one could make out the others' faces. The issue of slavery came up and all declared their opposition to it. When talk turned to colonization, the women supported it and one gentleman was "on the fence," while the "animal" supported colonization and raged against abolitionists because of their support for "amalgamation." Ruggles pointed out to the "animal" that amalgamation had nothing to do with the issue. Instantly, Ruggles's antagonist asked if he would marry a black woman. Ruggles replied that he would sooner marry a black than a white woman. This answer shocked the "animal." When the ladies were asked their opinions, they declared themselves unready to marry anyone. The colonizationist insisted against Ruggles's objections that abolitionism meant amalgamation. Ruggles retorted that marrying someone was a matter of taste and had nothing to do with principle. The colonizationist responded that Ruggles had "devilish bad taste, to marry a negress." That exchange chilled the conversation. Then the moon came out, and Ruggles opened a curtain to reveal his face. The "animal" was incensed to learn that he had been talking to a black man and fulminated that he had been tricked into revealing his feelings. He then sulked until they arrived at an inn, where he refused to allow Ruggles to sit at the breakfast table. When the others supported Ruggles, the "animal exhibited everything of the true PORK except the bristles." Angrily, the colonizationist refused to eat with the others and would not speak with anyone the rest of the journey. Ruggles got off at the next town to canvass and bid all adieus. When Ruggles arrived in Erie, Pennsylvania, a few days later, he found "the animal at home in the pen with the pigs."[46]

This interaction between Ruggles and the "animal" racist merits attention. The colonizationist complacently believed that the goal of abolition-minded blacks was to marry white women and was "shocked" to learn that Ruggles would consider marrying a black. He accused Ruggles of being a trickster, who intended to deceive innocent whites such as him. Patrick Rael has argued that blacks were very sensitive to such labels, because unscrupulous blacks had obtained cash from well-meaning whites by falsely pretending to be abolitionists. Ruggles, who was traveling as an agent and collecting funds for the *Emancipator*, could be vulnerable to such charges. Yet Ruggles's description of the "animal" indicates that he despised the racist for his beliefs and offensive statements and considered him to be less than human. Rather than be defined by racial accusation, Ruggles in fact turned it around, indicating through his description that he was superior to the racist. In another instance, Ruggles stated, "None but APES will doubt for a moment, that what man is man [is] everywhere." As Mia Bay has pointed out, black thinkers in the 1830s wondered whether whites might not be the inferior race. Ruggles's statements show that he did not just question but believed that racists were inferior. Ruggles was also unwilling to condemn interracial love. As someone who lived near the Five Points neighborhood in New York City, where mixed-race couples were common, Ruggles had routinely encountered respectable examples of such unions. He also noted that intermarriage was common in Latin America. In the American South, white and black infants suckled at the breasts of black nurses. To Ruggles, mixed-race love was repugnant in the United States only because prejudice taught that it was.[47]

Ruggles also showed considerable courage in confronting the racist. He traveled alone in a countryside where he was likely to receive very little sympathy. His antagonist, by Ruggles's description, had friends in Erie, Pennsylvania, not far from the Ohio border. Mobbing of abolitionists was common in these areas, and Ruggles was fortunate to avoid an attack.[48]

The insults Ruggles received in Pennsylvania were matched closer to home in January 1834. An incident involving a ferry ride from New York City to Newark, New Jersey, indicates the hazards blacks experienced on common carriers. Other black leaders, notably Thomas L. Jennings, had complained of mistreatment on omnibuses in the city. Ruggles was going on business by ferry to Newark; traveling on this route required first hiring a place on a stagecoach. The vehicle would then be ferried across the North (Hudson) River and would travel overland to Newark. Ruggles initially experienced trouble when a wily stagecoach driver tricked him into taking a later ferry. Ruggles waited, then took a seat inside the coach before it mounted the ferry. As he did, the driver motioned for him to sit up next to him so that white passengers could have seats. Ruggles declined and was told "you are a colored man and you must get out and ride outside, if you go to Newark with me." Ruggles argued forcefully with the driver, who said it was unfortunate "to be colored, it's true, but it is not customary and it is against my rules to allow colored men to ride inside." Ruggles demanded to get what he paid for: a seat inside. On the Jersey side, the driver told the other passengers to get out, then "entered the stage with the ferocity of a tiger, and with his hands like claws tore both clothes, buttons and skin and nature was at that moment prepared to give up even my heart's blood." The driver "trampled on my feelings, and he was robbing me of my RIGHTS, my LIBERTY, my ALL." The other whites assisted the driver and pushed Ruggles into the street. He then walked to Newark, lamed by the attack and sore at heart.[49]

Anger over the two incidents was seared into Ruggles's heart. The "animal" in Pennsylvania was a boorish racist who made baldly plain that he considered blacks to be inferior and lustful of white women. The incident on the Jersey ferry raised racism to a more painful level. The same denial of equality was there but was accompanied by nasty insults and physical abuse. It was a reminder that northern antebellum racism was more than ideological. Any black man who attempted to surmount its boundaries was liable to be beaten and thrown in the street. As an educated man, Ruggles had to be particularly aggrieved that a working-class coachman aided by middle-class patrons gave him a lesson in northern racial segregation. Born free, Ruggles could now feel the brutality and anger in the hearts of southern enslaved blacks.

Ruggles could find hope and succor from such abusive behavior in the work of other black abolitionists. Even among them, Ruggles found social relations were complex and at times frustrating. In addition to his tours as an agent, Ruggles attended the Third Annual Convention of the Free People of Color, held in Philadelphia from June 3 through 13, 1833. At the 1833 meeting, Ruggles played a small but visible role — moving or seconding propositions regarding temperance and a manual labor school; offering support for the Phoenix Society of New York, which promoted the liberal arts; asking the convention to help the new black colony in Wilberforce, Canada; and delivering a preamble to the discussion of the travails of Prudence Crandall, whose integrated primary school in Connecticut was under vicious attack. Appointments to committees gave him valuable experience. He gained a seat on the important committee regarding representation along with Thomas L. Jennings of New York, who appears to have sponsored Ruggles. Through this committee, Ruggles could reach out to delegates from other cities and thereby make new friends and become better known within the national movement. He stayed in the same boardinghouse with fellow New Yorkers William Hamilton and Henry Sipkins and with Nathan Johnson of New Bedford. Many of the delegates were former slaves, and Ruggles's shared experiences with them had to reinforce his earlier conviction that, once freed from an oppressive bondage, blacks could quickly take positions of leadership.[50]

As a member of the representation committee in 1833, Ruggles took part in one of the most important debates confronting the convention movement: whether to accept "irregular" delegates, who simply dropped by the meetings, voted with little knowledge of organizational debates, and might be bought off with a barrel of cider, as one Pennsylvania abolitionist complained to his friends. Should the convention be open to all, or should it restrict membership to maintain integrity of the electoral process? Such questions proved so vexing that Ruggles's committee resolved to develop "some more efficient plan of representation."[51]

The class nature of this debate must have been striking to Ruggles, who was well educated but not as prosperous as many delegates. Indeed, there was a bifurcation in social status and prosperity among the convention leadership. Many owned property, had savings, and worked in professional jobs. Others, however, claimed leadership because of community involvement, professional training, and commitment to action. Ruggles, who had ambitions to be a printer, belonged in the second, poorer class of leadership. Those among the propertied elite also differed from Ruggles: they were usually married, often to light-complected wives who represented status achievement. Such attitudes may have caused petty discrimination against Ruggles, who was single and, judging from surviving images, was dark-skinned. Beyond class and complexion lay the question of connecting with the ordinary black person. White men, for whom suffrage now reached far down the ranks of society, could legitimately claim to take part in a democracy. Free blacks, on the other hand, were virtually disenfranchised. Yet the convention meeting seemed to uphold an intraracial hierarchy. Were the conventions merely to be debate societies, or could they create racial unity and promote developments of black republicans? Such issues vexed Ruggles, who strived to find common ground with ordinary blacks.[52]

Ruggles attended the 1833 meeting as a delegate from Poughkeepsie, New York. This affiliation sheds light on Ruggles's whereabouts since the fire that destroyed his store in 1829. Although Ruggles did reestablish himself in New York City, it is likely that he had spent time in Poughkeepsie, a Hudson River port. From his comments on the Prudence Crandall case, it appears he had also spent time in Norwich. There he had family, but his associations in Poughkeepsie have remained obscure. Ruggles was connected to Nathan Blount, a Poughkeepsie abolitionist and teacher at the local school for children of color. Blount was one of the earliest black agents for the *Liberator*, beginning his duties in 1831.[53]

Ruggles could not support himself solely as an agent for the *Emancipator*. He returned to New York to take up residence on Lispenard Street in lower Manhattan. He took on duties as agent for the *Liberator* in New York City, becoming the only person to be agent for both antislavery papers.[54] He found other means to earn money through print. In May 1834 he opened a bookstore and antislavery circulating library at 67 Lispenard Street. This was further uptown than his old address on Cortlandt Street, but nearer to the center of the black community in the Fifth and Sixth wards. His immediate neighborhood included an elite residential enclave known as St. John's Park, or Hudson Square. Originally part of the Lispenard Meadows, this neighborhood had become, by the early 1830s, one of the most fashionable parts of town. Near Ruggles lived Mayor William Paulding, bank president John C. Hamilton, author Clement Moore (who wrote *A Visit from St. Nicholas*), and real estate merchant Anthony Bleecker. Most of the white residents worshiped at St. John's Chapel and sent their sons to Columbia College and their daughters to Mrs. Forbes' School for Girls. The elite, Episcopalian quality of the neighborhood brought Ruggles into contact with future allies and offered a degree of protection against mobs. At his shop, Ruggles operated his bookstore and did job-lot printing, letterpress work, and picture framing and also composed letters and bound books. Ruggles's new store was the first black bookshop in the United States. One of the many "firsts" in his career, the store, in addition to paper supplies, sold classics of the abolitionist movement. Soon, it was a designated place of sale for black writings. Maria Stewart, recently moved from Boston to New York, announced on the title page of her pamphlet, *Productions of Mrs. Maria Stewart*, that purchasers could find it at the bookstore of David Ruggles at 67 Lispenard Street. Her selection of Ruggles's store is further indication of his growing reputation among black abolitionists.[55]

Stewart surely influenced Ruggles more than as a client. Originally from Boston, she had been a powerful though unlettered voice for black female rights. She and her husband, James, a prosperous ship outfitter, were close friends of David Walker. After James's death in 1829 and Walker's in 1830, Maria Stewart stepped forth as a strong proponent of black women's rights. Though Stewart was illiterate, her command of the language so impressed William Lloyd Garrison that he published a number of her letters (which she apparently dictated) in the *Liberator* and her essays as a pamphlet. Stewart eventually became too outspoken for Boston and moved to New York City, where she became literate, joined the African Dorcas Society, and worked as a schoolteacher. Whether she lectured in New York City is unknown. That Ruggles carried her book is partly from Garrison's influence and from his openness to Stewart's message. One clear message from Stewart that surely rang home with Ruggles was her exhortation to black men to show their masculinity through resistance to slavery: "If you are men, convince [whites] that you possess the spirit of men," by fighting slavery. Eventually, her ideas appeared in his work.[56]

Ruggles's activism took a new direction in the spring of 1834. Since the late 1780s, agents of slave masters seeking to regain escaped chattel had come into the city with regularity, although the black community sometimes rioted against them. In the 1830s, an organized gang including slave catchers, constables, and a complicit judge terrified and angered New York's black population. At times, the New York Manumission Society had intervened. Often it did so only after the accused was shipped south, a process that made rescue difficult and expensive.[57]

During the spring of 1834, Elizur Wright Jr., a white abolitionist and officer of the American Anti-Slavery Society, initiated publication of a series of letters advocating greater resistance to the Fugitive Slave Act of 1793. Wright also became involved in aiding black children who had been seized as alleged slaves, put through a mock court of justice, and then shipped south for sale as slaves. Wright chronicled the actions of Richard P. Haxall of Richmond, Virginia, who had taken a seven-year-old schoolboy, Henry Scott, off the city streets and hauled him before Richard Riker, the city recorder, who was about to condemn the lad into slavery. Wright intervened and stopped the proceedings even after Riker ordered the boy to jail until the matter could be settled. As an officer of the city government, Riker served as a judge in such cases. Wright then convinced William Goodell, Arthur Tappan, and a group of black citizens to bail Henry out and allow him to live with the Wright family. Wright described other such incidents in his articles over the spring and summer of 1834. He also pointed out that slaveholders were misusing a writ of *homine replegiando* to claim possession of their alleged chattel without a jury trial.

Wright countered that according to English common law and New York State law, using such a writ required a jury trial to establish whether the accused was in fact a fugitive slave. Wright made his arguments public and thereby sharply raised awareness of such seizures, initiated a legal procedural battle that lasted the next few years, and inspired black New Yorkers to again resist kidnappers. One legal quirk that Wright advocated changing was that alleged runaways typically did not face judges, because technically they were not accused of any crime. They were simply errant property. Harboring runaways was, however, a felony with severe consequences.[58]

Doubtless inspired by Wright and by the anger and despair of victimized black New York families, Ruggles announced his intention to help save kidnapped New Yorkers in a brief notice in the *Emancipator* on March 25, 1834. Along with Philip A. Bell, Dr. Jonathan Brown, and William P. Johnson, who would all become his close associates in future resistance to kidnappers, Ruggles publicized a meeting to be held on March 28 at the Philomathean Hall on Delano Street to take up a collection to assist Henry Scott.[59]

As Ruggles moved into direct action, he maintained his presence in the American Anti-Slavery Society. At the first anniversary of the organization, Ruggles spoke before the opening session of the New York Young Men's Antislavery Society. He delivered a speech in the Chatham Street Chapel, indicating his growing presence in the movement.[60]

By the spring of 1834, David Ruggles had lived in New York City off and on for at least nine years. He had operated several groceries; had become heavily involved in reform movements, including temperance and free produce; and, most important, had become a new voice in promoting abolitionism. Though barely twenty-four years of age, Ruggles was an experienced antislavery agent, convention member, writer, and now bookstore owner. He had reached out to female abolitionists and worked well with the Tappan brothers, giants of the local abolition scene. In the rapidly developing world of black abolitionism, he had served an admirable apprenticeship. Now he was ready for larger responsibilities.

✻ ✺ ✻

CHAPTER THREE

Making Practical Abolitionism

New York City's simmering racial tensions burst into flame in the July 1834 riots against black New Yorkers. These riots against the black community were hardly the first. Rioters had trashed black churches, theaters, and small businesses and had set dogs against black students at the African Free School. But the 1834 riots were more coordinated, widespread, and dangerous. This time, racist groups accelerated broader battles to overpower and drive out the black community and silence white and black abolitionists, especially religious leaders. Months of incendiary articles in such Democratic newspapers as the *Morning Courier* and *New York Enquirer* and *Commercial Advertiser*, which labeled abolitionists as amalgamationists, fueled the riots. A racist novel about mixed-race love further inflamed violent actions. Anxieties about amalgamation were common in both the upper and lower classes and became a cover for acts of violence against blacks. A rally held on July 8 touched off the rioters' ire. That day, fifty free blacks of both sexes met with one hundred white men and women to discuss abolition. The *Morning Courier* and *New York Enquirer* warned against further meetings and specifically threatened black participants that, if they allowed themselves to become "the tools of a few blind zealots, the consequences to them will be most serious."[1]

During the riot, the mob roved through the Sixth and Eighth Wards, home to much of the city's black population; it destroyed several black churches and homes and attacked any blacks who fell into its path. In addition, the mob sacked the homes and stores of the Tappan brothers and the dwellings of pro-abolition clerics. Paul Gilje's careful identification of the rioters reveals that most came from the poorer working classes and from occupations where racial competition for jobs was common. At the same time, the upper and middle classes were involved through identification with the American Colonization Society (ACS) and by affiliation with the city's newspapers. This mixture of economic and ideological conflict indicates that white and black abolitionism was effectively challenging the racial status quo and motivating the Democratic Party, its partisan newspapers, and the ACS to act against the insurgent black activists and their white allies. The disorder was enough, however, to anger one of the staunchest opponents of black abolitionism, city recorder and judge Richard Riker. After the militia quelled the riots, Riker reminded the populace that the soldiers had live ammunition at their disposal and, had they been forced to use it to wound or kill, only the rioters would have been to blame. Riker found the mob more threatening to public order than abolition and, though he would later contradict such beliefs, he thanked God that the city's black population "was entitled to the protection of the laws."[2]

Few whites shared Riker's views. In the aftermath of the riots, the *African Repository*, the mouthpiece of the American Colonization Society, blamed the abolitionists for the rampage. Although the means by which the public "manifested its disapprobation of the conduct of the Abolitionists" deserved strong censure, the magazine found that the abolitionists were at fault. According to ACS critics, the abolitionists, reasoned its editor, abused their guaranty of freedom of the press by "endeavoring to inflame the public mind" against the South. The abolitionists deserved the violence they received. The *Emancipator*, in response, filled its pages with angry blasts from the Tappans and reports from other cities of the "disgraceful events" in New York City. For his part, David Ruggles blamed journalists, including William Leete Stone and Cornelius Webb, referring to them as "the editors of the most filthy prints in the country, which are more the organs of the Colonization Society than any other," for inflaming the mob.[3]

The riots discouraged many blacks whose homes and churches had been destroyed by the mob. Many worried they would suffer as did black residents of Cincinnati, Ohio. There in 1829, antiblack rioters nearby drove the population of free people of color out of the city. Many blacks abandoned the Queen City and left the United States to establish the Wilberforce Colony in Canada. Others remained behind to rebuild the black community and forged alliances with other free blacks through the convention movement. In the aftermath of the riot, New York's black population quickly dropped, beginning a slide to the smallest black presence in New York City since the early eighteenth century.[4]

A sad by-product of the ACS's campaign to assign blame to the abolitionists for the riots was the public humiliation of the esteemed black Episcopal cleric, Peter Williams Jr., by Benjamin Onderdonk, bishop of the New York Episcopal Diocese. That worthy churchman ordered Williams to quit any antislavery activity to avoid further violence against St. Philip's. In his classic reply, Williams accepted the edict but noted that his father had fought for the American Revolution and that, as a child, he had been deeply inspired by its egalitarian messages. Although he reluctantly resigned from the Phoenix Society and from the Anti-Slavery Society, Williams informed Onderdonk that he considered its members to be good men and good Christians. Although Craig Townsend's recent study reveals that Williams's reply to Onderdonk was more complicated, the latter tailored the public statement to make the black cleric appear abjectly servile. Williams was, in fact, simply obeying the orders he accepted when joining the Episcopal clergy years before. But to the black public, Williams's resignation and subsequent humiliation were testament to the growing unease in white churches over abolition, a tension that would cause major splits in a few years. To younger men such as Ruggles, the incident signaled the frustrations and dangers for blacks who attempted to work within the white establishment.[5]

Scholars have argued that the 1834 riots cowed white abolitionists and made them retreat from earlier, more radical positions on immediatism, on racial fraternity and equality, and on mixed marriages. Recently, Leslie Harris has argued cogently that the 1834 riot marked a split between white abolitionists, who now leaned toward a more conservative approach to abolitionism and to the goals of black equality. She contends that leading African American activists accepted the aims of black self-help in education as the best means to equality, thereby endorsing a more conservative stance.[6]

The abolitionist response to the riots, however, was not that simple. Harris argues that the Tappan brothers in particular emphasized education as the principal effort because they wanted to create an obedient black working class. It is true that the wealthy brothers took a more cautious stance. The Tappans, Joshua Leavitt, and William Goodell, joined by the black cleric Samuel Eli Cornish, signed a letter to Mayor Cornelius Lawrence outlining the objectives of the American Anti-Slavery Society. The stated goals were the abolition of slavery in the United States, black self-uplift, and opposition to the American Colonization Society. The letter vehemently disavowed any designs for interracial marriage and characterized newspaper stories about mixed-race marriage and adoption as unfounded. Lewis Tappan wrote to Theodore Weld two years later that he had attempted to "mix up the colors" on just one occasion, when he invited the choirs from churches of Peter Williams Jr. and Theodore S. Wright to sit with the white singers from the Chatham Street Chapel. Still, the Tappans routinely supported Ruggles's militant efforts by their presence and their money. To be sure, planning to create an obedient black working class certainly had been the desired outcome for philanthropists in New York since the early eighteenth century. But, by 1834, such thinking had to ignore the reality of racial prejudice in the city, which made black employment in most occupations rare. Even domestic work and seafaring, formerly safe jobs for blacks, became increasingly restricted to whites.[7]

One white radical refused to kowtow. Isaac T. Hopper, the aged abolitionist turned bookseller, showed valor during the riots by refusing the advice of friends to remove the display of abolitionist literature from his window. Hopper declared that he was not "such a coward as to forsake my principles . . . at the bidding of a mob." When a mob approached his shop intent upon ransacking it, Hopper walked out onto his steps and stared down the rioters, who then moved on without damaging his store. Born in New Jersey in 1771 to a family of Quakers and Presbyterians, Hopper attended the Society of Friends with his father but was not a member during his early life. As a small boy, he often visited an uncle in Philadelphia who made clothing for George Washington and Benjamin Franklin. Hopper met both luminaries and became a steadfast Patriot. By the early 1790s he was an active abolitionist and became famous for assisting runaway slaves and victims of kidnapping. He chronicled his exploits in a series of articles published in Philadelphia and New York City newspapers. Richard Newman has described Hopper as a utility man in the early abolitionist movement. Untrained in the law, men like Hopper did most of the groundwork of delivering writs to slaveholders and justices, apprising imprisoned blacks of their rights, checking on tips about fugitive slaves, and helping to identify kidnap victims. By the 1830s, however, when Hopper's confrontational style became more appropriate and attractive to black activists, the legal work of the white liberal establishment seemed pallid. By now a full member of the Society of Friends, Hopper found that he was more radical than others in the meeting were. More than personal glory, Hopper was interested in exemplary tales that might inspire other opponents of slavery. Hopper became an officer in the American Anti-Slavery Society when it formed in 1833. In Ruggles, he found a willing acolyte. Hopper surely found himself rejuvenated by the younger man.[8]

One important abolitionist argued that the riots had inadvertently helped the movement by pushing previously conservative whites into the abolitionist cause. William Goodell, the erstwhile editor of the *Genius of Temperance*, had now become a full-time fundraiser for the abolitionist movement. He later edited the *Emancipator*, the *Friend of Man*, the *Radical Abolitionist*, and other antislavery serials. On a speaking tour after the riots, Goodell found that whites in upstate New York were angry about suppression of speech and were now more open to fraternization with blacks. On the way north, Goodell stopped by to talk with Judge William Jay and found him hard at work on a book denouncing colonization, partly in response to the riots. Jay found the vigilante justice meted out by white rioters repugnant and blamed the ACS for the disorder. As Daniel Walker Howe has argued, Whigs such as Jay found popular sovereignty expressed in mobs affiliated with Andrew Jackson's Democratic Party to be a repulsive notion. In Jay's and Goodell's minds, the rioters were suppressing black rights, abolitionism, and free speech. In his travels upstate, Goodell found sentimental satisfaction in biracial religious harmony. He observed blacks and whites sitting together at a Sunday school in Catskill, New York, and ate dinner with a black man and his white host in Athens, New York. Later, Goodell found activists and college students' organizing with a greater fervor than before. The riots gave the Tappans and a few white abolitionists pause about their actions, but they stiffened the resolve of blacks and even radicalized other whites. To blacks, the riots were simply a sign that they had to fight harder for their rights.[9]

Rather than be intimidated by the rioters, Ruggles put more energy and commitment into the struggle. Ironically, the rioters missed his home, though they ransacked Arthur Tappan's nearby. Ruggles kept his antislavery bookstore open, a clear sign that he was not retreating from abolitionism. In an advertisement for Lydia Maria Child's latest book, *The Oasis*, Ruggles noted that many book dealers in New York City refused to carry it or any antislavery annual. Those who did, kept such works in unopened packages in their storerooms for months before returning them. Ruggles asked rhetorically: "By such means they would check the progress of Truth! Shall they succeed?" In addition to informing readers about materials available at his store, Ruggles's list indicates the ties he had formed with Lydia and David Lee Child, who would be of great importance to him in the future.[10]

His advertisement listed some of the titles that were available for purchase at the store or that could be borrowed through his circulating library. In addition to Maria Stewart's and Child's work, books and pamphlets for sale included Thomas Price's *Memoir of William Wilberforce*; *A Sermon by Reverend*

Mr. Dickinson of Norwich; and *The Address of the New York Young Men's Anti-slavery Society, To Their Fellow Citizens*. Delivered on the Fourth of July 1834 at the establishment of the Norwich Antislavery Society, Reverend Dickinson's speech combined temperance with pleas for equal justice and the right of literacy of enslaved and free blacks. Dickinson refuted claims by the ACS and by southern slaveholders that the extinction of slavery could not be immediate. Anything less than abolition now was, in Dickinson's sermon, sinful and un-Christian. In his sermon, Dickinson refuted the claim that not all slave masters were cruel by arguing that the "system [of slavery,] which occasionally leads to outrage, and which affords the slave no protection against it, is most cruel." Dickinson also recanted his lifetime membership in the ACS. Because of his recognized brilliance and reputation, abolitionists across the country reprinted Dickinson's sermon.[11]

Ruggles had to be pleased that the pastor of his home church was now an immediatist. His sale of the minister's antislavery sermon indicates that he was in contact with his hometown. Dickinson was one of many New England Congregationalists who had become dominant players in the antislavery movement by the 1830s. A descendant of a distinguished Montreal family and an 1826 Yale College graduate, Dickinson was considered to be among the most brilliant young clerics of his time. His acceptance of the pulpit at the Second Congregational Church of Norwich was a coup for the city. This was the church where the Ruggles family had worshiped at times and where its children, starting with David, were educated. Dickinson served the church between 1832 and 1835, before abruptly resigning to serve as a missionary to Singapore, where he remained until 1839.

Personal circumstances and a crisis over antislavery efforts in the church drove Dickinson from his church. Dickinson left his post after the sudden death of his wife in 1834 and because of rising anti-abolitionist fervor in Norwich, as well as Reverend Leonard Bacon's drive to ban abolitionism from Congregational churches.[12] Bacon was the influential pastor of the First Congregational Church of New Haven and a proponent of the American Colonization Society. Undeterred, the newly founded Women's Anti-Slavery Society quickly reprinted Dickinson's sermon locally. There was opposition to these efforts. In 1834 the pastor of the Norwich Presbyterian Church was drummed out of town and threatened with a tar and feathering if he returned to preach abolitionism. The following year, a mob drove abolitionist George Thompson out of Norwich, one of the many cities that evicted the Englishman.[13]

In New York, Ruggles, undaunted by the violence of the mob, developed plans to bring his campaign for literacy to a wider audience. In late May 1834, he sought and received permission from the Philomathean Society to rent its hall for Saturday afternoon meetings of the Garrison Literary and Benevolent Society. The Philomathean Society, formed in 1829 by members of the New York African Society for Mutual Relief, intended to host weekly debates and recitations on a variety of subjects. It included several youthful luminaries and members of the society, including Philip A. Bell as chair, the brilliant young physician James McCune Smith, Thomas Jennings Jr., and Henry Sipkins. By 1833 Bell and the board offered a lecture series out of the organization's hall at 161 Duane Street. Formed in 1833, the Garrison Society of New York was the strongest juvenile self-improvement society in the north. Previously, its students, whose ages ranged from four to twenty years, had met in a public school on Wednesday afternoons. Among its precepts were that students should not indulge in drinking or cursing. Despite every effort to ensure proper behavior, the public school trustees decreed that an organization bearing such a controversial name should not be allowed to use its facilities. Henry Highland Garnet, master of the school, led the boys in voting not to change the name of the organization, shouting "Garrison, Garrison, Garrison, forever," to voice their disapproval of abandoning their namesake. Ruggles then approached Philip A. Bell, as head of the Philomathean Society, who wrote Ruggles a warm letter granting his preliminary approval for holding the weekend sessions without charges.[14]

The members later used the Philomathean Hall for explicitly political purposes. In one of the first two such occasions, on August 1, 1834, at which Ruggles opened the meeting, members celebrated Great Britain's emancipation of slaves in its empire. William Hamilton Sr. was appointed president and Henry Williams and Thomas L. Jennings Jr., vice presidents. Ruggles declared that emancipation day was an "augury of the coming day when the glorious example of generous-hearted Britain will be followed by boasted 'free America' whose escutcheon is stained with the blood of three millions of her countrymen." As Jeffrey Kerr-Ritchie has pointed out, these celebrations, of which Ruggles was a principal sponsor for the next few years, were much more than community gatherings. They placed the local abolitionism movement into the context of the black Atlantic world's struggle against slavery. Early examples of celebrations occurring annually in black communities across the North and Midwest, these gatherings were significant as black cultural events, as transnational connections between West Indian emancipation and the American struggle against slavery, and in the mobilization of that effort. Experienced in the struggle and on familiar terms with sailors, Ruggles exploited those connections. That such celebrations often suffered from racist attacks and, in this instance, occurred soon after the infamous July riots in New York, seems not to have deterred Ruggles in the slightest.[15]

Ruggles was the contact person between the Garrison Society and the Philomatheans. Named in honor of William Lloyd Garrison, the society promised to encourage "the diffusion of knowledge, mental assistance, moral and intellectual improvement." By April 1834 more than "150 little ones attended the society" and engaged in "writing and delivering orations, reciting and composing." Ruggles worked with older black New York luminaries such as William Hamilton and younger ones such as Garnet and Smith. Such organizations, Craig Wilder has concluded, were part of a battery of voluntary associations that promoted a collective sense of black manhood. His membership brought Ruggles into a "spiritual community of personally independent and emotionally attached people" with an implied common fate and united goals of fighting slavery and demanding human rights for black New Yorkers. In addition, they demonstrate a fusion of self-help and radical politics.[16]

Soon, he had his own work to sell at the store. His first publication, a strident, Garrisonian critique of a white man's defense of the ACS and its attacks on black abilities, appeared in 1834. Ruggles's literary opponent was Dr. David M. Reese. An experienced physician from Baltimore, Reese moved to New York in 1820, became a highly successful medical administrator at Bellevue Hospital, and was subsequently appointed as city and county superintendent of public schools. Reese received favorable notice for recommending sawing wood to cure pulmonary diseases.

Reese could claim some abolitionist credentials. His name joined more radical opponents of slavery including Isaac T. Hopper, merchant Barney Corse, editor William Goodell, and publisher Gilbert Vale on a petition demanding the end of slavery and the slave trade in the District of Columbia. Despite his emancipationist attitudes, Reese declared himself disturbed over the actions of the immediatists in the American Anti-Slavery Society, whom he deemed mischievous and dangerous to the republic. Prominent in the New York branch of the American Colonization Society, Reese debated blacks at a mass meeting at the Broadway Tabernacle. Reese initially irritated the Tappan brothers by disavowing his contribution to the Magdalen Report, an indictment of prostitution in the city. Lewis Tappan reported that Reese first proclaimed, "They say it is the best thing I ever wrote," then denied responsibility after his home was threatened. By 1834 Reese had become anathema to antislavery activists because of his contemptuous dismissals of their opposition to colonization. In August 1834 he published an attack on abolitionism in a lengthy pamphlet criticizing the first annual report of the American

Anti-Slavery Society. The pamphlet sold more than twenty-five-thousand copies, a figure indicating that his arguments could not be safely ignored. Despite his profound disagreement with it, Ruggles carried the pamphlet at his bookstore. Reese's method was clever. In words aimed at moderate abolitionists, Reese avowed himself to be an uncompromising enemy of slavery and a friend to universal emancipation. Accordingly, he argued, discussion in the pulpits and congregation over slavery was entirely warranted, provided it was peaceably conducted and did not threaten the American government and union of the states.[17]

American unity, Reese argued, was more important than an immediate end to slavery. Comity between the states was at stake. Northerners could not ask southerners to ignore the laws of their own states that were the legal foundation of servitude. The anarchic demands by the Anti-Slavery Society stemmed from its inexperience. Reese ridiculed the society's claims that no one had mustered pity for the slave before formation of its society in 1832. Worse than their hypocrisy, Reese declared, was the immediatists' acceptance of amalgamation. This would be the result, he contended, of the abolitionists' practice of admitting blacks into Christian worship and into schools as equals. In shrill tones, Reese blasted the Anti-Slavery Society for acquiescing in the matter of interracial sex. The result of this, Reese argued, would be the expulsion of any white participants from their race. Reese quoted from one Charles Stuart in the *Phrenological Journal of Edinburgh* who "proved" that any encouragement of interracial sex by whites was stupid and against human nature.[18]

Reese then moved on to Garrison's attack on colonization. He summarized Garrison's positions that the ACS did little to reduce the numbers or power of slavery; that northern free blacks were universally opposed to it; that the colonies were not fit to Christianize Africa; and that nothing but white prejudice fueled the ACS. These conclusions, Reese asserted, were a misreading of the history of the efforts of such heroes as Granville Sharp, William Wilberforce, and Thomas Clarkson. Reese criticized at great length the speeches made by antislavery advocates at the convention; he found the arguments naively supportive of Great Britain's act of emancipation, overly critical of conditions in the southern states, and fiscally irresponsible in their claims to help enslaved peoples. Rather, he concluded, the society was anti-American, prejudicial against whites, and encouraged illegal thefts of human property that inevitably would alienate southern Christians and "involve this nation in the horrors of a civil rebellion, if not in the bloody tragedy of a servile war."[19] Reese's precognition of the American Civil War aside, his pamphlet was entirely an argument between whites, with no mention or consideration of the black abolitionist movement. Blacks were treated only as abstractions, or as threatening hordes eager for sex with white women, or as terrorists who intended to overthrow the American constitutional government. To Dr. Reese, the antislavery societies were misreading history and playing with social disasters. He could not imagine blacks responding in any civilized way.

Reese's calm, rational racism became a clarion call to Ruggles. His first publication was a historic event. Published less than two months after Reese's denunciation of the Anti-Slavery Society, *The "Extinguisher" Extinguished! Or David M. Reese, M.D. "Used Up." by David Ruggles, a Man of Color*, the forty-six-page pamphlet was among the first black American imprints, preceded by David Walker's *Appeal* and Richard Allen and Absalom Jones's protocol for the African Methodist Episcopal Church. This was no small accomplishment. Despite their frequent attempts, blacks had found publishing difficult. Printers would refuse jobs or did work anonymously to avoid criticism. Selling their work could be physically dangerous. The cost of a leather-bound book was often beyond the means of their intended readers. Accordingly, blacks chose the medium of pamphlets, which were smaller and cheaper to produce and allowed authors to maintain full control over their work. Ruggles likely received financial assistance from the Tappan brothers, who funded dozens of antislavery pamphlets in this period. Whether Ruggles printed the pamphlet at his residence and bookstore at what is now 65 Lispenard Street is not clear. Printers in New York City in the early 1830s commonly used iron hand presses, which were first introduced in England around 1800 and quickly replaced the wooden hand press. Iron hand presses required a number of employees including the master printer, an overseer, journeymen, apprentices, and specialists such as compositors, pressmen, and warehousemen. Ruggles never mentions any co-workers or the costs of printing, so it seems likely that he hired time and materials at a larger press, of which there were many in the city.[20]

Prosecutorial in tone, assertive, and openly contemptuous of Reese, Ruggles's pamphlet established his equal standing and right to a literary public space with the physician.[21] In the first paragraph, Ruggles asserted that he, as a black man, had a duty to refute Reese for the latter's deceptions. Early in the *Extinguisher*, Ruggles sarcastically remarked that he had waited for others to refute the doctor, but "they have said to me, 'great minds and great heads will not have any thing to do with such trifling productions of insignificant men.'" This was a time-tested method of rhetorical ploy used by black writers

THE

"EXTINGUISHER" EXTINGUISHED!

OR

DAVID M. REESE, M. D.

"USED UP."

BY DAVID RUGGLES,

A Man of Color.

TOGETHER WITH SOME REMARKS UPON A LATE PRODUCTION, ENTITLED

"AN ADDRESS ON SLAVERY AND AGAINST IMMEDIATE EMANCIPATION
WITH A PLAN OF THEIR BEING GRADUALLY EMANCIPATED
AND COLONIZED IN THIRTY-TWO YEARS.
BY HEMAN HOWLETT."

New-York:

PUBLISHED AND SOLD BY D. RUGGLES, BOOKSELLER,
65 Lispenard Street, near Broadway.

MDCCCXXXIV.

Title Page of *The "Extinguisher" Extinguished! Or David M. Reese, M.D. "Used Up." By David Ruggles, a Man of Color*. Ruggles's diatribe against Dr. Reese and his support for the American Colonization Society is strident and informed. It was one of the first black imprints. Courtesy of the Division of Rare and Manuscript Collections, Cornell University Library.

as far back as Richard Allen and Absalom Jones in 1794.[22] Worried about the "pestiferous effect upon the minds of the ignorant and uninformed," Ruggles decided to answer it. Considering the numbers of Reese's pamphlet in print, Ruggles's decision to combat its findings seems wise. As a leading defender of the American Colonization Society and disseminator of its cloaked racism, Reese, whose work was read by leading political and economic figures, could do more damage than the "bobolition" cartoons historians have spent so much time analyzing.

Ruggles's pamphlet was a strong act of self-assertion. In his approach, Ruggles placed himself as Reese's critic and intellectual superior. He demolished Reese's major and minor arguments with effective satire and sarcasm, both common tools of abolitionist literature, and debated several topics in the pamphlet: the New York Anti-Slavery Society, biblical justification for slavery, anxieties over "amalgamation," and black education.

First, Ruggles upended Reese's implication that the current crop of abolitionists in the New York Anti-Slavery Society was made up of "novices in philanthropy" who had little understanding of past heroes of the movement. Reese directed his criticism against the Tappans and other white leaders of the abolitionist movement. Ruggles denounced that claim as a "way of choking the truth." Reese claimed that the American Colonization Society had shown "greater pity" for the slave through its schools. To that statement, Ruggles responded, "Let the bloody whip of the slave master" speak of the pity of the oppressed. Ruggles thereby aligned the colonization society with the defenders of slavery by pointing out that northerners were as culpable as southern slave masters. Ruggles noted that Reese at one point claimed to be an opponent of slavery but shortly after had claimed that slavery was not a sin because it was "provided for in the Constitution." Ruggles also demolished the ACS claim that blacks were too degraded to be useful citizens. Although Ruggles acknowledged that blacks had suffered, fault belonged to whites who had created an environment of ignorance and crime. There was no evidence to "warrant the charge that [blacks were] but little above brutes."[23]

To Reese, the suggestion that blacks and whites should study together in seminaries was an "outrageous proposition" that would lead to amalgamation. Ruggles's response to Reese was that "amalgamation doctrine has turned your brain." Ruggles contended that he did not wish amalgamation, "nor does any colored man or woman of my acquaintance," but "I deny that 'intermarriages' between 'whites and blacks are unnatural.' Colonizationists often challenged abolitionists with the question, Would you be willing to marry a black wife?" Reverse this question, argued Ruggles: specifically, "you had better put this question to colonizationists in the south, who have been so long in a process of training." Ruggles contended that bias against mixed-race marriage is all about public opinion: "Nature teaches no such repugnance." Ruggles then used his own experiences from Bean Hill as evidence that black and white children play together without prejudice. Ruggles extended his experiences to encompass manumission schools for blacks in Maine, Massachusetts, Rhode Island, Connecticut, New York, New Jersey, and Pennsylvania. Those schools, Ruggles stated, produced "scholars who are so much *despised for wearing a sable skin*, may be found those who are not only able to speak without being 'told what to say,' but who are able to compete with even Doctor Reese himself, in science, literature, and especially in sound logic." In brief, these educated blacks were equal, often superior, to the smug physician.[24]

Showing a solid knowledge of the Bible, no doubt gained in his childhood studies, Ruggles argued effectively against Reese's use of sacred quotations. To Reese's claim that Jesus never once uttered a word against slavery, Ruggles replied that Jesus had also never condemned brandy, brothels, and running steamboats on Sunday, although each was now considered immoral. Reese pointed to the reference in the book of Paul to the obedience of slaves. Ruggles responded to Reese that Paul had not referred to skin color and that the servants held by the Israelites were captives, not permanent property. Reese had invoked Jesus as a justifier of slavery, even though he claimed to oppose human bondage himself. Ruggles pointed out the inconsistency of this argument and contended that Reese was creating a new doctrine that would vindicate the slaveholders.[25]

Ruggles took a radical position on intermarriage. He argued that, although he had no interest in it, there was nothing inherently wrong with the practice and that it had worked well in South America. He dismissed it as a minor issue that the ACS used to deflect concern from the more important topics of slavery and inequality.[26]

Although he did not reach the rhetorical heights of David Walker's point-by-point demolition in his famous *Appeal* of Thomas Jefferson's tortured racism, Ruggles had to be influenced by Walker's method. Ruggles refuted Reese's anxieties over mixed-race love, education, and his reference to the protection of slavery in the U.S. Constitution. Ruggles asserted that he had mastered the art of persuasion and pronounced Reese's work as "ridiculous nonsense."[27]

Ruggles reached out to a broader audience by placing a notice in the *Working Man's Advocate*, the newspaper of the fledgling white labor movement.

This gesture was not as farfetched as might be thought. Although historians have generally considered the workingmen to be hostile to abolitionism, recent work has suggested that the radical wing of the Workies was more sympathetic. Ely Moore, president of the General Trades Union, lectured at the Chatham Street Chapel on December 2, 1833, and praised the work of local printers. Ruggles, perhaps contemplating opening his own shop, may have been in the audience. Historian Jonathan Earle cites the example of William Leggett, the radical editor of the *New York Post*, as a fervent antislavery advocate who also espoused black rights. Infuriated by the 1834 anti-abolitionist riots, Leggett had moved recently from suspicion of abolitionist motives into full-scale antislavery and dispute with the Democratic Party about blacks' civil rights. Few black New Yorkers would argue with Leggett's denunciation of the 1821 New York State Constitution, which limited black votes. Leggett attacked the law: "May not the black man, who has only one hundred dollars, possess as much capacity, honesty, and love of country, as he who has twice the sum?" In his critique of slavery, Leggett connected antislavery and black civil rights with the equal rights doctrines of the Workies. Leggett's key associate was Theodore Sedgwick III, a young aristocratic lawyer, who would soon take up the cause of fugitive slaves.[28]

Dr. Reese penned another tract in 1835, this time an attack on William Jay's pamphlet, *An Inquiry into the Character and Tendencies of the American Colonization and Anti-Slavery Societies*. The Tappan brothers, fellow Presbyterians, had courted Jay, a social activist, because of the prestige of his family name and conservative reputation. Jay was a longtime sympathizer to abolitionism but had heretofore remained on the sidelines. His famous name and notoriety made him attractive to a movement anxious about its reputation as a gaggle of unpatriotic fanatics. Upset by the 1834 riots, Jay moved into the antislavery camp with his careful dissection of the ACS's methods and messages. In particular, he refuted the ACS's claims that the free black presence would result in slave revolts in the South and mixed-race love in the North. Rather, he argued in lawyerly terms that greater receptivity to the abolitionist movement would create greater clamor for the elimination of slavery. However naive, Jay's reputation and a successful sales run of ten printings mandated a response, again from Dr. Reese.[29]

On the surface, Reese was more tempered with Jay, the son of a Revolutionary War hero, than he had been with the abolitionists. Reese praised Jay's ancestry and, lamenting Jay's "unsophisticated fanaticism," beseeched him to recall his father's ownership of slaves and avowal of gradual abolitionism. After his initial display of politeness, Reese turned more condescending. He reprinted attacks on William Jay's antislavery position that had appeared in local newspapers. The local ACS leadership showered Reese with praise. Jay in turn argued in the *New York Commercial Advertiser* that Reese had badly misconstrued his father's attitudes and had failed to note a strong statement against slavery that the former chief justice and governor of New York State had made later in life. Jay argued that his father's abolitionism was gradual but was definite, certain, and compulsory.[30]

Jay contented himself with a letter to the editor. Sharper reaction to Reese came in a pamphlet published in Boston written by "Martin Mar Quack, M. D. L. L. D. M. Q. L. H. S. O. S. M. F. M. P. S. &c. &c. of that ilk." Attributed to Ruggles, the piece has the ring of one of his productions. Ruggles included an ambivalent message in *Extinguisher Extinguished!* that implied that he was the author. He noted that Martin was in Boston, but if the "Doctor cringes at anything I may say, here is David Ruggles on the spot, ready for an explanation and able to give satisfaction." Packed with evident satire on the pompous doctor's writings, it begins with a call to "Members of the New England Antislavery Society and other fanatics," asking them to turn their attention to the "dissection of a living biped, the strange qualities I recommend to your investigations." From the first page, the pamphlet is filled with ad hominem attacks. Reese, described as having all the "insolence, recklessness, and knavery of a Charlatan," is accused of writing his articles in order to raise his medical fees. The point of Reese's work is to target the abolitionists as "friends of sexual intercourse between the different races of mankind; and therefore they ought to be exterminated." Ruggles scores points by attacking Reese's claim that the abolitionists were at fault for the July riots, making them more criminal than the jailed rioters. Next to be ridiculed was Reese's claim that the rioters were merely defending the Fourth of July against the fanatical abolitionists. Ruggles blasted Reese for his intemperate attacks on Amos Phelps, Beriah Green, William Lloyd Garrison, S. S. Jocelyn, Samuel J. May, and other abolitionist leaders. While not the best of his work, the pamphlet established Ruggles as a defender of the abolitionist movement and demonstrated the fierceness and sureness of his attacks on abolitionism's critics and the ACS. Indeed, the pamphlet inverts class and race hierarchies as the impoverished black printer defends the elite New Yorker and other whites against attacks from one of the city's most prestigious physicians.[31]

David Ruggles continued his literary appeals for black support of the abolitionist press and made more attacks on slavery. In an address to the citizens of New York and elsewhere, published in a series of letters to the *Emancipator* in January and February 1835, Ruggles attacked black indifference to the anti-

A BRIEF REVIEW

OF THE

FIRST ANNUAL REPORT

OF THE

AMERICAN ANTI-SLAVERY SOCIETY,

BY DAVID M. REESE, M. D.

Of New York.

———

DISSECTED

BY MARTIN MAR QUACK, M. D. L. L. D. M. Q. L. H.
S. O. S. M. F. M. P. S. &c. &c.

OF THAT ILK.

———

Answer a fool according to his folly, lest he be wise in his own conceit.
SOLOMON.

————————

BOSTON:
PRINTED AND PUBLISHED BY CALVIN KNOX.
....
1834.

Title Page of *A Brief Review of the First Annual Report of the American Anti-Slavery Society, by David M. Reese, M. D. of New York. Dissected by Martin Mar Quack, M. D. L. L. D. M. Q. L. H. S. O. S. M. F. M. P. S. &c. &c. of that Ilk*. Boston: Printed and Published by Calvin Knox, 1834. This satire of Dr. Reese appeared after the physician attacked William Jay II for his support of the American Anti-Slavery Society. Courtesy of the American Antiquarian Society.

slavery press. He stated that black men and women were still "slaves whose condition is but a short remove from that of two millions of our race who are pining in their bloody chains." Their weapon, he claimed, was the press, which "we wield in behalf of our rights." Every black person should ask "if they had done enough to support the press rolling on the car of freedom." Any person with "one drop of African blood in his veins" should subscribe to and support the antislavery press. In a nation where so many rights of black citizens were circumscribed, the press remained "the liberty of OPINION — the liberty of SPEECH," which was guaranteed to all. Any black American who refused to pay four cents a week for a subscription and then spent more than that on tobacco showed only indifference to the plight of the slave and gave support to the insolent lies of the American Colonization Society. There was no such thing as neutrality toward the colonization society, for "No Man can serve two masters." For a young man who, only a few years before, had enjoyed frolics and festivals, the letters showed how intensely Ruggles had embraced the power of reading and writing and tied them to black self-improvement and to the antislavery cause. The letters also attest to Ruggles's developing skills at using abolitionist media to promote his ideas about the need for greater black participation in the struggle against slavery.[32]

His appeal was not only to blacks. Ruggles also wrestled with the specter of objectivity among white citizens toward slavery. Those individuals who sought to please all, he thundered, were slaves who "quickly degenerated into a poor, mean, fallacious sneak—a tool, a sycophant, and a fool." Neutrality corrupted the heart. Such individuals could be found among southern ministers, comparable to such biblical villains as Cain, Ham, and Judas. Southern clergymen might be beloved by their congregations, but that was only because they had studied their parishioners' support of slavery and tried to accommodate that evil love. Such obsequious support only confirmed cleric and congregation in the evils of slavery. Such people rejected the Bible in favor of slavish devotion to public opinion, which Ruggles called a fallacious position. This was not merely a problem among men but was also destroying southern white womanhood, a theme that Ruggles would address next.[33]

Ruggles broadened his moral appeal with a second pamphlet, *The Abrogation of the Seventh Commandment by the American Churches*, published on May 4, 1835. An extension of the claims the New York City Antislavery Society made about the vulnerability of black women, Ruggles's work was less sharp in tone than his attacks on Dr. Reese. *The Abrogation of the Seventh Commandment* is a reasoned appeal to women and the churches of the northern states to take a careful look at their complicity with slavery over the issue of mixed-race sex. Ruggles went quickly to the heart of the matter by pointing out the rising number of mixed-race peoples born in the slave South, a pattern that shows "the wide spread and incessant licentiousness of the white population," because, he continued, black females could not offer any resistance to their masters or expect any protection from the law. More mixed-race babies were born because of the unceasing demands of the internal slave trade. These sins of the southern states were corrupting the region's churches, which had to ignore the prostitution and adultery rampant among slave owners and their wives. When slave masters and mistresses visited the North, they implicated the "Christian ladies in New England" who entertained them. Neither group could ignore the problem. The solution, Ruggles contended, could be found in I Corinthians 9–13: "Not to company with fornicators." Ruggles beseeched northern women to abandon racial and gendered solidarity with southern women and shun them. In so doing, northern women could gain their voices on the issue of slavery—a right denied them by politics. He asked northern women further to sign protests against the admission of any slaveholders to the pulpits of churches; if a slaveholder preached or held some ceremony in the church, they should withdraw immediately. Ruggles asked northern ladies to recognize that "there are 500,000 women in this republic exposed to the most fearful tortures your sex can suffer." Ruggles appealed to white northern women to unite and drive out the slaveholders from the churches and from the region. Failure to do so would mean accepting that they were the "Christian associates of men who systematically justify the most outrageous and scarlet colored infractions of the law of God, which prohibits adultery and theft."

As important as his goals were, Ruggles's proposed methods were revolutionary. At a time when American Protestant churches were splitting apart over the issues of slavery and abolitionism, Ruggles was not seeking a truce but demanding that northern congregations shun their southern communicants. He aimed his words right at women, who formed the majority of loyal members in most American churches. Women had also formed a significant part of the antislavery movement, though their contributions were rarely given the credit they deserved. From the Free Produce movement to the petition drives, women's roles were couched in personal choice. Perhaps Ruggles wanted to harness some of the growing force of the female petition movement, which now had turned to antislavery demands. By emphasizing the connections between enslaved black women and free white women, Ruggles's plea commanded more committed activism. Ruggles urged women to unite in organizations, to drop the deferential position commonly taken in the petitions, and to shun slaveholding women. That was far beyond what any other contemporary male abolitionist advocated. Ruggles's combination of abolitionism and women's rights appeared sixteen years before the revelations of Harriet Beecher Stowe's *Uncle Tom's Cabin*.[34]

In his pamphlet, Ruggles attempted to infuse two white organizations with antislavery attitudes. The first was the American Seventh Commandment Society and the second was the New York Female Moral Reform Society, which had met at the Chatham Street Chapel on May 15, 1835. Moral reform in this instance meant prostitution, a volatile issue in New York City. In 1832 the Magdalene Society, under the leadership of Reverend John R. McDowall, published a study that counted more than ten thousand female prostitutes in the city. There was immediate furor over his numbers and over the project itself. In the winter of 1833, the American Seventh Commandment Society formed to help McDougall, followed first by women's missionary efforts to convert prostitutes and then in 1835 by the formal organization. Ruggles's attempt to combine moral reform of prostitution with abolitionism did not have immediate impact, although the constitution of the women's movement declared that it was important for "virtuous females to look down on licentious men and virtuous men to look down on licentious women." Two years later Angelina Grimké, the most radical of female abolitionists, wrote an extensive appeal to southern women in the *Antislavery Examiner*. She did not go as far as Ruggles wanted and asked southern women to reform themselves and their husbands, a method Ruggles plainly felt unworkable.[35]

Two older women had strong influence on Ruggles. The first was Maria Stewart. Her productions and probable conversations with Ruggles focused on black women's organizing power and use of the scripture to create a liberation theology. Stewart encouraged the mobilization of black women to resist slavery; Ruggles adapted her ideas to convince white women to do the same by following biblical commandments. Rather than focus on black women's need for social uplift, Stewart and Ruggles extended the need for moral reformation and action to white women. Ruggles was additionally influenced by Lydia Maria Child's 1833 book *An Appeal in Favor of That Class of Americans Called Africans*. As Carolyn Karcher observes, Child's book provided the abolitionist movement with its first full-scale analysis of the slavery question. Author of popular domestic manuals aimed at the rising middle-class woman, Child took a big risk in publishing her attack on slavery. In addition to its solid historical grounding and fine-tuned logic, Child's book presented a white woman's perspective on slavery. Karcher argues that Child's comments on the fate of black women in bondage were convoluted, but her analysis of

THE

ABROGATION

OF THE

SEVENTH COMMANDMENT,

BY THE

AMERICAN CHURCHES.

"When thou sawest a thief, then thou consentedst with him, and hast been partaker with adulterers."—PSALM l. 18.

NEW-YORK:

DAVID RUGGLES, 47 HOWARD STREET.

1835.

Title Page of [David Ruggles], *The Abrogation of the Seventh Commandment*. New York: David Ruggles, 1835. Ruggles strived in this pamphlet to convince northern women of both races to shun their southern counterparts because of their complicity with southern male sexual abuse of enslaved women. Courtesy of the Library of Congress.

the destructive effect of slavery on white women was acute. As black women took on all the responsibilities and burdens of motherhood, the plantation mistress became a caricature of a lady. Child did not create this argument, which had its origins in the work of Philadelphia Quaker Elizabeth Margaret Chandler, editor of the female department of the antislavery newspaper the *Genius of Universal Emancipation*, and of Maria Stewart. What Child did was to popularize such notions and make room for Ruggles's extensions of her ideas. If plantation women did not realize their culpability, Ruggles demanded that they be ostracized.[36]

Ruggles's pamphlet hit a nerve. American women created innumerable societies in the 1830s and many of them centered on abolitionism. Although many men in the antislavery movement opposed female officeholders, a flash point that would lead to division in the crusade a few years later, female membership and contributions were vital. By raising money, circulating and signing petitions, and lobbying legislatures, women were the "silent army of abolitionism." Such actions enabled white women to hone political skills as they created a movement for improved civil rights and the franchise. The Ladies' New York City Anti-Slavery Society formed in 1834, the year before Ruggles published his pamphlet. Members were characteristically wives or daughters of prosperous merchants, were new arrivals from smaller towns and cities in New England, and were attracted to abolitionism through evangelical revivals. Most were members of the Chatham Street [Presbyterian] Chapel. They viewed slavery as a sinful violation of female chastity and the sanction of the Christian family. Ruggles's pamphlet matched their anxieties. That the New York Society and Angelina Grimké largely ignored Ruggles's ideas is not surprising; white female abolitionists wanted black endorsements of their goals more than their actual contributions.[37]

If *The Abrogation of the Seventh Commandment* did not gain adherents among its intended audience of white women, it appealed to the emerging black feminist organizations. Almost alone among black male abolitionists, most of whom held patriarchal attitudes about women's place in the movement, Ruggles worked directly with the African Dorcas Society of New York City. Organized in 1827, the African Dorcas Society provided Ruggles with a venue for a public talk in 1833. A second group of middle-class black women supporting Ruggles was the city's Colored Ladies Literary Society, which ostensibly sought to "acquire literary and scientific knowledge" but did not hesitate to pledge money to help fight for black rights in the city. Unfortunately, the same barriers of race that existed in male organizations also divided black and white women. Ruggles's efforts opened small cracks in the walls that separated black and white female activists but could not surmount them.[38]

Given Ruggles's success with fundraising at black female organizations, it is surprising that he could not find a mate in one of them. Females were always a majority of the black population of New York City. Historically, they had worked as domestics, though Irish women were quickly supplanting them. With the rise of Irish domestics, black females were increasingly relegated to lesser roles as washerwomen. Downgraded in work, they found solace in the church. Educated black women had to retreat from the public world to the private sphere or to volunteer activities in the Dorcas Society or similar organizations. Given that Ruggles came from a large family with a strong mother, attended church, worked well with women's associations, and seemed to have a knack for finding good housing, it is surprising that he did not marry. In his mid-twenties at this time, Ruggles would seem a prime candidate for marriage. One can only speculate that his constant labors, the intensity of his activism, or perhaps the anger he often showed made a suitable match impossible.[39]

Perhaps, too, no woman wanted to bear the pressures Ruggles faced. Anti-abolitionists took note of Ruggles's activities. Newspaper attacks on Ruggles rose in the autumn of 1835. One public notice referred to his bookstore as an "incendiary depot" at the corner of Broadway and Lispenard. There, Garrison's *Liberator* is distributed by "David Ruggles, a black amalgamator who lately married a white wife." Such verbal assaults were usually precursors of more violent measures. On September 4, someone set fire to the store. The following week a mob organized in front of Ruggles's shop on three nights. Undaunted, Ruggles published a notice in the *Liberator*, refuting one charge and embracing another. He declared that he had never been married to any woman. He did state proudly that he sold the *Liberator*, which he called a "herald of light and truth." He then placed a reward of fifty dollars for identification of the arsonist and twenty-five for the names of any of the mob members. After the blaze, Ruggles had to relocate to a more downscale address at 165 Chapel Street, not far from where he had begun his New York City residency.[40]

The anti-abolitionist press reported the fire with undisguised glee. A racist satire published first in the *New York Star* chortled that New Yorkers should observe the memory of "David Ruggles of 67 Lispenard Street." The blaze and the implied threat in the article did not silence Ruggles, who continued his battles with kidnappers. He reported on November 7 the case of a black man named Brown who was seized by a slave catcher from Philadelphia named Hall. This "demon in human shape," as Ruggles termed him, gained access to Brown by pretending to be a friend of an uncle of Brown's wife. After Brown warmly received him in his home, Hall asked the man to walk with him, then turned him over to Tobias Boudinot, the constable for the Third Ward, who was gaining an unsavory reputation as an ally of kidnappers. Before Brown or his wife could do anything, the husband was taken south in chains. As Ruggles and Thomas Van Rensellaer reported regularly in the city's newspapers, such seizures were becoming commonplace in New York. Ruggles denounced Boudinot in print as pretending to be an abolitionist, while actually being a man-stealer.[41]

Ruggles did not limit his activities to New York City but began to enlarge his contacts around the state. While doing so, he experienced still more violent opposition. Ruggles had firsthand experience with riots in Utica, New York, in October 1835. He was one of several black men to answer the call by the Utica Anti-Slavery Society for a convention to form a statewide movement. Organizers held the meeting in Utica to widen abolitionist appeals beyond New York City and perhaps to entice greater involvement by Gerrit Smith, a wealthy land baron who lived about twenty miles southwest of the city in the village of Peterboro in Madison County. Alarmed at the prospect of hundreds of abolitionists visiting their city, opponents of the movement, including the Utica Democratic Party, and Joshua Danforth, who was the ACS's most zealous local proponent, mustered opposition to the convention. The city was also the home of the author whose racist novel about interracial love had sparked violence in New York City the year before. As the date of the conclave neared, angry citizens denounced the antislavery society in public meetings for allegedly publishing incendiary materials. On the eve of the convention, Congressman Samuel Beardsley, a staunch Jacksonian, blasted the abolitionists as anti-Unionists and proclaimed that they were intent on turning Utica into Sodom and Gomorrah. Another public speaker argued that slaves in the South lived better than farmers in the North. The Utica Common Council, to its credit, supported the right of the convention to meet. At the meeting, mobs from all ranks of society disrupted the ceremonies by tearing up petitions and shouting down speakers. Although the fracas did not descend into harmful violence, antislavery advocates had to abandon the city; members then reconvened at the local Presbyterian church near Smith's home in Peterboro. Ruggles had already experienced more violent mobs in New York City.

Although Ruggles is not recorded as a vocal participant, the entire affair increased his status among upstate abolitionists and widened his circle of contacts. Accompanied by New York City antislavery stalwarts Lewis Tappan, Joshua Leavitt, and the black grocer J. W. Higgins, Ruggles met dozens of upstate abolitionists who would later become supporters of his effort. These included men who lived in upstate towns such as Fayetteville, Warsaw, and New Hartford, or in such counties as Ontario and Jefferson, all hotbeds of antislavery petitioning and rallies. Many of the abolitionists were from Connecticut and other New England states, so Ruggles shared origins with them. He and the other conventioneers would in time be pleased with their efforts in Utica. Antagonistic toward the convention in 1835, the majority of the city's voters within six months listened peacefully to sixteen lectures by Theodore Weld. More than six hundred citizens joined the Utica Anti-Slavery Society and twice that number sent abolitionist petitions to Congress.[42]

Religious conviction underlay the shared abolitionism of Ruggles and other delegates to the convention. The New York State abolitionists were commonly Congregationalists who had joined forces with stronger Presbyterian parishes to create "Presbygationalist" churches. The Plan of Union of 1801 formally unified the two denominations to limit conflict and facilitate missionary works. Identifying slavery as the greatest sin of its time, these Presbygationalists combined radical perfectionism with direct challenges to institutional power to create a dynamic ecclesiastical abolitionism. As Congregationalists such as the Tappan brothers and Ruggles poured into the Presbyterian churches in the city, they extended New England theologies and attitudes about slavery into the denomination. Until his plan was vetoed by Reverend Gardiner Spring of the Brick Presbyterian Church in New York City, Lewis Tappan wanted to create a chain of Congregationalist churches across the metropolis and thereby extend abolitionism. Although unpopular with more conservative theologians, Tappan's proposal reflected the views of many evangelicals. Unlike conservative abolitionists whose principal concern was the protection of "white labor," ecclesiastical abolitionists insisted upon full civil rights for black Americans and were fully involved in the women's rights movement from its beginning. Finding their truths in the Bible, ecclesiastical abolitionists, as argued by historian Douglas M. Strong, were motivated by their experience of Christian holiness to stand up against the dominant institutions of church and state. Such beliefs were compatible with those expressed by Ruggles.[43]

Upon his return to New York, Ruggles directed more of his energies to combating the kidnapping of fugitive slaves and free blacks from New York City's streets. Kidnapping had been a problem since the early days of the republic, with numerous outrages occurring in New York City over the years.

Now, with the loss of black political power and the rise in slave prices in the South, kidnapping incidents soared. The city's highly public street life made theft of children all too easy. As well, southern slave owners had used agents to arrest and return fugitive slaves from the North. Slave agents and kidnappers found it easy to confuse runaways with free blacks or to treat free blacks as if they were runaways. Much of the city's white population, tied to the South by business connections, still regarded blacks, just a few years after the end of slavery in New York State, as chattel and, profoundly racist in attitude, were willing to ignore kidnapping. Aggressive kidnappers, abetted by an indifferent white population and assisted by complicit magistrates, could steal black people off the streets with little risk. Richard Riker, the New York City court recorder, frequently sanctioned kidnapping of free blacks. Although he had condemned the 1834 riots, this official favored slavery and was willing to accept any white man's testimony against an accused black person or supportive witness. Corse and the Manumission Society had access to sympathetic legal talent in the city, which enabled them to protect some accused African Americans. Agents of slave masters were unconcerned about the actual identity of the black people they seized and often took any person with even a vague resemblance to their intended prey.[44]

Historically, the city's black community had strived to resist such depredations. Since the early years of the century, the black community of the city had mobbed such agents, known popularly as kidnappers or "blackbirds," to prevent such seizures. Helping protect accused fugitives was the New York Manumission Society, which since the 1780s had provided legal counsel to accused people and at times even took part in street confrontations. After a hiatus of several decades, the radical wing of the Manumission Society, under the leadership of Barney Corse, resumed in the late 1820s the active defense of self-emancipated bond people and of victims of careless identification. Corse was the heir to a venerable local tanning company and had married into the family of Samuel Leggett, the first president of the New York Gas Light Company. By the mid-1830s, Corse had become chair of the standing committee of the New York Manumission Society and thereby had access to sizable funds for legal defenses of free blacks accused of being slaves. Corse was an ally who could grant Ruggles access to the very elite of New York City society.[45]

The Manumission Society sought to attack other privileges enjoyed by slave masters. Despite the abolition of slavery in the state in 1827, visiting slave masters retained rights to bring their human chattel into New York. Legislation dating back to 1801 allowed nonresidents to travel in and out of the state with their enslaved people. The 1817 legislation dooming slavery after July 4,

1827, reaffirmed permission to nonresidents to bring slaves in; two years later, a new law permitted owners who resided part of the year in the state to carry away and bring back slaves. New Jersey had not expanded upon its gradual emancipation statute of 1804, which meant that slavery was very close by New York City. Bergen County, just across the Hudson River, was home to 584 enslaved blacks according to the census of 1830.[46]

Ruggles used public forums to build momentum for the movement against kidnappers and to alert the black community to traitors. In an emotional rally in late October 1835, Ruggles described at length how state laws aided slave masters and man-stealers, and how ship captains and "even colored persons" were employed in "kidnapping clubs." He identified several blacks working for slave agents, specifically naming David Holliday, who walked through the city identifying runaway men, women, and children. Ruggles also cited two other black men, John Wallace of Staten Island and Ned Shores, who had several aliases. Wallace tried to entice Eliza Drummings onto a ship with promises of love and a kiss. When she fled, he had her property seized, sold it, and left for New Orleans with the money; she "suffered grievously." A fourth infidel, Thomas Tallibut, tried to have a young woman from the South arrested and taken aboard a ship. At the end of the meeting, Ruggles, along with Thomas Van Rensellaer, John J. Washington, William Thomas, and Henry Butler, went in search of Tallibut to "bring him justice."[47]

In a significant advance of his own activities and one with national ramifications, Ruggles next moved to create an organization to battle kidnappers and to provide practical support for self-emancipated slaves. On November 21, 1835, Ruggles and other "Friends of Human Rights" organized the fabled New York Committee of Vigilance. A group had been meeting informally on a weekly basis for more than a year. Its executive committee included William Johnson, Robert Brown, George R. Barker, and J. W. Higgins, as well as Ruggles, who became its secretary. The officers of the group were a mix of blacks and whites and included a restaurant owner, a broker, a grocer, and two career abolitionists. Several of the white members worked nearly full time as abolitionists. William Johnson, born in England, was a career abolitionist and served as the committee's treasurer from its inception into the 1840s. George R. Barker was a second lifetime abolitionist. The committee, the nation's first of its kind, stated that its mission was "practical abolition," which would offer direct assistance to "protect unoffending, defenseless, and endangered persons of color, by securing their rights as far as practicable." The committee emphasized that it would help fugitive slaves obtain "such protections as the law will afford."[48]

To enlarge membership and to help support its actions, the Committee of Vigilance officers formed an Effective Committee of about one hundred men and women. Each person was a fundraiser, entering into a small book the names of ten or twelve persons from whom the member had solicited a penny or more a week, bringing the total number of people involved to more than one thousand. Some members simply gave fifty cents per month; others contributed pennies at a time. As Leslie Harris has pointed out, the size of the Effective Committee was far larger than any gatherings of the antislavery societies or the black convention movement. The frequency of solicitations also gave the committee a constant presence in the black community. Ruggles and his committee were able to attract support from almost 10 percent of the city's black residents. Their methods gained quick approval from William Lloyd Garrison and other white abolitionists.[49]

The committee was by far the most radical response any abolitionist group had made to the problems of kidnapping and easily the most overt demonstration of support for self-emancipated slaves, inspiring the Philadelphia society, which formed the next year. By declaring itself beyond legal authority, the committee opened itself to criticism and violent reaction. Its defiant words showed it did not care. Although not an insurrectionary movement such as the rebellions of Denmark Vesey or Nat Turner, members used direct confrontation to oppose slaveholders and their agents seeking fugitive slaves. It thereby stood in defiance to laws and beliefs about property rights common in the United States. It was also an indication that committee members were willing to use tactics stronger than the patient methods urged by other abolitionist groups to protect children swept up by kidnappers.

The committee became a crucial method to give disenfranchised blacks, male and female, middling and poor, a voice for their anger. The committee determined to circulate information on protecting free blacks by any means necessary and became a beacon of help for fugitive slaves. Steven Hahn has argued that northern black communities regarded themselves as "under siege," an apt term for how the embattled blacks of New York City viewed attacks by kidnappers and slave traders. The Committee of Vigilance was an organized method of self-defense. Hahn uses the New York City black community, refreshed continually by newly arriving fugitives from southern slavery, as an example of a nineteenth-century maroon society, with its own leadership, rules, and governance. Rather than live apart in the countryside, as did earlier maroons, these clustered in cities and small towns of the North. They did not seek to restore the past, but to push hard against slavery and for freedom.[50]

Hahn's argument is a pregnant notion. Certainly fugitive slaves, among those whom the committee wanted to help most, were petite maroons because they escaped from bondage. Beyond that clear link, Hahn's discussion broadens the importance of northern black communities by linking them to a national concept of slavery and resistance. It veers sharply from standard community studies that emphasize the growth of such benevolent institutions as churches, schools, and fraternal organizations that seek black uplift and strive to battle discrimination and slavery. Hahn's idea fits well with black nationalist studies that focus on African culture in urban black neighborhoods. By linking black districts to maroons, Hahn makes violence a characteristic of northern black response to slavery and racism, a method that, despite David Walker's *Appeal* and the example of Nat Turner, was still being debated in the 1830s.[51]

A major difference between black communities, its abolitionist workers, and maroons, was race. The Committee of Vigilance had close ties with major abolitionist organizations, included white members and, as we shall see, reached out vigorously to sympathetic whites and blacks throughout the North and Canada, even if people of color largely ran the organization. Rather than create an insular world, the Committee of Vigilance sought to form a network that coalesced as the Underground Railroad.

Ruggles was easily the most visible member of the group. His home at 165 Chapel Street was the headquarters for the committee. As secretary, he recorded its actions and reported them to newspapers; in his performance, he went far beyond the others in fighting kidnappers. The need for the committee may be measured by the fact that in early 1837, the committee was involved in an average of one new case per day.[52]

Ruggles connected the central role of the committee to the larger struggle in a remarkable statement printed in the group's annual report. In the preface, Ruggles stated that, while he respected greatly the work of the American Anti-Slavery Society, the Committee of Vigilance had a special task that only threatened blacks could understand. Ruggles argued that in a city where "much oppression and injustice was practiced against our colored brethren," where so much discrimination occurred, and where pestilential slave catchers roamed freely preying on innocent blacks, only an organization devoted to stopping kidnapping would suffice. Although the efforts of the American Anti-Slavery Society were laudable, it would take time to achieve the revolution it sought in society. If the American Anti-Slavery Society could take the larger view, the Committee of Vigilance tackled the daily task of protecting liberty and fighting slavery in New York. It vowed to direct its attention to the arrival of fugitives from the South, to the presence of slave vessels in New York's port, to the proceedings of slave agents and kidnappers including their abduction of innocent people, and the recovery of persons and property detained in the South. This work would not be cheap. The committee proudly announced protecting 335 people from slavery. The costs of such efforts had already put the organization into a deficit of nearly four hundred dollars. This debt troubled but did not deter Ruggles, who declared:[53]

> To effect a mighty revolution, such as the general abolition of slavery, requires agents, and funds, and time, and influence . . . but while we long and labor for the accomplishment of this noble cause, let us not lose sight of the minor evils, which tend in the aggregate to make up that monstrous system of inequity; let us in every case of oppression and wrong, inflicted on our brethren, prove our sincerity, by alleviating their sufferings, affording them protection, giving them counsel, and thus in our individual spheres of action, prove ourselves practical abolitionists.[54]

In his appeal, Ruggles beseeched the antislavery movement to move beyond sterile discussions into direct action, which would aid those who needed it most: fugitive slaves and the free black victims of kidnappers. Attention to the "minor evils," he argued, would not overburden the movement but would broaden it. Practical abolitionism would make the struggle against slavery and racism more immediate and, he hoped, appealing to the larger population of sympathetic whites and aggrieved blacks.

Ruggles extended his practical abolition on many fronts. Enumeration of his activities in the winter of 1835–36 reveals how broadly Ruggles worked in the antislavery movement. He was agent for the *Liberator* until he had to resign because of the complexity of delivering the newspaper in a city where subscribers moved constantly and often neglected their bills. Working as the agent of the *Emancipator* also proved onerous as numerous subscribers failed to send in payments, forcing Ruggles to demand cash in advance. He served as secretary for a meeting welcoming Nathaniel Paul as agent for the fledgling colony of Wilberforce in Upper Canada (Ontario). A few months after that he joined Samuel Eli Cornish, Thomas Downing, Charles B. Ray, and other notable members who disavowed themselves from Israel Lewis, who claimed to represent the Wilberforce Colony in Lower Canada (Ontario), a black utopian community. Lewis was waging a public relations battle with the head of the colony, the venerable black abolitionist and businessman Austin Steward. Ruggles and the other signers clearly supported Steward, who had been active in the movement for more than a decade. In addition, Ruggles continued his newspaper campaign against kidnappers by publishing their names and violations against the civil rights of black New Yorkers. Such a method inverted the racial methods of the past used in runaway notices. Now whites were the ones who abused the law. In a similar inversion, Ruggles listed the kidnapping of an eleven-year-old boy in early December and described his clothing precisely before declaring that the city was "infested with kidnappers."[55]

The Committee of Vigilance enlarged its mission over the course of its first year. At its first annual meeting, held just six months after its creation, chairman William Johnson argued that the committee was essential because New York City was a "SLAVEHOLDER'S HUNTING GROUND." Johnson listed a number of abuses of the rights of black people in the state. He proclaimed that fugitives and free people of color were exposed to the terror of slave catchers and noted that New York State denied people of color the vote, right to trial by jury, and access to public schools, academies, and colleges. Its churches were closed to all except black domestics. All this, he argued, was done to show support to the system of southern slavery and its ally, the American Colonization Society. The committee's actions and statements began to attract followers from upstate New York. Alvan Stewart of Utica claimed that its meetings were the first time that he had ever been present in such an "assembly of colored people." Through the committee, benevolent whites could interact with numerous people of color, rather than the occasional black they might encounter in other antislavery societies.[56]

Ruggles did not abandon his efforts to start black schools. Ruggles and his fellows in the Phoenix Society tried to establish a high school for black children in New York to teach them "the Classic Mathematics, and higher department of English courses of Study," in the spring of 1836. One donor gave a library of more than 350 books on religion, modern literature, and the classics. Shortly after, Ruggles, Lewis Tappan, and Thomas Van Rensellaer announced the opening of an evening school for adults. Such efforts needed funds. Appealing to philanthropist Gerrit Smith, whom he had met during the Utica riots the year before, Ruggles, as agent for the Phoenix Society, asked for funds to support lectures that would help young black people "rise in the scale of intellect." Without education, Ruggles argued, blacks would remain "depressed and degraded," but with learning they could prove to whites that their minds were as capable of "indefinite Expansion" as their own. Several black leaders, including Samuel Eli Cornish and Peter Williams Jr., previously targeted the philanthropist, and doubtless Ruggles wanted to build on the connections made in 1835 at the organizing meeting of the New York State

Anti-Slavery Society. Whether Smith gave money is unknown, but the school prospered for a while. By early 1837 it had enrolled sixty scholars taught by a man and a woman. They also instructed adults in the evening school. Ruggles and his colleagues may also have planned to create a school in New Haven, Connecticut. In September 1836, silversmith Isaac L. Dimond, a Connecticut native, one of the most successful real estate investors in New York City, and financial backer of the Broadway Tabernacle, gave Ruggles a plot of land in New Haven for a dollar. The eventual result of this benevolent transaction is unknown, but it does indicate that Ruggles had expansive plans.[57]

Ruggles's other activities continued unabated. In early May he was one of ten leading black citizens of New York who spoke out about the financial troubles of the Wilberforce Colony in Ontario, Canada, and blamed Israel Lewis for them. In August he addressed a celebration of British Emancipation at the Baptist Church in Catskill, New York. Ruggles used the occasion to rally support for the Committee of Vigilance and its efforts to end slavery and to help fugitives escape the clutches of slaveholders and evil city officials.[58]

As the controversy over kidnapping heated up, more and more of Ruggles's time was spent on fighting it. In late July 1836, Ruggles angrily reported the forced removal of a black man named George Jones. Summoned by police officers to answer an accusation of assault and battery, Jones, urged by his employers, went with the city police to the Bridewell prison. After several hours there, he suddenly was placed before Judge Richard Riker, who pronounced him a fugitive slave and ordered him shipped to the South. In his report of the kidnapping, Ruggles lifted his rhetoric, saying "We have no protection in law—because legislators withhold justice. We must no longer depend on the interposition of the Manumission or Anti-Slavery Societies, in hope of peaceable and just protection," but ominously demanded that a "remedy be prescribed to protect us from slavery." He proclaimed: "Whatever necessity requires, let that remedy be applied. Come what may, anything is better than slavery." Moving beyond civil disobedience, Ruggles was clearly calling New Yorkers to adopt if necessary the violent methods of antikidnapping mobs of the past.[59]

In his condemnations of kidnappings, Ruggles flouted danger. A few days after the abduction of George Jones, Ruggles identified in an article "Boudinot, Bowyer, Huntington, Smith, Bell, Ridell . . . to be what the southerners call a 'negro-catcher.'" By listing these white men by name, Ruggles was warning black New Yorkers to avoid them. He continued naming names in every article about kidnapping from then on, effectively creating a kidnapper's directory. Doing so was necessary for reasons beyond the obvious. Tobias

Boudinot, for one, was prone to describing himself as an abolitionist, when meeting naive blacks. This man, Ruggles thundered, "Wolf-like . . . comes in sheep's clothing, before pouncing on an innocent person and dragging him before the Recorder [Richard Riker] who is ever ready to sacrifice him upon the altar of slavery." He also reached for larger themes of white injustice. In an August 3, 1836, article, Ruggles asked how black New Yorkers could account for the "alarming decrease of the black population in this city." He calculated that the black population of New York was eighteen thousand in 1830, but that total had slipped to fifteen thousand five years later. Much of this, he reasoned, could be blamed on kidnappers, who acted with impunity, seizing young and old on spurious pretexts, jailing them, and then, with cooperation from Riker, shipping them South into slavery. Indeed, Ruggles argued, it was safer for kidnappers to operate between New York and Texas than it was for pirates to board ships on the ocean because the man-stealers did not have to contend with the British navy. Though his population calculations were high, he was correct that the city's black populace was endangered.[60]

Ruggles and his fellows at the Committee of Vigilance continued to hold public meetings to rally black New Yorkers against the kidnappers. On October 6, 1836, Thomas Van Rensellaer, Jacob Francis, and Ruggles led a "very large adjourned meeting of the colored citizens of New-York" to consider the kidnapping, shipping, and sale of three people to southern slave masters. The committee lamented that it could not trust the city recorder, Richard Riker, to administer the law fairly. Moving in a more radical direction, the meeting resolved that it was in vain to look to the courts for succor, "where every advantage is given to the slaveholders and to the kidnappers." Rather, the participants declared "humanity and justice dictate, that every colored citizen unite his every effort . . . and continue those efforts in every proper and legal manner." While arguing for legal methods, Ruggles and his group stated that they could not trust the white legal establishment to uphold the law and protect citizens of color.[61]

Discussion of kidnappings, the primary subjects of the monthly meetings of the New York Committee of Vigilance, attracted larger and larger numbers of people. At the November meeting, chaired by Robert Brown and attended by an overflow crowd at Ruggles's home at 165 Chapel Street, Ruggles impressed the audience "with the alarming fact that any colored person within this state is liable to be arrested as a fugitive from slavery, and put upon his defense to prove his freedom, and that any such person thus arrested is denied the right to a trial by jury."

These grass-roots methods spread allegiance and avoided the noxious def-

Kidnapping. From [Jesse Torrey], *A Portraiture of Domestic Slavery in the United States Proposing National Measures for the Education and Gradual Emancipation of the Slaves, Without Impairing the Legal Privileges of the Possessor and A Project of a Colonial Asylum for Free People of Color Including Memoirs of Facts on the Interior Traffic in Slaves, and on Kidnapping.* 2nd edition. Ballston Spa: Published by the Author, 1818. Torrey's book highlighted the kidnapping of free blacks as part of the corrupting influence of the internal slave trade. The illustration shows how kidnappers terrorized black families. Courtesy of Division of Rare and Manuscript Collections, Cornell University Library.

erence often necessary when applying to white benefactors. Ruggles used rallies to report successes and to plead for money. At one, he stated that the committee's efforts had saved "THREE HUNDRED PERSONS," in the past year "from being carried back to slavery." Though the treasury was now depleted, Ruggles contended that he had never seen the "colored people" of the city "pay their money so freely and promptly." It was, he concluded, because the committee offered "practical abolition." William Johnson then described three more cases of kidnapping of small children. Ruggles returned to the floor to discuss the methods used by Boudinot, D. D. Nash, a city marshal, and their lawyer, to seize unwary children and sell them into slavery.[62]

Antislavery celebrities began to frequent the meetings. Beriah Green of the Oneida Institute, an integrated school in upstate New York, attended the November gathering. William Lloyd Garrison spoke at the December congregation. He informed the audience of five hundred blacks that other blacks and whites were watching their efforts with approval. Garrison identified fully with the crowd, noting, "Great efforts are making among the whites for their moral improvement. We (you perceive that I speak as a colored man)

Making Practical Abolitionism

must try to keep up with them." Garrison reminded the assemblage that the struggle against slavery was not the work of any man; rather, "Your obligation to God requires it." Not to be outdone, Lewis Tappan came to the next committee meeting. He echoed Ruggles by identifying a merchant on Pearl Street who bragged that he could get fifteen hundred dollars in Virginia for a young black man named Paul.[63]

Building upon the excitement of Garrison's visit, Ruggles and Philip A. Bell held a second meeting. On December 5, 1836, Ruggles acted as secretary for a meeting of a new local organization, the United Anti-Slavery Society of New York, held at the Phoenix Society Hall on Chapel Street. "Those who manifested that they remembered those in bonds, as bound with them," soon overcrowded the hall. Speaking at the meeting were Charles B. Ray and Samuel Eli Cornish, who lavished praise on the American Anti-Slavery Society. Ruggles and Philip A. Bell spoke warmly of the *Liberator*, which had for six years rejected the attacks of its opponents and was "sustained mainly by individual effort." Then Ruggles spoke eloquently of how the *Liberator* helped remove the gloomy years when the "spirit of expatriation" held sway, when the American press cried, "Away with them!" in an effort to sweep "the free colored population" across the Atlantic. The *Liberator* came to the rescue of the abused and oppressed. "And now witness (said Mr. R) the pleasing change in the attitudes of the American press and churches about slavery."

Garrison and the *Liberator* were doubtless grateful for such remarks, but most extraordinary was Ruggles's command of the crowd. In one instance, the unnamed reporter noted "the audience was completely electrified"; in a second instance, Ruggles's words "produced a thrilling effect." Ruggles spoke directly to those in the audience who "had felt the iron hoof of slavery upon their neck." Recall that slavery in New York had ended but nine years before. Many in the audience may have come from the slave state of New Jersey or from points south where human bondage was prided as the social and economic order of society. Ruggles could touch those husbands in the audience whose families had been torn from them, or mothers who had daughters "writhing in chains," thereby "exciting deep emotion" in the audience. After a collection and subscription drive for the *Liberator* and a swelling series of hymns, the meeting closed with an elegy by Reverend Timothy Egan of Methodist Asbury Church. In his speech, Ruggles, not a preacher himself, touched the hearts of his audience by direct appeals to their memories of slavery, their anxieties about families in the midst of waves of kidnappings, and their hopes for a community of benevolent whites and activist blacks. The speech's theme of the abused black family echoed the most personal statements in David Walker's *Appeal*. The description of his contact with the audience matched those used later to describe Frederick Douglass.[64]

In late 1836, Ruggles turned his attention to an equally dangerous foe: the illegal slave trade. In early December, Ruggles identified the presence of a Portuguese slave ship, the brig *Brilliante*, captained by I. C. A. De Souza. Rebuffed in his initial attempts to inform the newspapers of the slaver's presence, Ruggles eventually convinced the *Evening Post* to publish an article about the illicit vessel. The ship was then at berth in New York harbor and, alleged Ruggles, held several blacks with Spanish surnames on board as slaves. In fact, he learned about the slaves from one of the sailors. According to Ruggles, with information published in the *New York Sun* and the *New York Evening Post*, the ship had sailed from the Gambia Coast in Africa six weeks before, "with 12 or 13 Africans on board." Although the New York authorities, he claimed, were aware of the presence of the Africans, several had already been transported for sale in the southern states. Ruggles visited the vessel several times during daylight to confirm rumors that slaves were aboard the ship. He may well have known that de Souza was a notorious slave trader, information that had been publicized in American newspapers in 1831, including one in Norwich, Connecticut.[65]

Ruggles had de Souza arrested, and the slaves were also taken into custody. On Friday, December 16, the case came before the U.S. District Court with Judges Thompson and Betts determining the verdict. William Jay prosecuted the case against de Souza. The captain protested that his arrest was illegal under a treaty between the United States and Brazil of 1828. He declared that he had no intention of selling the slaves locally but was only making a brief stop in New York port. Eventually, de Souza was discharged, but the slaves remained in jail. Ruggles demanded their release but was rebuffed. Another judge determined that the slaves were not free because they were the property of a foreign national, not an American captain. Ruggles was not allowed to testify in the case. Eventually, the police escorted the slaves to the ship to prepare for departure.[66]

Aroused by this information, black New Yorkers made a dramatic move. As the New York newspapers reported the incident, on December 24, "a gang of negroes, some of whom were armed," went aboard the ship, assaulted the crew, and took away "two of the five slaves who were in the crew." The crew put up no resistance, but when a mate came from below and tried to stop the raid, "one of the gang cocked a pistol at him, and threatened to blow his brains out." Two hours later, the gang returned, intending to rescue the other three slaves. This time, they were repulsed, though they threw stones at the crew. The newspapers demanded prosecution but argued that the "gang was comparatively innocent, having doubtless been led on by the abolitionists." Regardless of the condescension implicit in the last remark, the event was stunning. A group of black men had boarded a ship, used force, and threatened to shoot a white man if he interfered with their rescue. The action was a major escalation of violence and unprecedented in a northern city. Ruggles denied being part of the gang, although he strenuously defended its behavior, in line with his position that blacks had the right of self-defense.[67]

His opponents viewed the incident as proof that Ruggles's departure from New York City was overdue. Between one and two o'clock on the morning of December 28, Ruggles was asleep in his home. Hearing loud knocks, he went to his door, which several men tried to force open. Ruggles demanded to know who was outside. One of the men responded "Why — Why it is Nash; I have come to see you on a matter of importance." Ruggles told Nash to come back at eight o'clock in the morning. Angered, Nash went off in search of High Constable Hays. When the intruders returned, they forced open the front door, menaced the landlady with knives and pistols, and attempted to grab Ruggles. They yelled at Ruggles that they would teach him to publish the names of kidnappers. Fortunately for Ruggles, the watch arrived and arrested Nash and the mate of the *Brilliante*, a sailor named Joseph Michaels. A search produced a writ to seize Ruggles as a slave, take him to the *Brilliante*, and ship him for sale in the South. Nash exclaimed that, had he caught Ruggles outside, "I would have fixed him." The mate claimed that Ruggles had assaulted the captain of the ship. The next day when Ruggles went to City Hall to press his case against the housebreakers, Tobias Boudinot arrested him for assault, and, despite the lack of a warrant, had him transported to Bellevue prison. Ruggles remained there a short time before being released.[68]

Boudinot arrested Ruggles using a writ he had obtained from Governor Marcy in 1832, enabling him to grab any black person identified rightly or wrongly as "Jesse, Abraham, Peter, or Silvia," names that were commonly used by local African Americans. Boudinot bragged that this warrant enabled him to arrest any person of color, then send him or her to the South, without even an appearance before a magistrate. Clearly the city officer viewed any black, even Ruggles, who was born free, as meat for the slave market. To demonstrate Boudinot's evil nature, Ruggles cited a recent case involving a kidnapped black youth named Peter John Lee, from Rye, New York. From what Ruggles understood, Nash, Boudinot, and another slave agent named Waddy had planned to do the same with him "for some two or three months past." Such depredations, concluded Ruggles, were happening in the city of

New York "while Humanity and Justice continue to sleep!" It was characteristic of Ruggles's courage that he would use this terrible threat against his own freedom to remind readers of a recent kidnapping. Ruggles, knowing that he was fortunate to still be free, wanted only to "take fresh courage in warning my endangered brethren against a gang of kidnappers, which continues to infest our city and country."[69]

Peter's plight allows evidence of how Ruggles worked with some of the most eminent New Yorkers. William Jay first discussed Peter's situation in a letter of December 3, 1836, with Theodore Sedgwick III, a young New York lawyer. Jay was incensed that a New York City police officer could travel up to Westchester County and seize Peter without a warrant. The officer had told local people that he had a general warrant given by the governor to capture any "fugitives from justice." Jay wrote Sedgwick to determine, if possible, whether any warrant existed and, if not, expressed that the barrister should move to prosecute the officer. Jay used strong language to describe the seizure, calling it base and wicked. Jay then turned to Ruggles. On December 10, 1836, Jay agreed that Peter's case could be resolved positively if Ruggles could provide him with proof of the victim's freedom and, if that was unavailable, then surety of length of his stay in the North, his family ties, and the method by which he was abducted. Jay told Ruggles of three affidavits sent up by the lawyer Theodore Sedgwick III. He wanted to know more about Nash in order to prosecute him. Finally, he offered Ruggles ten dollars against expenses. This offer appears to be more an acknowledgment of Ruggles's strained finances than a payment. Certainly Ruggles had a very independent mind about methods.[70]

Ruggles used the case to rally support for the Committee of Vigilance. Lewis Tappan recorded the first anniversary meeting of the committee chaired by Reverend Theodore S. Wright on January 16, 1837, held at the First Colored Presbyterian Church at Thompson and Houston Streets. Lewis and his brother Arthur Tappan observed that the audience was in rapt attention throughout as Wright and then Reverend John T. Raymond, pastor of a black Baptist church in the city, spoke about racial discrimination. Raymond, a free black, had been banished from his native state of Virginia because he had delivered a speech in New York praising the Wilberforce Colony in Canada. Tappan then recorded that Ruggles presented "the afflicted wife of Peter John Lee (a colored man who had been recently kidnapped from Rye, New York)," along with her "two fatherless little sons. The audience was deeply affected." Lewis Tappan later used this incident to show why Arthur and other abolitionists supported the Underground Railroad. Arthur had realized, his brother argued, it was a duty to help "men in efforts to obtain their liberty, when unjustly held in bondage." Ruggles surely agreed with those sentiments. His method was to appeal again and again to the sorrowful feelings of the black community about kidnappers' disruption of families and thereby to rally them to support the Committee of Vigilance. Certainly it worked with the Tappans.[71]

Ruggles became more radical about resistance to kidnappers and slave traders. An indication of this came in his rousing dissent from the resolutions declared by a public meeting of citizens reacting to a local judge's decision to return a fugitive slave into bondage. The meeting of a number of white abolitionists, who were joined by Ruggles, declared a deep sympathy for "our brethren in bondage" but could not accept the need for resistance. Rather, the committee argued that "[we should] fling ourselves upon the magnanimity of our country to deal with us as with one blood with them" and to entrust in the Creator. How such hopes could be sustained during the administration of the proslavery Martin Van Buren remains unclear, but Ruggles disagreed sharply. He complained "with much warmth" that the resolution "neither advocates resistance or non-resistance." To the slaveholders he argued that "our complexion is presumptive evidence of slavery" and that no one present could seriously promote nonresistance "when our houses are invaded and we are carried off by avaricious kidnappers."[72]

The black abolitionist community regarded Ruggles highly. That esteem is evident in a statement preceding Ruggles's report about his near-abduction. The writer, "B," referred to Ruggles as "one of our most worthy and useful fellow-laborers in the common cause of Human Freedom." The writer connected the failed kidnapping with a statement of how laws were administered in the city and warned black city dwellers, "Beware of these Slave-catchers"; he advised them to "imitate the conduct of Ruggles, and be as one man in the firm and unalterable determination to maintain your just rights and to defend your property and persons against all attacks . . . of notorious Slave-catchers." In short, in a time of crisis, Ruggles's behavior was right. His methods may have been controversial, but in late 1836 they were the vanguard of efforts to rally the mass of black New Yorkers.[73]

In two packed years, David Ruggles had moved into the forefront of abolitionism in New York City and made significant impact on a national scale. He worked as an organizer and wrote intelligent and forceful pamphlets and letters. He found in the battle against kidnapping a cause that resonated with local blacks and many whites. Kidnapping and the linked slave trade were issues that hit the city's black community hard, and in his tough confrontational approach, David Ruggles struck an emotional chord with an ever-growing audience. His role in founding and prosecuting the work of the New York Committee of Vigilance was far-reaching. Benjamin Quarles has deemed the committee the greatest black self-defense organization of the antebellum era. Ruggles interviewed black victims, questioned whites who were holding blacks illegally, and acted as an advocate for endangered blacks. At the same time, Ruggles reached out successfully to black women and attempted, however unsuccessfully, to do the same with white female abolitionists. His energetic struggle against kidnapping and the slave trade was making headlines and changing the methods of the fight against slavery. But all this activity cost him deeply and personally, as the next chapter reveals.[74]

＊ ✿ ＊

CHAPTER FOUR

Melding Black Abolitionism and
the Underground Railroad

David Ruggles had argued strenuously for support of abolitionist newspapers and pamphlets. He was among the movement's most active authors. In early 1837, New York's black community and the black abolitionist movement in particular received an enormous boost with the establishment of the city's second black newspaper. Edited by Robert Sears and Philip A. Bell, the *Weekly Advocate*, soon renamed the *Colored American*, started publication in January 1837. The weekly fast became a leading forum for the Committee of Vigilance and for Ruggles's letters and editorials. He supported the venture from the beginning. When Samuel Eli Cornish was named editor of the *Colored American*, Ruggles was one of seven men who pledged five dollars a year to help pay his salary. Ruggles also prepared a petition to the state legislature to grant agents of the *Colored American* the right to canvass the state for subscriptions. Ruggles's old friend, Charles B. Ray, worked as an agent for the newspaper and traveled throughout the upstate New York region, spreading word about the publication and simultaneously finding willing participants to provide safe houses for those escaping slavery.[1]

Ruggles continued his own barrage of publications. In early January 1837, the Committee of Vigilance, for which Ruggles served as secretary and principal author, published the *First Annual Report of the New York Committee of Vigilance*, a pamphlet of eighty-four pages. In addition to the preface in which he outlined the goals of the committee, the book was a compilation of kidnapping cases in New York and elsewhere in the United States over the past year. Ruggles carefully developed each case using newspaper articles to demonstrate the correct goals of the committee. Ruggles and the committee did not rest on their achievements. He called special meetings every time a new kidnapping occurred in the early months of 1837 or announced rewards for the return of the children in the newspapers. Gradually these events developed into regular monthly meetings. Ruggles highlighted the kidnapping of children, understanding that such actions would provoke white sensibilities as well as black anger.

There was a sense of present danger. The Panic of 1837, caused by a national financial credit crunch and the country's dependence on foreign credit, created a desperate quality in New York City. Need for cash, the opening of the Texas slave market, and the high price of cotton pushed the numbers of kidnappings to higher and more brazen levels.[2] In March 1837 a New York City constable kidnapped and transported a free black woman named Morgan and her six children to Maryland and sold them to a slave catcher for shipment south.

Though such kidnappings had occurred many times before, this seemed a particularly egregious example. John Stauffer has argued cogently that the Panic of 1837 and such abuses shattered the beliefs of abolitionists in normative social structures and magnified their self-conceptions as outsiders. Even the actions of so-called friends made black New Yorkers feel marginal, a sensibility that became evident in a dispute over a legacy that would have kept open the Phoenix School for girls. The school trustees regretfully had to close doors when they were unable to pay rent of three hundred dollars per annum from their own pockets. Particularly galling was the knowledge that an endowment of more than six thousand dollars bequeathed by William Turpin of New Haven lay unused in banks. Israel Corse of the Manumission Society and Arthur Tappan were executors of the bequest and refused, because of the panic, to turn the cash over to the school. The *Colored American* bitterly concluded that if the "trust had been left with colored men," they would have used it properly and saved the school. The following year, the literary society attached to the school also fell on hard times.[3]

With his actions against kidnapping, Ruggles rose into leadership in New York's black community and his name became known among northeastern abolitionists. In New York City he moved in the company of men with education and skills much like his own. Black activists in northern cities tended to be well-educated, entrepreneurial figures. Although ministers predominated,

The Underground Railroad

For Beriah Green "—
of Oneida Inst.

THE

FIRST ANNUAL REPORT *Compliment*

OF THE

NEW YORK COMMITTEE OF VIGILANCE, *of*

FOR THE YEAR 1837, *(D. Ruggles)*

TOGETHER WITH

IMPORTANT FACTS RELATIVE TO THEIR PROCEEDINGS.

The cause that I knew not, I searched out.
Yea, I brake the jaws of the wicked, and plucked the spoil out of his teeth.
—Job xxix. 16, 17

PUBLISHED BY DIRECTION OF THE COMMITTEE.
For sale at the Bookstores—Price 12 ½ cents single—$8 per hundred.

NEW YORK:
PIERCY & REED, PRINTERS,
7 Theatre Alley.

1837.

Title Page of *First Annual Report of the New York Committee of Vigilance, for the Year 1837, Together with Important Facts Relative to Their Proceedings.* New York: Piercy & Reed, 1837. Ruggles edited this compendium of cases that the Committee of Vigilance prosecuted in defense of free blacks and fugitive slaves. Courtesy of Division of Rare and Manuscript Collections, Cornell University Library.

other leaders worked as teachers, lawyers, doctors, dentists, shop owners, and artisans. Most were born free, although former slaves often became anti-slavery leaders. New York City black leaders were especially well educated. Contemporaries of Ruggles included Charles B. Ray, Theodore S. Wright, and James McCune Smith, all college graduates. Another close associate, James W. C. Pennington, known as the fugitive blacksmith, attended Yale Divinity School.[4]

Ruggles's name also spread throughout the southern states, where slave masters regarded him with fear and animosity. His notoriety can be discerned from an incident in Savannah, Georgia, on April 28, 1837. John Hopper, son of Isaac T. Hopper, was visiting the South for commercial reasons. The younger Hopper declared that he did not belong to any antislavery organizations but was mobbed and nearly lynched shortly after his arrival in Savannah. D. D. Nash, a New York City marshal, who was also visiting the southern port, had identified Hopper as "a friend to abolition." Nash was drunk at the time and shouted to the mob, "This same Hopper, his brother, and damned old father, Arthur Tappan, Barney Corse, and David Ruggles, a damned n____, who they treat as a brother—I'd give my own life to have him here—are the very leaders of abolition in New York City." A member of the mob then kicked Hopper and a fifteen-year-old boy spat in his face. Only after Hopper convinced the local sheriff that he had no abolitionist goals in Savannah was he able to escape the mob without further harm.[5] It took time for John Hopper to gain satisfaction from New York City magistrates. When William Jay visited Mayor Cornelius Lawrence to protest against Nash's behavior after the incident, he was blandly assured that Nash was then "absent on a mission from the sheriff of this county in Georgia." Only when Nash returned to New York did the mayor summon the agent to his office and remove his powers as a marshal. In his words and misdeeds, Nash inadvertently revealed the extent of Ruggles's reputation as a dangerous radical.[6]

Ruggles and the Committee of Vigilance pushed another fugitive slave case into public notice in the spring of 1837. William Dixon's case became a focus over the issue of the right to a trial by jury for fugitives. In a sensational moment, a large crowd, estimated at more than one thousand persons, gathered outside the jail where Dixon was being held. As police escorted Dixon down the courthouse steps, the crowd, hearing that the proceedings had gone against him, aided his escape and provided him with "a large dirk and a Spanish knife." Dixon was quickly recaptured. Samuel Cornish condemned the use of violence, charging that "an ignorant part of our colored citizens," had caused the riot and damaged the movement. He beseeched the mob to allow the "Intelligent and efficient Committee of Vigilance" and its "eminent lawyers to handle the case." Cornish demanded that the "ignorant mobs" cease "going to the Courts at all, or assembling in the Park, on the occasion of fugitive trials—you can do no good, but much harm." The following week, the *Colored American* presented more details of the riot and blamed Judge Riker as "Justice Bloodgood" for saying that he regretted not having a gun with him to send "a few of these damn n_____ to hell." The newspaper condemned the magistrate for his vulgar and violent behavior and concluded that his actions showed why alleged fugitives needed jury trials.[7]

Richard Riker's court became preoccupied with the Dixon case for months as witness after witness stated that Dixon had been a resident of New York City since the early 1830s and had been unlawfully arrested as a slave. Smart, tough young lawyers appeared on Dixon's side. Notably, John Hopper was able to convince Riker that the testimony of free blacks should be allowed in Dixon's case. A second attorney, Horace Dresser, who represented Dixon, was able to cast doubt about whether Dixon had ever been a slave, to the anger of the southern press. Such legal work was not cheap. In November the Committee of Vigilance pledged to raise one thousand dollars in Dixon's defense. Only a few months later, Ruggles was forced to advertise that the committee was in default of about twenty dollars. The committee was not the only party to experience financial difficulties. Walter P. Allender, Dixon's alleged owner, was required to pay two dollars a day for the man's stay in jail, costs that he eventually found onerous. Dixon was discharged but, fearful of the owner's retaliation, left the city for safety in the countryside. He later returned to New York City, where he encountered another fugitive from Maryland. Meanwhile, the Committee of Vigilance continued to raise money to pursue the case, hoping to establish a fugitive's right of trial by jury. Eventually, it was successful in gaining Dixon's freedom and obtained a seaman's protective certificate for him, which identified him as free. Such certificates shielded free blacks, at least in theory, from kidnappers. Even after its legal victory, the committee continued to pursue the case in hopes of ensuring trial by jury for fugitive slaves and other accused blacks. Particularly significant was the cross-racial cooperation that Ruggles and other black New Yorkers maintained with the white lawyers and abolitionists.[8]

The announcement of Dixon's release reveals the financial methods of the Committee of Vigilance when helping blacks under duress of the law. Dixon was held in jail with a bail of five hundred dollars, a sum roughly equal to a skilled laborer's annual salary in the 1830s. The Committee of Vigilance raised three hundred dollars through donations and collections from different churches and by its own appeals. "A friend," probably Arthur Tappan or another wealthy white, loaned the rest. Dixon was responsible for paying back the loan, which would mean large sacrifices for him and doubtless continual contact with and attendance at committee meetings. Whether he was legally liable is unclear; even if he was, the problems of collecting funds due from him were large and eventually would cause difficulties for the committee, especially for Ruggles.[9]

Despite their contempt for the slave catchers, Ruggles and the Committee of Vigilance sometimes found it necessary to deal directly with them and to pay for the freedom of those ensnared in their clutches. Such was the case of John Davis, a family man in New York City, whom Boudinot and Nash seized in May 1837. Several churches quickly raised about three hundred dollars to pay for his freedom. The committee reluctantly agreed with the method, though it argued that Davis's case had to be an exception to avoid making New York City into a slave market and supporting such barbarous wretches as Nash and Boudinot. Giving money to slave masters in this and other such cases marked a departure from the methods of William Lloyd Garrison and his followers who forbade such transactions.[10]

The breadth of Ruggles's energetic activities can be seen in the short announcements he made in the abolitionist press. In one, he made known the Committee of Vigilance's celebration on July 29, 1837, at the Broadway Hall of the third anniversary of British emancipation of enslaved West Indians. Expanding the appeal of the New York Committee of Vigilance, Ruggles announced that participants would be offered the chance to sign petitions demanding the abolition of slavery in the District of Columbia and against the admission of Texas into the Union. Continuing the practice of linking local efforts with the international struggle, Ruggles introduced James A. Thome, fresh from a lengthy visit to the West Indies, who argued vehemently for more than an hour against the opponents of immediate abolition of slavery.[11]

In early August, Ruggles joined in a campaign to collect petitions across New York State to make voting more open to blacks. Two years after the collapse of the black convention movement, New York City blacks pushed to regain their lost civil liberties. At this point, this drive was largely confined to blacks and had no ties to organized political parties. The campaign used classic religious and reform methods to gain support. Philip A. Bell prepared to tour across the state to collect massive numbers of petitions to "DELUGE the legislature" and convince state lawmakers to restore the vote to black citizens. Bell and Charles B. Ray soon experienced discrimination when they attempted to drink tea on the steamboat *James Madison*, while sailing up the

Hudson River. Ordered to take tea in the kitchen with the deck hands, the two abolitionists protested. "Palmed off" by a series of ship officers who seemed ashamed of their racist policy, the pair had to go without tea. Editorials in the *Colored American* linked the incident with the incessant cry of amalgamation and blasted critics for exciting needless anxieties about race mixture to justify denying equal use of transport facilities. One article, probably penned by Ruggles, noted that amalgamation was growing fastest in the slave states and that the local anxiety of it was merely the "mean, dishonest, ungodly resort of colonizationists, knaves and fools."[12]

While Ruggles devoted some attention to political rights, his main energies remained in protection of fundamental human rights. He advertised about the plight of kidnapped black children taken by slave agents, or the actions of southerners who used New York laws to bring enslaved people into the state temporarily. He listed each new kidnapping as it occurred. Reversing the purposes used in runaway notices, Ruggles identified the clothing and other physical appearances of kidnapped children. He reported the abduction of John Robinson Welch, a boy of eight or nine years of age, from his home on Mulberry Street; in the same announcement, he reminded readers of the fate of Thomas Bryan, a local boy, now confined in jail in Vicksburg, Mississippi, and about to be sold to satisfy prison fees. On May 20, he reported the disappearance of Frances Maria Shields, a girl of about twelve years of age. By November 1837 the Committee of Vigilance was involved in fifty-two new cases. Every time, Ruggles disclosed his residence, now located at 36 Lispenard Street, as the source for information about abducted people, making public that his home was an open refuge for enslaved people intent on liberty and to families seeking help recovering their loved ones from illegal bondage.[13]

Ruggles also continued naming names in his denunciation of slave traders or covert masters. He reminded readers of the loophole that allowed masters who sought to evade the laws requiring that slaves kept in the state for more than six months would be automatically freed. The practice was to take them out of state, to New Jersey, for example, then return immediately and reregister the enslaved person. While technically legal, the practice violated antislavery morality in New York State. Ruggles identified one master as Mr. David Stanford of Brooklyn; Ruggles added that Stanford was a member of the Methodist Episcopal Church, a clear notice that its congregation should reprimand and perhaps ostracize him.[14]

Ruggles's duties began to take a toll on his health. In mid-August 1837, he announced that he was "compelled to retire from the city and take refuge in the country."[15] The rigorous demands of his post with the Committee of Vigilance were adding to an already stressful work life. Money problems emerged and worsened his physical condition. In August 1837 he reported in an audit of the committee treasury, which was twenty-two dollars in debt, that he had been forced to retire to the country.[16] Ruggles's illness highlights the solitary nature of his personal life. At twenty-seven, he was still unmarried. Bachelorhood was common in 1830s New York City, where many young men spent their early adulthood in boardinghouses, going to brothels, and living sociable lives. Ruggles fit none of these descriptions. The gravity with which he conducted his life suggests that he had little in common with the clerks and working-class B'hoys, many of them new to the city, and who made up the sizable subcommunities of bachelors around the Bowery and Five Points.[17]

Despite his highly public role, Ruggles seemed to have many associates but few close friends. As noted, he belonged to churches. Many of his colleagues in the struggle were members of the New York African Society for Mutual Relief, an important cog in black New York Society. Ruggles was not on its membership list, nor is there any record that the organization helped him out during his bouts of illness. Leslie Harris has pointed out that the Society for Mutual Relief was filled with ministers but no chimney sweeps. Ruggles was well educated, but perhaps his role as printer and activist kept him out of this important community safe harbor.[18]

Ruggles apparently had friends upstate, and it is likely that he retreated to convalesce in Poughkeepsie, where Nathan Blount headed the Lancastrian School for black children. In late September after his return to New York, Ruggles advertised for a teacher to take charge of the school.[19] Ruggles also maintained contact with his Norwich family and on October 30, 1837, traveled to his hometown to purchase land for its use. On that date, Ruggles paid $425 down on a mortgage of $800 to purchase a small plot of land on the Plain Hills Road. The lot was not far from where one of his brothers owned land. For a man living in near poverty and wholly involved in political action in the nation's largest city, it was an unusual move. Perhaps Ruggles was investing some money for his family or seeking a place where he could rest his sickly body. No further record remains of this transaction, and it appears that a few years later someone else owned the property, indicating that Ruggles defaulted on the rest of the mortgage.[20]

Ruggles's zeal and multidirectional energy made him vulnerable to accusations of fraud. In October 7, 1837, a sailor named Joseph Galvino wrote Ruggles about the slave-trading activities of John Russell, a local black boardinghouse keeper. According to Galvino, three Africans from the Gambia region arrived in New York City and were briefly housed at Russell's sailors' lodge. Russell, said Galvino, forced the three men onto a ship captained by John Shepherd, who then tried to sell them as slaves, with Russell's knowledge. Galvino claimed further that Russell had pocketed the wages of the men and had treated them as "if they were in a slave country." Ruggles claimed that he interviewed Galvino thoroughly and was convinced of the veracity of what he asserted. So sure was he of the truthfulness of Galvino's statement that Ruggles rushed the story into print in the *Colored American* without reviewing it with Cornish. In defense of Ruggles, it should be noted that Russell's establishment had a bad reputation for "pandering to the bad taste of certain of his black customers." There were fights at the bar among white and black seamen that attracted the attention of the night watch. Russell also had a bad reputation for dishonesty, especially with sea captains.[21]

Despite his rowdy reputation, Russell did not hesitate to sue the *Colored American* and Ruggles for libel. Ruggles claimed that the newspaper had done nothing more than report the incident and that Russell could contradict the story in its pages, should he so desire. To cause distress to the newspaper was unmanly and mean of Russell. The story did not go away and eventually caused a major rupture between Ruggles and Cornish.[22]

In early September, Ruggles, continually active in the fight against kidnappers, informed New Yorkers of the kidnapping of a young apprentice from Jamaica. The boy's master sold him to a South Carolina slave trader. When Ruggles took a writ of habeas corpus to a local judge named Ulshoeffer, the magistrate refused to receive it because he was at dinner. When Ruggles told the judge that the ship would sail soon, the magistrate ordered him out of the house. Warned of Ruggles's efforts, the slave trader then took the boy overland to the South.[23]

While allies showed signs of concern about the more aggressive direction of the Vigilance movement, in May 1837 the Anti-Slavery Convention of American Women held a mass meeting in New York City. Kidnapping was a key issue discussed. In a direct appeal to "Free Colored Americans," the ladies expressed their sorrow at the "forcible seizure and consigning to cruel bondage [of] Native American citizens." The women were horrified at seeing black residents "manacled and guarded by officers armed with weapons of death—guiltless of crime and accused of none, but forced to prove that they are men and not beasts." Despite such crimes against humanity, the ladies' movement beseeched "our colored friends" not to use violent resistance, as such attempts would end only in disappointment and infuriate public sentiment and "furnish your blood-thirsty adversaries with a plausible pretext to treat you with cruelty." Patience was the watchword.[24]

Gradually, Ruggles became more radical on other issues in opposition to fellow committee members and, indeed, the abolitionist movement. A frustrating dispute arose over an adverse decision in December 1837 that returned a black man named Henry Merscher into slavery. One Judge Betts of New York City refused to consider a writ of *de homine replegiando* or Merscher's own evidence before condemning him to bondage. At a public meeting held at the Asbury Church on December 7, 1837, Ruggles, who had previously been appointed chair of a special committee to report "resolutions expressive of an unprotected and aggrieved people," listed ten statements for the meeting's considerations. Among them were resolutions opposing violence in support of slavery, upholding temperate behavior, protecting children from kidnappers, and looking to the Creator for guidance. It was the fifth resolution that spurred animated debate. Ruggles therein offered sympathy for "our brethren in bondage, whether they be white men in Morocco, or men of all colors in the Brazils, the West Indies, or U.S.," and pledged the meeting to carry on their cause by every lawful means. Ruggles then proposed a controversial clause that "we cannot recommend non-resistance to persons who are denied the protection of equitable law, when their liberty is invaded and their lives endangered by avaricious kidnappers." The case at hand could easily be seen as such an occasion for armed resistance, as could the numerous instances over the years in which kidnappers snatched small children off the city streets and sold them into slavery in the South.

Quickly objecting were Reverend Theodore S. Wright, Jacob Mathews, Charles B. Ray, and William P. Johnson, all of who were normally in solidarity with Ruggles. They asked that the clause be excised because "it was inconsistent with the peace principles advocated by the members of the A.S. Society, and to the spirit of every other resolution." Johnson, Bell, Garnet, and the others were doubtless influenced by the series of articles William Whipper of Philadelphia had published in the *Colored American* espousing nonresistance. Ruggles warmly responded that they misunderstood and that there was not a "gentleman in the house that could recommend submission under such appalling circumstances, when our houses are being invaded and we are carried off one by one by avaricious kidnappers." The question, he argued, was not over resistance or nonresistance. Because blacks were by definition of the laws of the United States presumed enslaved, any of them should, "when pounced upon by a kidnapper, not only use words implying resistance, but should resist even unto death." After a long and protracted discussion that was not reported in the proceedings, the clause was excised by a vote. Though defeated in the ballot by the ministers and other committee members who opposed his resolution, Ruggles, whose ear was closer to the ground, was undoubtedly expressing the anguish and anger of much of the black community over the kidnappings. For Ruggles, the issue was not so much the philosophy of antislavery as communicating the despair of the families wrecked by theft of a child, father, or mother. That the wrangle occurred as news emerged of the murder of the abolitionist newspaper editor Elijah Lovejoy by a mob in Alton, Illinois, made Ruggles's opinions seem more apt. Although they did not evince support for Lovejoy's shooting of an assailant or his resistance to the mob, in December black New Yorkers, including Van Rensellaer, Cornish, Theodore S. Wright, and Ruggles, mourned Lovejoy and took up a collection for his widow.[25]

Ruggles's dispute marked a significant transition in the antislavery movement. As one who was visibly active in direct struggle against the agents of slavery in the nation's largest city, Ruggles took a strong stance in favor of personal resistance to enslavement. As a core part of his "practical abolitionism," personal resistance made common sense to ordinary people, especially those beset by villainous kidnappers. As he plunged ahead with the work on the Committee of Vigilance, Ruggles became better known and his actions spoke louder.

Despite the dispute over nonresistance, Ruggles had to be pleased with the success of his organization. He had to remind members to pay monthly dues and turn over their subscriptions, but progress was on the horizon. The committee announced in its New Year's Greeting that it had opened correspondence with friends throughout New York State to help support the Dixon case now wending its way through the state's superior courts. Ruggles made a lengthy personal appeal for funds to keep the case going.[26]

In the midst of this flurry of activities, Ruggles announced that an eye illness, probably the onset of the cataracts that would eventually blind him, would keep him out of the city for a short while. While Ruggles tended to his health, fellow black abolitionists initiated a new organization whose focus differed from helping fugitive slaves and victims of kidnappers. The 1821 New York State Constitution had practically stripped blacks of the right to vote via a $250 property bond requirement. In the late 1830s, black state residents chafed at this onerous law and viewed it as a principal obstacle to improved civil rights. New York City blacks were surely aware of the Pennsylvania legislature's new restrictions on voting by introducing the word "white" before "freemen" as a qualification for the franchise. Anxious to ensure that the New York State lawmakers did not adapt a similar measure, Philip A. Bell and Charles B. Ray went on a second tour of upstate New York to canvass for support of a resolution restoring black suffrage. In New York City, a drive mounted to organize to remove the bond. A substantial number of black New York leaders joined the movement at a meeting on June 7, 1838, at which they elected officers and created committees to organize the general populace. Plans were made to send a delegation to the state conference to be held in Albany. Unassailable by intention and unquestionably needed, the organizing drive meant a diversion of energies from what the Committee of Vigilance had done the previous year.[27]

Ruggles continued working in his own pathways. When he returned to the city in early 1838, he published a lengthy appeal for support of the Committee of Vigilance's drive to win, via the William Dixon case, the right to a jury trial for self-emancipated slaves. Should that right be gained, Ruggles assured his readers, "man-stealers and kidnappers would invade the rights nor depopulate the state of its human inhabitants no more." Gone would be the "shrieks of wives for kidnapped husbands—the groans of husbands for their kidnapped wives," and children for their abducted parents. Ruggles directed that all correspondence about the case be forwarded to his home.[28]

Ruggles worked at a feverish pace. On March 1, 1838, he published a survey of the committee's 173 ongoing cases. Families who escaped from Virginia were found homes in New York. Ruggles reported on a case of a freeborn woman and two children whom the overseer and keeper of the Brooklyn Alms House had incarcerated with the intention of sending them South into slavery. Ruggles interrogated overseer Lance Van Nostrandt about his activities at his home. "Your correspondent" waited on the overseer, questioned him about the family, and demanded that the good citizens of Brooklyn "vindicate the honor and humanity of their city by requiring the immediate restoration" of the family's freedom.

Further in his report Ruggles announced suits against Judge Richard Riker, Tobias Boudinot, "the kidnapper," and E. R. Waddy, the sheriff of Northampton County, Virginia. According to Ruggles, these men engaged in kidnapping black people and selling them to dealers in New Orleans. Shortly after, Ruggles proclaimed that the "Kidnapping Club" was back in action in New York City. Ruggles reported on other kidnappings and then gave an update on the libel suit against him for slandering a boardinghouse keeper. Ruggles seemed resigned to losing the case because the judge was overheard to say that "your secretary has too much to do with the newspapers and should be stopped." Ruggles foresaw the glee that anti-abolitionists would have if he

The Author Noting Down the Narratives of Several Freeborn People of Color Who Had Been Kidnapped.
From [Jesse Torrey], *A Portraiture of Domestic Slavery in the United States Proposing National Measures for the Education and Gradual Emancipation of the Slaves, Without Impairing the Legal Privileges of the Possessor and A Project of a Colonial Asylum for Free People of Color Including Memoirs of Facts on the Interior Traffic in Slaves, and on Kidnapping.* 2nd edition. Ballston Spa: Published by the Author, 1818. In this image Torrey captures the retelling of the sagas of free blacks who had been kidnapped. Replace the white man with Ruggles, and it is not hard to imagine this scene replayed countless times at 36 Lispenard Street. Courtesy of Division of Rare and Manuscript Collections, Cornell University Library.

was convicted but promised that he would "establish the whole truth" about the letter.[29]

His writing pace may be discerned by his rapid response to David Reese's newest attack on the abolition movement. The *Emancipator* reported the publication of Reese's new pamphlet on February 24, 1838. Two days later Ruggles wrote that he was working on a reply. Two weeks later, he apologized to the public that his retort to Reese was not yet in press, but, he explained, given that Reese's appeal was several hundred pages long and that the doctor had published a second book entitled *Humbugs of New York*, the "welfare of the community required that I should stop the presses and dissect them both." Ruggles's efforts were applauded. "Philos" from Philadelphia argued that the proper method to deal with the misleading propaganda from the American Colonization Society was to refute it immediately as "David

The Underground Railroad

Arrest of the Slave George Kirk. This later cartoon intended to lampoon the efforts of abolitionists to help fugitive slaves. Beyond the racist imagery, it helps capture the controversial nature of such arrests. Courtesy of the American Antiquarian Society.

Ruggles does upon David M. Reese." By mid-March, Ruggles, although he was "sick, and almost blind," announced the planned publication of his latest attack on Dr. Reese.[30]

His timing was right. The American Colonization Society remained a force in New York politics. Supporters of the New York City branch of the ACS soon reorganized the local organization with a new constitution, which allowed it sizable autonomy. Although subsequent efforts by the national board in Washington reduced that independence somewhat, efforts made in New York City to convince free blacks to move to Liberia were determined locally. The New York City branch also understood that its greatest opponents were local abolitionists. Dr. Reese contended that the city's abolitionists formed the biggest obstacles to the society's progress. While he targeted Lewis Tappan and Gerrit Smith, the most immediate responses to Reese and his colleagues were from blacks.[31]

On April 2, Ruggles published a reply to Dr. Reese's critique of abolition titled *"Humbugs."* Ruggles named his work *An Antidote for a Poisonous Combination, Recently Prepared by a "Citizen of New-York," Alias Dr. Reese.* Published by William Stuart, this pamphlet was for sale at Stuart's Bookstore, 108 Nassau Street; at the Anti-Slavery Society Office, 143 Nassau Street; and at John Carter's store, Church Street, next door to Zion's Church.[32] That Ruggles did not publish it himself perhaps attested to the strains on his finances of fighting a continual war against kidnappers. Rather, the American Anti-Slavery Society executive committee, which included the Tappan brothers, Samuel Eli Cornish, Theodore S. Wright, Joshua Leavitt, and others, voted to advance Ruggles thirty-five dollars against an initial press run of one thousand copies at eight cents each, a sum less than the usual subventions ordered by the committee. As the cover price was twelve and a half cents each, the society purchased about four hundred copies at a wholesale rate.[33]

Much of the pamphlet dissected Dr. Reese's complaints about the New York Anti-Slavery Society and his apologies for slaveholders. Reese argued that slave masters were involuntary participants in the slave trade and the institution itself. Dr. Reese contended that the antislavery society threatened, by attacking the slaveholders, to "overthrow . . . liberty, law, and religion." Reese argued that abolitionists were thereby "rash, violent, and anti-Christian," words that, Ruggles responded, would not delude northerners who knew far better. Ruggles challenged Reese's contentions that the system rather than the slave owner was sinful, claims that Ruggles found fallacious. Just as bad, Ruggles continued, was Reese's argument that the act of slaveholding was not a sin, whereas emancipation would be cruel and inhuman. This, Ruggles noted, referred to examples of "aged, decrepit, insane, blind, deaf and dumb and idiotic servants." His response to Reese was that government could not impose conscience upon slaveholders and that the argument was often extended to maintain slavery for married couples, when the emancipated partner would be forced to leave a southern state. Therefore, Reese argued, emancipation would be cruel. Slave masters in the South often used such an argument to indicate how they would like to free their chattel, except for obstacles that prevented it, Ruggles pointed out. These thoughts were previously used in the South, Ruggles stated, until abolitionism gained ground in the North. Since then, southerners were more concerned with defying what was perceived as meddling with their patriarchal authority.

Following this useful analysis of proslavery ideology, Ruggles moved on to the primary focus of his publication: Reese's criticism of efforts taken against kidnapping by the Committee of Vigilance. Ruggles stated there was no connection between the Anti-Slavery Society and the Committee of Vigilance. The committee was the only "combination organized" to address the refugee problem. Emphatically proclaiming independence, Ruggles informed

The Underground Railroad

AN ANTIDOTE

FOR

A POISONOUS COMBINATION

RECENTLY PREPARED BY A " CITIZEN OF NEW-YORK,"

ALIAS DR. REESE,

ENTITLED,

" AN APPEAL TO THE REASON AND RELIGION OF

AMERICAN CHRISTIANS," &c.

ALSO,

DAVID MEREDITH REESE'S " HUMBUGS"

DISSECTED, BY

D A V I D   R U G G L E S ,

AUTHOR OF " THE EXTINGUISHER EXTINGUISHED," &c.

NEW-YORK:

PUBLISHED BY WILLIAM STUART,
No. 108 NASSAU-STREET.
1838.

PRICE $9 PER HUNDRED,—12½ CENTS SINGLE.

Dr. Reese that the committee "is an organization deriving no power, authority, or instruction from the American Anti-Slavery Society, and having no connection with it at all." In a footnote, Ruggles included the Manumission Society as a second organization devoted to helping slaves seeking freedom. He then challenged Reese to prove that the committee had violated any law in helping fugitive slaves.

After dismissing as ludicrous Reese's complaint that slave masters seeking return of their escaped bond people were being mobbed in New York City, Ruggles justified the legality of opposing masters' efforts. Ruggles quoted Dr. Reese saying that members of the American Anti-Slavery Society "organize combination for this purpose [for rescuing fugitive slaves] as well as for *clandestinely concealing* ['the shady shadow of the umbrageous tree'!!] and abducting into Canada or elsewhere, fugitive slaves, knowing them to be such, and publicly glory in their success in these lawless acts of *kidnapping* and *manstealing*, in defiance of the Constitution of the United States, and our own laws."[34]

Ruggles's response affirmed the slaves' rights both to consideration as equal citizens of the nation and to free movement: "Now when a portion of our citizens at the South wish to change their residence for a more northerly clime, for sake of their health or happiness, shall we contravene their honest intentions? Ought we not rather to assist them, especially if they are poor, and helpless, and friendless, as some of them are? Who is there in this land so brutish as would lay his clutches upon a poor slave just escaping from bondage? Not one, I trust, save a Nash, a Boudinot, or perhaps our order-loving author?"

Ruggles then stated that "the slaveholder has no right to any human being residing or sojourning temporarily or otherwise in the State of New York." The state did not recognize slavery; "therefore every slave who strays from bondage is the proper subject of our kindness, humanity, and protection from kidnapper," and that procuring the escape of a slave from bondage to liberty is "a violation of no law of the land, and I am sure if my opponent has ever read his Bible he will not contend that it is contrary to the precepts and spirit of that blessed book." Ruggles then referred Reese to Deuteronomy 23:15: "Thou shalt not deliver unto his master the servant which is escaped from his master unto thee."[35] Ruggles's supple use of biblical quotations with state law would appeal to most northern citizens, white or black, male or female.

Ruggles was especially adamant in refuting Reese's claim, reminiscent of arguments following the 1834 riots, that abolitionists were responsible for mob behavior, punctuating his comments with a rhetorical question: "Who ever heard of mobbing a slaveholder?" Ruggles found the doctor's arguments dated. He noted that northern attitudes had changed, and Reese's contentions, already stale in 1834, lacked any merit. Ruggles had justification for what he was saying. The gubernatorial election of 1834 indicated that abolitionist sentiment had grown stronger. The winning candidate, William Seward, skirted the issue of kidnapping, but moved quickly after the election to ban the return of self-emancipated enslaved people to their masters. Ruggles's pamphlet, the assurance with which he argued his case, his open contempt for Reese, and the resonance with which his arguments were received in the political realm are indicative of how much the actions of the Committee of Vigilance were affecting state politics and society. Soon after its publication, dissident members of the New York State Presbyterian Conference read Ruggles's pamphlet aloud in a heated dispute over participation in abolitionist activities. Ruggles's words, one dissident argued, demonstrated that abolitionism was on the right side of piety. Even so, Ruggles did not accept compromise from candidates. He refused to endorse Seward as a candidate because such a position was a pure and simple compromise with evil.[36]

Simultaneously, the Committee of Vigilance celebrated its second anniversary. The festivities, held at the Third Free Presbyterian Church in New York with George Tracy presiding, commenced with a prayer by Reverend George Storrs of Utica. Two members from Schenectady, New York, made a lengthy report on activities in their city. Lewis Tappan publicly promised financial support and urged all present to canvass for contributions. Also present and reporting were Hiram Wilson from Canada and Amos Dresser from Tennessee. Alvan Stewart, the noted activist from Utica, recommended that "organizations should be established as auxiliaries throughout the state," an indication that Ruggles's methods for creating an Underground Railroad were spreading and gaining support rapidly. The organization's constitution, published in the *Emancipator*, significantly opened membership to both males and females.[37]

At the celebration, Ruggles promised to publish the activities of the Committee of Vigilance. The previous year, he had done so in a lengthy pamphlet. For the second year, he chose a novel format. The annual report of the New York Committee of Vigilance was included in a new magazine, entitled the *Mirror of Liberty*, which made its first appearance in July 1838. Ruggles's publication of the *Mirror of Liberty* was an important historic achievement. It is generally accepted as the first magazine produced by a black American in the United States. It was printed and sold at his home, at the antislavery bookstores, or by subscription. Ruggles compiled nearly the entire issue. It consisted of reports of local cases, reviews, the Committee of Vigilance's report, poetry, and an essay on women's rights. According to the prospectus, the magazine was "consecrated to the genius of liberty" and would be beholden to "no sect, association, or company of men," but would expose those evils that blocked the progress of a "scattered, peeled and downtrodden people." Ruggles received high praise for his new venture. The *National Reformer* of Philadelphia lauded him as a "thorough-going abolitionist—one that works by day and by night, with his hands, feet, and pen. . . . He is the most success-ful, as well as the most inveterate enemy of the slaveholder. In fine, he may be termed the Granville Sharpe of the New World." To be compared with the Briton who was at the head of the English abolitionist movement was high praise, indeed.[38]

Ruggles made a direct appeal to women in this first issue. He wrote a poem titled "Woman's Rights," which included the verses: "Was woman formed to be a slave—to sink in thralldom to the grave, and Freedom never know! Say, must she toil and sweat, and bleed, A pampered lordling's pride to feed, And every joy forego." Clearly aimed at ordinary women, Ruggles's poetry was the latest in his appeals to females. Abolitionists, especially Garrison, used poetry to appeal to women. Locally, Patrick Reason wrote poetry to express his abolitionism and to promote his crusade to reclaim black suffrage, yet Ruggles was alone in demanding political power for women.[39]

Women answered with financial support. At the end of the *Mirror of Liberty*, Ruggles listed contributions to the Committee of Vigilance from January 16, 1837, to July 6, 1838. The familiar names are present. Arthur Tappan donated $50.00; Joshua Leavitt gave $10.00. J. W. Higgins submitted $25.00 on behalf of the Colored Presbyterians. Barney Corse supplied $50.00 on behalf of the Manumission Society to help pay for the Dixon case. Ruggles him-self gave $60.00, a sum that indicates that he placed the cause above his own welfare and perhaps explains his own poverty. Along with smaller donations from men were numerous cash contributions from women. Mary Halsey gave $16.00, Mrs. Theodore S. Wright offered $10.00; Mrs. P. Russell provided $25.00. Twenty women donated smaller sums ranging from $.10 to $1.25.

The Committee of Vigilance also benefited from the largess of churches and antislavery societies. William P. Johnson, the treasurer, compiled dona-tions in the first six months of 1838 totaling $531. Numerous collections at the Broadway Tabernacle netted about $50. Donations in excess of $40 came from the Asbury Presbyterian Church. The Abyssinian Baptist church gave $6. Third Presbyterian extended $22. Individual contributors included Mrs. Wedge-wood of England, who sent $26 through Elizur Wright. F. A. Perkins of Nor-

For the Pres. & Sec. of the Boscawen Anti Slav. Soc

THE

MIRROR OF LIBERTY,

FOR JULY, 1838.

VOLUME ONE. NUMBER ONE.

CONTENTS.

Introductory Remarks,
New York Gazette and the Brooklyn Affair.
N. Y. Committee of Vigilance.
Importing a Slave into the United States.
Dr. W. W. Sleigh's Book.
Our Subscribers.

What are we Doing?
Ex-Recorder Riker.
Who will Reject our Claims?
Poetry—'Woman's Rights.'
Second Annual Report of the New York Committee of Vigilance, with receipts.

Edited and Published by David Ruggles, at the corner of Church and Lispenard streets, New-York.
Printed by Gilbert Vale, Jr. No. 9 Peck Slip.

Title Page of *Mirror of Liberty* 1, no. 1 (July 1838). Ruggles's magazine was primarily composed of reports on the activities of the New York Committee of Vigilance. The first black-owned and black-operated magazine, the *Mirror of Liberty* was one of the many signal achievements in Ruggles's meteoric career. Collection of the author.

wich sent $2, probably at Ruggles's suggestion. His list amounted to $482. Listed as contributors in the first half of 1838 were Gerrit Smith and Arthur Tappan as well as subscriptions from churches and societies in Skaneateles and Otsego, New York, and $5 given by David W. Ruggles of New Bedford, Massachusetts. Ruggles asked the New England Anti-Slavery Society for a donation, but his request was tabled. Despite that rebuff, in all the committee took in more than $1,500. Fifty dollars came from sales of the *First Annual Report*. Johnson and an auditor listed expenditures, which were not detailed, amounting to nearly $1,700, creating a deficit of almost $200, a substantial sum for the time. The deficit was alarming, but even more worrisome was the lack of records over the total contributions and their destination, both indicators of the ad hoc nature of the committee's finances. Money came in regularly but went out in response to the many personal crises of the free blacks and self-emancipated slaves whom the committee helped. It is important to note that Johnson and Ruggles strived to account for incoming cash but seemed to have little control over the outflow.[40]

In the middle of the summer of 1838, however, Ruggles and the committee benefited from the faith and enthusiasm of white and black, male and female, and individual and institutional supporters from across the city and region. Despite successful fundraising, these infusions of cash could not meet all the pressing needs of the committee and the fugitives it protected. The committee's "want of funds" meant that it occasionally had to refuse requests. The secretary's and the treasurer's accounting did not list sizable expenditures. Given that the committee, by its own count, was involved in 187 cases in 1837 and early 1838 (522 since its formation), Ruggles, Johnson, and the others were simply handing out cash to those in need of food, shelter, and transportation to safety. Just as Ruggles had urged seating newcomers to the conventions back in 1833, he now spontaneously accepted the words of fugitives and provided them with needed cash. It was ultimately virtuous, republican, and dangerous.[41]

Ruggles constantly took on new assignments. One demonstrates how he strived to help those who backed him. On February 2, 1838, Ruggles headed an investigation into a charge that Hester Lane, a free black woman and philanthropist, had engaged in slave trading. For years, Lane, a pillar in the black community, had "purchased" enslaved individuals and even whole families from southern slave owners, brought her acquisitions to New York City, and then freed them. A few weeks earlier, Ruggles, Thomas Downing, Samuel Eli Cornish, Samuel Hardenburgh, and others had heard Lane was charged with attempting to sell a woman named Martha Johnson into slavery. Ruggles visited Johnson, who was ill, and gained from her a deposition denying that Lane had tried to sell her. Ruggles wrote in the conclusion of a "Committee of Investigation" that Lane had been slandered.[42]

In response, the black women of New York City continued their support for Ruggles and the Committee of Vigilance. Although they admitted that their expenses left little for contributions, the Ladies' Literary Society of New York held a fair in early 1838 to gather donations for the committee and for the *Colored American*.[43] A few nights later, Ruggles, Henry Highland Garnet, and others led a "Free Discussion" on February 6, 1838, to promote petitions to the state legislature to remove hindrances to black suffrage.[44]

By now, Ruggles's home had become the city's central depot on the Underground Railroad. Runaway slaves coming north already knew or were quickly informed that David Ruggles's house was the most welcoming place in New York. Fugitives who stayed free as far as Philadelphia were invariably directed to Ruggles's house. John Thompson worked for some time in Philadelphia, then, worried about slave catchers, traveled to New York. Ruggles advised him to go to New Bedford to get work on the sea. James L. Smith arriving in New York, asked a black woman if she knew "where I should find Mr. Ruggles." She took him to the house. There, he gave Ruggles a reference letter from Philadelphia. Smith remembered, "We had a great time rejoicing together." He stayed with Ruggles over the weekend, and then Ruggles provided him with letters to friends in Hartford and Springfield and cash for the trip. Ruggles repeated this procedure with William Green, a fugitive from slavery in Maryland. New England ministers hailed his work. For freedom-minded blacks in Maryland, David Ruggles was the North Star.[45]

Another Maryland black who made his way to Ruggles's home was Basil Dorsey. His saga demonstrates the extent of Ruggles's contacts in Philadelphia. Basil Dorsey was enslaved to Tom Saulers of the town of Liberty, Frederick County, Maryland. Dorsey contested his bondage and arranged for his own sale to a man named Richard Cole, but Saulers reneged on the agreement. Dorsey then fled with his three brothers in May 1836 on a route that took them through Gettysburg, Harrisburg, Reading, and finally to Bristol, Pennsylvania. Three of the brothers succeeded, but Basil was arrested the following year in Doylestown, Pennsylvania. The Philadelphia Committee of Vigilance secured Thomas Ross, a prominent Philadelphia lawyer, to help defend Dorsey. At the hearing, Ross was able to convince the judge that the slave master's claim was invalid because the alleged owner used a revised version of the statutes of Maryland to prove that slavery was legal. Ross argued successfully that the book presented was not published by the state of Mary-

36 Lispenard Street, New York City. Ruggles's home and the headquarters of the New York Committee of Vigilance, this still-extant building was the place of refuge for Frederick Douglass and hundreds of other self-emancipated slaves. Photograph by the author.

land and was therefore not an authenticated copy of the laws of that state. The judge ruled that Dorsey should be free. Dorsey walked out the courthouse somewhat bewildered. On the steps, Robert Purvis, the famed Philadelphia black abolitionist, extended his hand. A large crowd had gathered at the courthouse in anticipation of the judgment. Suddenly a wagon appeared "surrounded by a crowd that no slaveholder could penetrate. And after it had escorted the man to the precincts of the village," the crowd returned to the courthouse to rejoice and praise Purvis, the Committee of Vigilance, and the judge. The wagon carrying Dorsey sped on to New York City, where Dorsey was lodged in Ruggles's home. After a few days, Ruggles, helped by David Lee Child, sent Dorsey on to refuge in Northampton, Massachusetts.[46]

During the Dorsey rescue and on many other occasions, Ruggles was openly public about his welcome to freedom-seeking blacks. By mid-1838, he had rented better lodgings and an office across the street at 36 Lispenard Street, a block from Broadway, the busiest street in the nation's largest city. As did the famous Reverend John Rankin of Ripley, Ohio, who constructed a hilltop home where he sometimes housed as many as a dozen self-emancipated people waiting for wagons to carry them further north to the next station, Ruggles opened his home to enslaved people on the run. Along with private homes in Brooklyn, Ruggles's lodgings were among the strongest local beacons for travelers on the Underground Railroad.[47]

Ruggles used a wide network of contacts constructed from his years as an agent for the *Emancipator*, from attendance at antislavery gatherings and conventions in several states, and even from his seafaring days. The extent of his contacts can be seen in his report of the Second Anniversary Celebration of the New York Committee of Vigilance. Speakers hailed from upstate New York (Utica and Schenectady) and Canada (the Dawn settlement). Ruggles had broad support from abolitionists. The closing speaker was Amos Dresser, a student from Oberlin noted for having been whipped in Nashville for distributing antislavery materials. Dresser introduced William Dixon, the fugitive slave claimed by Dr. Allender of Maryland and the focus of the important case. Lewis Tappan offered a resolution that "it is the privilege and should be esteemed the duty of every abolitionist, to aid the New York Committee of Vigilance by liberal contributions." Alvan Stewart pronounced at the meeting that "the man, who delivers a slave from his pursuers, does an act upon which Heaven will smile." Gerrit Smith, also in attendance, affirmed the need to help slaves escape. Reverend Theodore S. Wright pronounced the benediction.[48]

There were several major strands to his network. One used coastal vessels from New York City and Long Island to New Haven, Norwich, Newport, Rhode Island, and Providence and beyond. New England passages ran overland through Hartford, where Reverend James W. C. Pennington was a close ally of Ruggles. From there, freedom seekers could find refuge in the Berkshires and then north into Vermont and New Hampshire. A third route ran up the eastern side of the Hudson River, with stops in towns with Quaker meetings and with black settlements, then to Poughkeepsie and Albany, New York. There, such movement stalwarts as Abel Brown and Stephen Myers insured that freedom seekers received a warm welcome. Some fugitives may have taken the difficult route through the Adirondacks with a likely stop at Rokeby, a farm in northern Vermont, before setting out for the wilds of Canada. Stemming west from Albany was a second powerful limb along the Erie Canal to Utica, Syracuse, and then on to Oswego, New York, and across Lake Ontario to Ontario, Canada. Many more went through the western part of New York State. If dangers lay along these routes, freedom seekers could find succor through the Catskill region into the Chenango Valley and the home of Gerrit Smith in Peterboro and then further north. In all of these towns and cities, including remote Peterboro, a combination of sympathetic whites and determined blacks, many of them former fugitives, was eager to help. In numerous small towns in New England and New York, a black person armed with a letter from David Ruggles quickly found warmhearted sympathizers who would help out on the way to free soil. As an indicator of the receptivity to his message, Ruggles received testimonials for his magazine from supporters in such rural towns as Cazenovia, New York; Brandon, Vermont; Haverhill, Massachusetts; and such seaports as Newburyport, Massachusetts, and Kennebunk, Maine. One may easily surmise that the commendations were implicit promises to enable freedom seekers sent their way from New York. Ruggles had become perhaps the most significant knot in these cords of benevolent conspirators and was so long before the better-remembered activities of Harriet Tubman and William Still.[49]

Ruggles kept up a steady drumbeat against kidnappers. He warned city residents in March 1838 that the "kidnapping club" was back in business. Identifying Boudinot, Nash, Wilder, and "the Recorder" (Riker) as the culprits, Ruggles contended that they had stolen another young man without even bothering to go into a hearing. Rather, the decision to send Henry Roberts southward was made in the comfort of Riker's home. Ruggles worked very hard to free blacks caught in the devices of the slave catchers.[50]

One situation indicates how hard Ruggles and the Committee of Vigilance worked to free those who fell into the hands of slave catchers and did so by using the testimony of aggrieved black family members. The case of Captain James Dayton Wilson of the steamer *Newcastle* is indicative. Stephen F. Dickerson, a free black man living in New York City, informed Ruggles, in June 1838, that his son, Stephen, and two other young men, Isaac Wright and Robert Garrison, all of them sailors, had been tricked by Captain Wilson, while the ship was docked in New Orleans the previous November. The captain had ordered the three young men to carry some hemp into the city but none of them had returned. Young Dickerson wrote his father that he had been sold into slavery along with the other two. Ruggles gained corroborating evidence from white sailors on the *Newcastle* who worked out of New Bedford, Massachusetts, and were now willing to testify against Wilson. Informants in Philadelphia supplied Ruggles with valuable testimony from the purchasers of the boys in Louisiana. The slave owners offered to free the young men provided that they were reimbursed for their original payments and that the enslaved men were proved to be free. Both masters identified Captain Wilson as the original supplier of the young men.[51]

Armed with this evidence, Ruggles ordered Wilson arrested for slave trading. He even pledged fifty dollars to the court to ensure his testimony. Wilson's deposition in the case reveals much about Ruggles's behavior in such circumstances. Corse, Hopper, and Ruggles went to Wilson's lodgings on Cortlandt Street. After they were admitted into Wilson's rooms, the trio sat down in chairs. Wilson, believing that Ruggles was a servant, told him not to sit in his presence. Thereupon all three men arose from their chairs and stated that they were equals and had come to "make enquires about the three boys who were sold into slavery." The three men stated their names, which was when Wilson learned Ruggles's identity. Wilson became very angry that Ruggles was in his house. Wilson ordered Ruggles to leave but was astonished when "the black man refused and . . . looked at him in an insolent manner" and then resumed questioning him about the kidnappings. Wilson then pushed Ruggles out of the room and kicked him down two flights of stairs, causing serious injuries to his liver. After this, Ruggles went to the police and had Wilson arrested, this time for assault.[52]

Ruggles's signature on the arrest warrant was strong, bold, and forceful, a good representation of his identity, fiery anger, and inner strength. A modern reading of his signature indicates that his writing was a blend of copybook styles taught in schools from the late eighteenth to early nineteenth century and that Ruggles clearly had a style of his own. Modern analysts of Ruggles's handwriting find much resentment in his stroke, which would fit his temperament after Wilson's physical attack on him. Other comments suggest

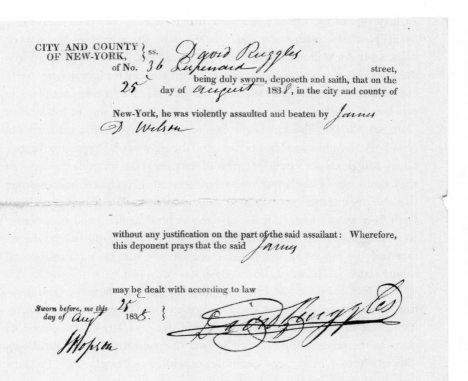

that Ruggles was a highly creative and intelligent person who was a fluid
thinker, very capable, and not shy when confronting opponents. His motives
were morally based. He could also be irritable and outright angry at others.
Certainly, Ruggles was correct to be hostile with Wilson and others involved
in one form of the slave trade or another. Beyond that, analysts contend,
Ruggles could be rigid and would quickly resist any adversity he encountered.[53]

After Ruggles had the sea captain confined in jail, Wilson's lawyers attempted to get the motion for arrest quelled, arguing that Ruggles was mistaken about Wilson's identity and that the true villain was a man named
Thomas Lewis, then in jail in New Orleans. Wilson garnered some sympathy from the press. The *New-Yorker* argued that he was "undoubtedly innocent." More important was judicial leniency. The magistrate, Oakley, hearing the case, gave Wilson seven weeks to restore the young men to liberty.

At least one of the jurors was a slave master who spent much of the year on his plantation with many slaves. In this case, the purchaser of the three boys, a Mr. McMahon of New Orleans, had signaled his willingness to free the boys. Ruggles, in a public announcement, pleaded for fifty dollars to pay the judicial fees to extricate the boys from bondage. In a poignant plea, he proclaimed, "What is to be done, must be quickly." He sought funds from churches. Ruggles also linked the case to an older deposition made by the New York Manumission Society to extend the right of trial by jury to fugitive slaves. Ruggles reported the progress of the case at the monthly meetings of the Committee of Vigilance. At the same time, Ruggles had to acknowledge that the organization's funds were exhausted and asked churches to help. Cash flow was an issue, but the case shows how far-flung and cooperative were Ruggles's network of contacts and how forcefully, quickly, and courageously he moved against malefactors. Despite Ruggles's efforts, several months later, all charges against Wilson were dropped.[54]

Ruggles's actions attracted the sponsorship of major figures in the abolitionist movement. William Lloyd Garrison's visit to New York City to commemorate on August 1 the anniversary of the complete emancipation of slaves in the British Empire surely helped. Garrison spoke at the Broadway Tabernacle to a "very large assembly" of whites and blacks. Free Produce food and temperance drinks were available for purchase. The tabernacle had become an all-purpose gathering spot for interracial, antislavery gatherings. Under the leadership of Lewis Tappan and Samuel Eli Cornish, the church housed several schools for blacks and was the venue for meetings on black suffrage, nonresistance, and emergency meetings for new causes and anniversaries for antislavery societies. Built to house the ministry of Charles G. Finney, the sanctuary architecture used theatrical seating plans, which ensured that everyone present could view the rest of the congregation. This had worked well at the Chatham Street Chapel. The Broadway Tabernacle changed paths when Finney abruptly moved to Oberlin College. Lewis Tappan and Samuel Cornish filled the vacuum with antislavery services. Finney wanted segregated seating, about which the *Colored American* had complained bitterly. Using the model established in the Chatham Street Chapel, where classes and races mixed easily, and where audiences had powerful impact on the conduct of the services, the combined Presbyterian and Congregational memberships at the Broadway Tabernacle established a dynamic fusion of personal responsibility for public sins within a democratic forum. When a movement star such as Garrison came to town, contact between the audience (which included Ruggles and other local antislavery activists) and the preacher achieved an almost hallucinatory quality. Ruggles came out of such meetings refreshed for battle. The effect on the Tappans was equally electric. Inspired by the experience, in late 1838, Lewis Tappan rebuffed charges of heresy and established an antislavery society right in the church.[55]

Ruggles pushed his pursuit of the kidnappers far beyond New York City while confronting very dangerous men. Ruggles learned through his contacts that Thomas Lewis, who had previously been in custody in Louisiana for cutting off a man's head with a Bowie knife, was on board a revenue cutter that traveled from Philadelphia to New Bedford, Massachusetts. Ruggles quickly went to Philadelphia, obtained the necessary papers implicating Lewis, and then pursued the felon to Newport and New Bedford. Lewis was leaving New Bedford in two hours when Ruggles arrived with a summons. With the "prompt assistance of the Sheriff and other officers," Ruggles had Lewis arrested and jailed. He then took the extraordinary step of writing to the governor of Florida, R. K. Call, to inform him that Lewis was now in jail in New Bedford. Call replied to Ruggles, asking that Lewis be kept in custody and that a reward might be forthcoming.[56]

In pursuit of Lewis, Ruggles suffered two indignities. On the steamboat from New York to Providence, he paid the clerk for a full ticket and then was forced to sit on the open deck. Following that, he was removed forcibly from the regular rail car on the Stonington Rail Road and pushed into the "pauper or Jim Crow" car. When Ruggles asked why he was so treated, the conductor told him it was "because you are a damned abolitionist." Ruggles described this outrage in several articles in the next week, advising readers to avoid the Stonington Railroad, or "you are liable to be defrauded and lynched on the route to Boston."[57]

After this frustrating incident, the tireless, courageous Ruggles sped back to New York City to preside over a "very large meeting of the Committee of Vigilance." Ruggles had learned from dockworkers of three Africans who had been imported into New York City as slaves from Rio-Nunez on the west coast of Africa by a Captain Eben Farrell. Ruggles accused the captain of holding the three men against their will and planning to sell them into slavery. Ruggles used this information to have Farrell arrested for enslaving the sailors. The Committee of Vigilance had forced the captain to free the trio. Ruggles sarcastically noted that to his knowledge there had been "twenty-two native Africans imported into the port of New York" in the past year, or more black Americans than the American Colonization Society had convinced to migrate to Liberia. He then addressed the case of the three kidnapped boys to the large crowd. Several others spoke at the meeting, but it

Frederick Douglass

Frontispiece of Frederick Douglass. From *Narrative of the Life of Frederick Douglass, an American Slave. Written by Himself.* Boston: Anti-Slavery Office, 1845. After the young fugitive slave arrived at Ruggles's home at 36 Lispenard Street in New York City, the abolitionist taught him early lessons about antislavery methods. Eventually, Frederick Douglass became one of Ruggles's strongest supporters. Collection of the author.

is clear from the report that Ruggles's dynamic courage and relentless activism were animating the abolitionists. Another meeting on September 1 celebrated the second issue of the *Mirror of Liberty*.[58]

In early September, Ruggles's arduous experiences in New England helped benefit a young runaway slave. William Green was not the only self-emancipated young man from Maryland who followed the word-of-mouth news about the kindness of Ruggles. Another from Maryland who seized his liberty was Frederick Augustus Bailey, later known as Frederick Douglass. In addition to the moving story Douglass narrated in his three autobiographies, there are additional aspects worth keeping in mind of this famous tale. Later, Douglass would become one of the greatest Americans of the nineteenth century. That noble stature was not clear in 1838. Though Douglass was already literate, he was not erudite. Although Douglass strives in his carefully painted self-portrait in three autobiographies to present himself as fully formed at the moment he leaves slavery, the truth was harder. When he encountered Ruggles, the fugitive from Maryland was a troubled young man who had fought with his master and an overseer and had been jailed and nearly sold into the Deep South for running away. Later describing himself as an "Old Soker," Douglass drank heavily at this time. In September 1838 Douglass was like many of the other frightened black men who came to Ruggles's house on Lispenard Street. Douglass recalled that Ruggles and he discussed practical matters about his future. The young fugitive wanted to go to Canada, but Ruggles convinced him to try New Bedford, Massachusetts, a decision with enormous ramifications for Douglass's and black America's destiny. Ruggles did not simply pack his charge off into the night but housed him for about a week (during part of which Ruggles was in jail) and gave him money, letters of recommendation, and names of sympathetic abolitionists in Newport, Rhode Island, the first stop on Douglass's voyage to liberty. When Douglass left for New Bedford, he had already learned much about life in the north from Ruggles. Anxious about money, Douglass received assistance from two white friends of the New Yorker who lived in Rhode Island, who "gave us such assurance of their friendliness as to put us fully at our ease." In such fashion, Douglass and his wife, Anna Murray, received full immersion into radical abolitionism.

Much has been made of the influence of William Lloyd Garrison and, later, Gerrit Smith and Abraham Lincoln, on Douglass's intellectual and political development. Douglass famously commented: "I have been asked where I got my education. I have answered, from Massachusetts Abolition University, Mr. Garrison, President." It is important to recognize, however, that Douglass's career as a free man began in Ruggles's home, where he learned firsthand the hazards and inspirations of the antislavery movement and comprehended the networks of white and black abolitionists. It was at 36 Lispenard Street that the fugitive changed his name, obliterating his past and self-identifying as a free man. He married his fiancée Anna Murray at Ruggles's home. Ruggles doubtless lectured the younger man about slavery to the bottle and perhaps helped Douglass overcome his aversion to temperance. At the house on Lispenard Street, the younger man could see Ruggles hard at work, prosecuting slave catchers, working on his press, and laboring as an equal with white comrades. Douglass could spend time in Ruggles's reading room. The pastor who presided over his wedding, James W. C. Penningon, who had fled from Maryland in 1828, was a successful example of self-

(FAC-SIMILE OF THE ORIGINAL AUTOGRAPH.)

Frontispiece of James W. C. Pennington. From Wilson Armistead, *A Tribute to the Negro* (Manchester, England, 1848). Ruggles and the fugitive blacksmith, as Pennington called himself, probably influenced each other. Ruggles inspired Pennington with his zeal for black rights, and Pennington uplifted Ruggles with his affecting tale of escaping from slavery. Courtesy of Division of Rare and Manuscript Collections, Cornell University Library.

emancipation. Pennington worked as a blacksmith in Brooklyn, New York, before becoming an ordained Presbyterian minister in Hartford, Connecticut. Pennington and Ruggles worked closely, as the New York Committee of Vigilance sent the minister as many as twenty-five fugitives a day. The days that Douglass spent with Ruggles were his baptism into the fiery battle against slavery and northern racism. Ruggles gave the younger man far more than the blessings of a five-dollar bill and a letter of introduction. Douglass's time with Ruggles was the pivotal moment in his life, as he left slavery behind on his way to becoming an abolitionist.[59]

The Underground Railroad

Douglass, whose thirst for knowledge is well known, had to be impressed by what he found at Ruggles's home. The house was now the city's first reading room and circulating library run by a man of color. Located in Ruggles's home, which was also the office of the New York Committee of Vigilance, the lending library gave readers access to "the principal daily and leading antislavery papers, and other popular periodicals of the day." Ruggles opened the library in part because blacks were excluded from most "Reading Rooms, popular lectures, and all places of literary attraction." Ruggles hoped that the reading room would be a literary attraction for "all young men whose mental appetites thirst for food" and would help them avoid the constant presence of vice. Annual subscriptions cost $2.75, though "strangers visiting this city can have access to the Reading Room, free of charge," an open invitation to fugitive slaves needing spiritual and intellectual uplift.[60]

Douglass's memory of Ruggles's generosity is also useful for charting stops on the Underground Railroad. After leaving New York, Anna and Frederick first took a steamboat to Newport, Rhode Island. Ruggles directed them to contact a Mr. Shaw there. Excited about getting to New Bedford, the couple decided, encouraged by two men they met en route, who "seemed at once to understand our circumstances," to go by train immediately to New Bedford, where they were directed to the home of Mr. Nathan Johnson. One problem was that the young couple did not have sufficient cash to pay for their train ride; fortunately the two men they met paid the rest of their fare. Douglass became immediately aware of the vast contacts Ruggles had throughout the northeast for securing fugitive slaves to freedom.[61]

Frederick Douglass arrived at Ruggles's home in the midst of one of the most sensational antislavery cases of the 1830s. The facts of the Darg case, as they came out in the subsequent trial, were as follows. On August 25, 1838, John P. Darg, a Virginia slaveholder, arrived in New York City accompanied by his slave Thomas Hughes. The issue of southerners bringing their human chattel to a free state was under intense negotiation between the governors of New York and Virginia, but Darg apparently felt confident about securing his servant. A few days later, however, Hughes came to Isaac T. Hopper's house, seeking refuge. The Quaker was initially reluctant and asked Hughes to leave his home. The next day, the *New York Sun*, the most vitriolic of the penny press newspapers, published a notice offering a reward for the return of Hughes and the approximately seven thousand or eight thousand dollars he had taken with him. Hopper, Barney Corse, and perhaps Ruggles served as go-betweens for Darg and Hughes. The latter no longer had all the money, having given some of it to others who helped him escape and losing a portion to some local gamblers. Corse and Ruggles decided that returning the cash was moral, but turning over Hughes was not. They convinced Darg to free Hughes provided that the enslaved man gave back as much loot as he took. When the sum turned out to be far less than Darg wanted, the slave master ordered Corse and Ruggles arrested for grand larceny. Critics of abolitionism labeled the trio as extortionists and lampooned them in a widely distributed cartoon.

Corse quickly found bail, but Ruggles was jailed for three days with common criminals, even though he had not been charged with anything. Ruggles testified about his involvement in the case on September 5, followed by exculpatory testimony by Corse and Hopper. While Ruggles languished in jail at the mercy of police bullies and common criminals, a "very large and respectable Meeting of colored citizens" again hailed the editor of the *Mirror of Liberty*. As he related later, Ruggles was tossed in a "dirty and loathsome cell, eight feet long and four feet wide." At one o'clock in the morning, he was joined by "four drunken, half crazy, infamous wretches, who increased the filth of the damp, underground hole." Ruggles had to stand the entire time he was in the cell. On September 9, after he had spent three days in jail, Arthur Tappan and J. W. Higgins—a black grocer, an officer of the Committee of Vigilance, and treasurer of the Dey Street (Presbyterian) Church—posted three thousand dollars for Ruggles's bail, a sum about six times the average annual wage of a skilled worker. It was an act of extraordinary generosity on Tappan's part, as he had lost much of his wealth in the Panic of 1837, and an act of faith on the part of the church. Without their sincere goodwill, Ruggles would have rotted in jail until his health failed or his jailors found a propitious moment to ship him south into slavery. Ruggles was only twenty-eight years old and, despite his health problems, would command a decent sum on the slave market.[62]

H. R. Robinson, a local printer, published a satirical cartoon about the dispute. In the image, Hopper, Ruggles, and Corse stand arms locked in the reception room of Darg's home. The slave master is wielding a chair in one hand and holding a bag containing almost seven thousand dollars. He angrily denounces the trio as extortionists looking for a illicit reward. Darg denounces their "damned pieces of impudence" and proclaims "the only reward you deserve is the halter or the States Prison. You scoundrels!" Hopper is pictured telling "friend Darg" that he is there to claim the one-thousand-dollar reward. He also absolves Corse of any responsibility for acting as his agent. Corse seeks to evade blame, as he was only helping "Brother Hopper and Brother Ruggles." The cartoonist puts the most damaging words in the black

Isaac T. Hopper

Frontispiece of Isaac T. Hopper. From L. Maria Child, *Isaac T. Hopper: A True Life.* Boston: Published by John P. Jewett, 1853. The venerable Isaac T. Hopper taught Ruggles many methods of fighting kidnappers and struggled alongside Ruggles in several battles. Collection of the author.

abolitionist's mouth. Ruggles is depicted as worrisomely saying "I don't like the looks of this affair. I am afraid my pickings will not amount to much." Hopper and Corse appear to be tangentially guilty, while Ruggles is caricatured as a thief and extortionist.

The clothing of the four men tells much. Hopper is garbed in an eighteenth-century Quaker outfit, as befits his faith. Darg and Corse wear businessmen's suits of the 1830s style with regional variations. Darg's coat and hairdo reflect southern tastes. Ruggles, on the other hand, is portrayed wearing a long double-breasted jacket, white pants, stovepipe hat, a cravat, and thick eyeglasses. Save for the spectacles that he needed because of his fading eyesight, Ruggles wore a mixture of fashion appropriate for a "dandy," an antebellum sport with loose morals and interest in the fast life. A chalk portrait probably from this era of Ruggles is a bust and head image of similar appearance. Sean Wilentz has discussed the Bowery B'hoy as a symbol of antebellum working-class consciousness and assertiveness. While there were many contemporary black dandies, nearly all of the images of them are racial satires. Free men of color appear as thick-lipped, low-browed, apelike black buffoons. While the cartoonist's aim was doubtless to signify Ruggles as inappropriately dressed, the abolitionist seems dignified, even as he voices anxious words. While racist whites reveled in the extravagant, foppish clothing in other "bobolition" cartoons, this one had to vex them. As Shane and Graham White have argued, a smartly dressed black striding through the street was an act of provocation almost too great for any white to bear. To incense racists further, Ruggles was a street dandy who dared to enter the home of white slave masters, challenge their property rights, arrest them, and behave with a profoundly superior moral air. Ruggles was a black radical dandy.[63]

At the hearing to determine if the black abolitionist should be released on bond, Isaac T. Hopper testified in defense of Ruggles and related his knowledge of the Darg incident. Hopper swore that Hughes had come to his home late at night, that he had allowed him to stay in the home only until daylight, and then asked him to leave. Upon reading the advertisement in the *New York Sun*, Hopper realized that this was more than a fugitive slave case. He and Corse learned that "a very respectable man" now held the money taken by Hughes from his master Darg. At first Hopper refused to give the name of the respectable citizen, then later relented and identified him as Henry (last name unknown), who lived somewhere nearby and who worked as a waiter in a public garden on Broadway, near Leonard Street. After this vague account, Hopper testified that he had never seen Ruggles with Hughes and considered him innocent of any involvement.

In an astonishing procedure, Ruggles then cross-examined Hopper, making him one of the first blacks to act as a lawyer in the history of the United States. Ruggles asked a series of questions of Hopper about his identification with the antislavery cause and elicited from him a statement that Hopper had never seen Ruggles and Hughes together and that he never had the slightest idea that the latter was a criminal. Watching the proceedings in the audience was Frederick Bailey (Douglass), the young man whom

The Disappointed Abolitionists. New York: H. Robinson, 52 Cortlandt Street and 11½ Wall Street, 1838.
This evocative print states the proslavery and anti-abolitionist sentiment that Hopper, Corse, and especially
Ruggles were no more than extortionists. Courtesy of the American Antiquarian Society.

Ruggles was sheltering. After this testimony, Ruggles was finally released on
bail, though the charges of being an accessory to theft remained. If Hopper's
testimony was correct, then the city of New York was holding Ruggles in jail
under false charges and without any proof.[64]

Ruggles's judicial hearing took seven hours. In addition to the remarkable instance of his self-defense, other noteworthy details speak to Ruggles's
methods and influence. Ruggles not only examined Hopper but also cross-
examined Mrs. Amaranth Darg about her knowledge of the affair, which
proved to be slight and damaged the value of her testimony. A number of
witnesses exculpated Ruggles. Arthur Tappan testified that he had never
had any conversations with Ruggles about Tom Hughes and had never seen
them together. Seth Benedict, a prominent New York City publisher, told
the magistrate that he had known Ruggles for some time as editor of the
Mirror of Liberty and had no knowledge of any involvement by Ruggles in
the Darg case. Moses Y. Beach, the famous editor of the *New York Sun*, stated
that he knew Ruggles as editor of the magazine and testified that he had advised Ruggles not to publish articles about the case, as they might injure him,
but believed that Ruggles had done nothing wrong. Agreeing with that was
Dr. Daniel E. Stearns, a prominent homeopathic doctor. The doctor sympa-

The Underground Railroad

thized with Ruggles, yet warned him that pursuing the case could be dangerous to the cause. What becomes clear is that Ruggles was acquainted with and consulted leading journalists and physicians about his activities. They advised him, though he seems rarely to have listened. Plainly, Ruggles was not shy about going to some of the city's most prominent men and to his legion of supporters in the black community for help. Arthur Tappan and J. W. Higgins were willing to put up thousands of dollars to secure Ruggles's release.[65]

Higgins was one of several black men attesting to Ruggles's innocence. During his testimony, Higgins and William P. Johnson of the Committee of Vigilance identified Ruggles as a member of the Dey Street (Presbyterian) Church. Johnson noted in his testimony that he had known Ruggles for thirteen years and that they "go to the same church." The Dey Street Church had recently combined with the Chatham Street Chapel, home of many antislavery meetings, to take over the Broadway Tabernacle, site of innumerable antislavery meetings.[66]

The trial was followed in newspapers around the country. Some journals were unsympathetic to Corse, Ruggles, and Hopper. The *Hudson River Chronicle* argued that while no one could blame Hughes for wanting to be free, Corse "undoubtedly instigated the negro to steal the money." The newspaper slammed Corse, stating that "he merits the severest rigor of the law" for robbery and conspiracy. Ruggles was consistently referred to as the "colored agitator." Other journals reported the incident as a strange case of robbery.[67]

The Darg case continued to take unusual twists. Hughes sought to extricate himself from freedom. On September 26, Darg, after hiring the venerable New York attorney Ogden Hoffman, initiated suits against Ruggles, Corse, and Hopper. By November, Hughes declared that he was willing to return to Virginia and slavery. After Hughes returned to Virginia, he was clapped in jail until he could be sold south. The enslaved man claimed that Darg had tricked him, saying that he would reunite him with his wife, Mary. When back in Virginia, Darg informed Hughes that he had sold Mary and was about to sell him. Hughes then changed his mind and declared a desire to be free. Hopper and the other abolitionists hired Horace Dresser to litigate the case. They published Hughes's new statement that he wished to be free, acknowledging his shame at taking the money, and claiming that he had always intended to return it. Hughes further stated that the police had urged him to implicate the abolitionists, but he insisted that Corse, Hopper, and Ruggles knew nothing of the cash "until I had left my master and if any man is guilty, I am the one." Fortunately for Hughes, the abolitionists were able to secure his release.[68]

Ruggles's activities were energizing local abolitionists. An editorial on September 15 in the *Colored American* derided the city's case against him as a "farce."[69] Saluting his efforts, three black women, whom he had recently helped, honored Ruggles in October with a gift of a cane with a golden knob. The bearers of the gift lauded Ruggles, stating that the cane was recognition of "your meritorious and untiring zeal in the cause of human freedom." Two weeks later, another meeting hailed the new issue of the *Mirror of Liberty* and suggested that the magazine should appear monthly rather than quarterly. The following month, Lewis Tappan extolled the actions of the Committee of Vigilance and Ruggles in particular. Most important, Arthur Tappan, William P. Johnson, S. S. Jocelyn, John Brown, George Tracy, and J. W. Higgins signed up for six subscriptions each.[70]

Sadly, the struggle was taking its toll on the valiant Ruggles. Only twenty-eight years old, he was now nearly blind and was afflicted with severe bowel disorders. Information printed years later indicates that he was consulting with a doctor named Swain about his maladies. During this period, Dr. Swain was well known for his "Vermifuge," which was applied to diseases stemming from intestinal worms. Common among American children, worms caused extensive misery and, if left untreated, could be fatal. Living on the edge in New York City, Ruggles was easily susceptible to such an ailment and would not have had the financial resources to combat it. In addition, the stress of his work added to his woes. As an antislavery worker, Ruggles met with even more intense racism and personal hostility than other blacks did. He was constantly physically threatened and verbally abused by slave catchers, city marshals, and judges. In time, these threats worsened. His living conditions were a third factor. All of his money and time went into the movement. Nonetheless, there is no indication that he was abandoning his efforts. If anything, he pushed himself and New York's black community into stronger radicalism.[71]

Ruggles had few sympathizers outside of the abolitionist community. His arrest of Captain Dayton, his part in the Darg case, and his open defiance of slave catchers drew angry responses in local newspapers. The *New York Daily Express* ventured that Ruggles should be "hammering stones on Blackwell's Island (prison) the rest of his life." The paper went on to describe him as a "sooty scoundrel" who made the writer wonder if he was living in Africa or America. Ruggles, the writer scolded, was the "official ourang-outang of the 'Antislavery Society.'" The only complaints about all this came from the *Emancipator*. Members of the Manumission Society, in contrast, objected to the newspaper's association of their group with Ruggles, assuring the public that he was not a member. Ruggles, ever courageous and believing that exposure of such racist arguments would defeat them, published all of them in the second issue of the *Mirror of Liberty*.[72]

Controversies emerged within the committee itself in the aftermath of the Darg case that revealed widening splits within. During the regular quarterly meeting of the committee held on October 10, much of the discussion centered on Ruggles's imprisonment. William P. Johnson spoke long and thoroughly about the ill treatment Ruggles had received. Ruggles addressed the "malicious prosecution" of Barney Corse and himself. All was agreeable until Ruggles alluded to the vacillation of a certain person to sign the bond that would have discharged him without going to jail. When Johnson and Theodore S. Wright remonstrated with Ruggles and demanded he not name the person, Ruggles abruptly declined to speak further. Standing up then was Augustus Hanson, the financial agent of the committee. Hanson, who stated in testimony that he had known Ruggles only a few weeks, now proclaimed that he had been in the police station continually with Ruggles and that it was only the latter's obstinacy that kept him in jail after the first evening of his arrest. Apparently, the unnamed person, probably Hanson, given the ensuing debate, had asked Ruggles to get bail from Corse, Tappan, or someone else and questioned whether Ruggles would honor the bond and not flee. His pride deeply hurt, Ruggles then refused to accept bail from the mysterious individual, to the consternation of Hanson and even of the police officers. At the meeting, Ruggles angrily stated that he would "go to prison and remain there during my natural life rather than to be bailed out by an individual who would tell me that he was afraid that I would deceive him." Hanson again took the floor, exclaiming that such was the obstinacy to which he had referred. He also pleaded that the real enemies were not each other but the city government and the slave catchers. Discernible among these debates are growing tensions between Ruggles and other members of the committee over his tactics and his personality.[73]

Worse afflictions were on the way. Just as he was healing from the abuse suffered during his arrest and jailing, Ruggles suffered a new and unexpected problem. John Russell, the boardinghouse keeper whom Ruggles had described as a slave dealer in an article months earlier, won a libel case against Ruggles and the *Colored American* for damages of $220 plus court costs of $300 and legal fees of about $80. Initially, the newspaper dismissed the victory and left collection of the money up to Russell's conscience. In the same issue, the newspaper reported a meeting held the night before at which Ruggles addressed the evils of seamen's landlords who collaborated with slave catchers.

Other than that, it was business as usual, as Ruggles helped form a new organization known as the New York Association for the Political Elevation and Improvement of the People of Color, which was designed to agitate for better civil rights and enhanced suffrage in New York State. The following week Ruggles headed the monthly meeting of the New York Committee of Vigilance. He received moral support from those in attendance, who were described as "a highly respectable number of colored citizens of this city," for his activities and for the *Mirror of Liberty*.[74]

This flurry of activity did not alter the troubling fact that the *Colored American* needed $500 to pay Russell. Cornish began canvassing wealthy white sympathizers for contributions. In early November, he wrote William Jay, asking for $150. Cornish also reprinted the letter from Joseph Galvino to Ruggles in which Galvino contended that Russell had helped ship out the captured blacks to New Orleans. Cornish expressed full support for the Committee of Vigilance and in an editorial referred to it as "one of the most honorable, benevolent, and important institutions among us." Still, Cornish argued, the suit was the responsibility of the committee, not of the newspaper. In November the Committee of Vigilance came up with $100 by bits and pieces from contributors around the state and thereby gained a short grace period. In mid-December, Ruggles published an editorial in the *Colored American* that the committee was still short $300. In early January, Russell's lawyer informed the newspaper that it expected the remainder without delay.[75]

A second case that gave ammunition to Ruggles's enemies was the affair of Charity Walker. She and two other blacks named Jesse and Jim were enslaved people who had been brought up to New York City by their owners, the Dodge family. In the spring of 1838, Mrs. Dodge told Walker that she planned to take the three of them back to South Carolina, in part to avoid passing six months' residence in New York, an anniversary that would automatically free the slaves. Alarmed about this return into the land of slavery, Walker contacted Ruggles, who went to the Dodge's house, informed the mistress that the three servants were now free and that they had a right to wages for their work in New York City. After a heated dispute, Charity Walker left with Ruggles and went to live and work for the landlady in his building on Lispenard Street. Walker formed a liaison with another employee there and was soon pregnant. Ruggles arranged for her to live elsewhere, unsuccessfully attempted to get her lover to marry her, and then billed the Dodges for back wages that he hoped would support her through her confinement.

The Dodges refused to help, stating that once she had left their house, they severed ties with Walker. Newspapers were quick to condemn Ruggles for inveigling Walker out of her home, allowing her to lapse into immorality, then evicting her from his house, and finally dunning her former masters for her support. One referred to him as the "notorious and impertinent meddler" and labeled him the "black [Daniel] O'Connell of the slaves," a reference to the Irish radical.

Ruggles retorted that Walker had lapsed back into the ways of slavery and that he had done no wrong but only had helped someone incapable of living a free life. He contended that he had helped fourteen people escape from slavery in Brooklyn in the past two years and that Walker was the only one who "has suffered the pernicious influence of slavery to blight her prospects in the enjoyment of liberty." There were, he concluded so many slaveholders in Brooklyn that it should be called the "Savannah of New York." Still, his miscalculation of Walker's character indicated that Ruggles could not always lift an enslaved person into full free status.[76]

Ruggles's method of assistance for Charity Walker shows his boldness in dealing with proslavery whites. His exchange with a Doctor McClennan at the Brooklyn house, highlighted by Fergus Bordewich in his portrayal of Ruggles in *Bound for Canaan*, reveals Ruggles's quick wit, sense of purpose, and composed interaction with angry whites. Ruggles went to Brooklyn to inform Charity Walker of her rights. McClennan arrived to help the home-owners evict Ruggles as an intruder. Ruggles responded that it was the doctor who was the intruder, with no right to interfere "against liberty and the laws of the state."

"I am here to remove a disorderly person," McClennan declared.

"Find such a person here, and I will aid you in his removal," replied Ruggles. "I was invited here to relieve humanity."

"I wish you would *leave*, sir," McClennan repeated.

"I wish you would leave, sir," said Ruggles.

"You aggravate me," said the doctor.

"You don't aggravate me," replied Ruggles.

The doctor realizing that Ruggles was bigger and stronger than he, asked the abolitionist to wait until the man of the house arrived. Ruggles responded that if Charity were ready to leave with him, he would protect her. Although the case ended badly, Ruggles plainly had no fear or deference toward the white physician.[77]

In the midst of this furor, Ruggles decided, on the advice of his eye doctor, that he should temporarily withdraw from the excitement of battling against this "slaveholder's hunting grounds" and take a trip to Paris, France. There, with proper remedies, his eyesight might improve. It is curious that Ruggles did not mention the New York Eye Infirmary, which was founded in 1820. City hospitals did treat blacks, provided they could pay room and board, so Ruggles simply may have exhausted the infirmary's methods. He asked the friends of the *Mirror of Liberty* to allot him a brief vacation and promised that the next issue would come out with a full account of the Darg case. Ruggles informed his public that his ailments, especially blindness, derived largely from "seasons of mental anxiety," which were "frequently caused by interesting scenes of action in which we have been called to conflict." Specifically, physicians advising Ruggles, particularly Dr. Swaim, contended that his blindness stemmed from excessive "flow of blood to the head," perhaps a sign of hypertension. Ruggles quickly gained financial help. Supporters for Ruggles's travel plans included Arthur Tappan, Gerrit Smith, J. W. Higgins, Reverend Simeon Jocelyn, William S. Jinnings, President George M. Tracy of the Committee of Vigilance, and others who offered to pay for the expenses of a voyage and an operation to correct Ruggles's eye problems. One of the largest donors was John P. Williston, an indelible ink manufacturer from Northampton, Massachusetts, and a fervent supporter of abolitionism. Williston came to New York City to adopt William Howard Day, a black youth, so it is likely that the two printers met each other. Notwithstanding his physical problems, Ruggles called the regular monthly meetings of the Committee of Vigilance for November and December as well as a special meeting to rally against the resurgent American Colonization Society.[78]

Personality clashes and the tensions over the libel suit cause the ten-year alliance between Ruggles and Cornish to fray. On December 15, 1839, while they took part in a call for a meeting against the American Colonization Society, the battle over the libel suit and the missing funds raged in the background.[79] Soon Cornish went public with a denunciation of Ruggles for endangering the *Colored American* through costs of the libel suit. Ruggles responded to his accuser in a lengthy letter to the rest of the Vigilance Committee on January 9, 1839. Infuriated, Cornish attacked Ruggles again in print. Although wealthy benefactors soon paid the libel award, Cornish campaigned to have Ruggles driven out of the movement. In a nasty attack printed in the *Colored American* on January 26, Cornish accused Ruggles of bankrupting the movement through costs of his legal problems, his land speculations, and "his public fame, which is bitter against him." In response, Ruggles's defenders demanded an accounting from Cornish of the costs of the libel suit. His audit indicated a shortfall of several hundred dollars from legal expenses. The public list of contributors indicated fairly modest sums of fifty dollars or less from such philanthropists as the Tappan brothers, Gerrit Smith, and William Jay and from smaller donors around the state. Ruggles apparently borrowed fifty dollars from J. W. Higgins to help defray the debt.[80]

Ruggles, aggrieved by Cornish's attack, responded with an anguished plea. How, Ruggles asked, could Cornish have published the innuendo about missing funds from the Committee of Vigilance? Ruggles, apparently giving up hope for a rest cure in a European hospital, declared that, as in the Darg case, he would pay for his own costs, even if he had to "sell my old socks for the money." After a careful accounting, it appeared that the committee's funds were short four hundred dollars. Ruggles pleaded that the Committee of Vigilance, hurt by the costs of prosecutions, had been forced to cut his salary over the past two years by five hundred dollars, a sum that would have allowed him to pay all debts and go to Europe for rest and medical treatment.[81]

Sick in body and wearied in mind by the public attacks, Ruggles submitted his resignation as secretary and agent for the New York Committee of Vigilance on February 12, 1839. He declared, "Nothing but a proper sense of my own inability to perform the duties of the position" is responsible for the resignation, which he attributed to his "opthamalia" and to the "perplexing personal difficulties with which I have to contend." Ruggles reported that he had consulted "Dr. Saunders, the German Oculist," and optimistically forecast that the doctor's skill could save his sight. He did maintain his reading room at 36 Lispenard Street. Ruggles's ailments and the strident controversy over the libel suit and his management of the Committee of Vigilance's finances so distracted him that he had no comment on the *Amistad* Affair as it developed over the summer of 1839.[82]

Even after his resignation, charges against Ruggles flew thick and fast. "An Abolitionist" wrote in the *Colored American* of his sorrow that the "little article 'self' was so prominent." In fact, "Abolitionist" opined the magazine was all Ruggles: "Him first—him last—him middle—him without end." The writer continued with cruel wit that Ruggles might have poor eyesight but the public did not. In fact, Ruggles, he suggested, was like Cardinal Woolsey: "Great in Promises and in performance, nothing." The writer concluded by comparing Ruggles further with a viper, which delights most on feeding on the blood of the virtuous. Former allies in Philadelphia chimed in with criticism. The *National Reformer* castigated Ruggles for mislabeling its efforts as a "Reform Convention," a very unpopular term in Pennsylvania because of its use by the state government the previous year to disenfranchise blacks. A more personal attack came from another former supporter. Despite Ruggles's regular accounting of his bills, one major donor to the movement cast doubts on his ability to handle money. Lewis Tappan, writing to Gerrit Smith, declared, "Like most every colored man I have ever known, [Ruggles] was untrustworthy in money matters. I do not accuse him or others as deficient in integrity, but no regular account appears to be kept of moneys received or paid." Thus, a key financial resource of the abolitionist movement used Ruggles's predicament to explain why he would never employ blacks in his counting office, an example of paradoxical racism among white abolitionists.[83]

Ruggles demanded a public hearing on his own conduct and to refute the accusations.[84] The meeting was postponed several times until July 18. In an editorial published a few days later, the *Colored American* reported the proceedings. With tangible sarcasm the writer recounted a lengthy speech in which Ruggles blamed Cornish for all the persecutions. In addition to the libel suit, Ruggles apparently blamed Cornish for the troubles he suffered from "land companies" and the Vigilance Committee. According to the report, these accusations came solely from the "heated imagination and fever distempered brain of David Ruggles." Worse, William P. Johnson, the head of the Committee of Vigilance and an old friend, refuted Ruggles. The *Colored American* reported that after the Committee of Vigilance made its donation toward paying for Ruggles's libel, the newspaper was still two hundred dollars short. A month later, the temporary alliance between Cornish and the committee fell apart after Johnson denied that the suit was entirely the committee's responsibility. The newspaper then retorted that meetings had been held by the committee the previous November to pay off the suit. The only item on which Cornish and the committee seemed to agree was that no further contributions could be expected of Ruggles.[85]

Ruggles attempted to maintain a public image. He attended the annual meeting of the American Anti-Slavery Society in New York City on May 7. He voted with the majority on the question of sending delegates to the national convention called for by William Goodell, Joshua Leavitt, and others.[86] Yet the attacks cost him energy and time. In late August 1839, Ruggles published his last pamphlet in New York City, *A Plea for "A Man and A Brother,"* in which he tried to refute Cornish's indictments. Published at the office of the *Mirror of Liberty*, the entire document involves the spirited public exchange on July 18 between Ruggles, Philip A. Bell, and William P. Johnson. Cornish, Theodore S. Wright, and William Johnston, the treasurer of the committee, were invited to attend but declined. Ruggles spoke first, explaining carefully how he had been cheated out of his salary and was paid less than a fundraising

A PLEA

FOR

"A MAN AND A BROTHER,"

BY

DAVID RUGGLES,

Made on the 18th July, 1839,

BEFORE A PUBLIC MEETING HELD AT THE HALL

245 Spring Street.

ALSO, EXTRACTS FROM THE SPEECHES OF MESSRS.

PHILIP A. BELL & WILLIAM P. JOHNSON;

WITH NOTES AND REMARKS.

NEW-YORK:

PUBLISHED AT THE OFFICE OF THE MIRROR OF LIBERTY,
36 LISPENARD STREET.
1839.

For sale at the Book Stores, and at the Stand in Nassau-st., cor. Fulton.

Title Page of *A Plea for "A Man and A Brother,"* by David Ruggles. New York: Published at the Office of the *Mirror of Liberty*, 1839. In this pamphlet, Ruggles published his defense against the accusations of mishandling of funds made by his erstwhile allies, Samuel Eli Cornish and the New York Committee of Vigilance. Courtesy of Division of Rare and Manuscript Collections, Cornell University Library.

agent, Reverend C. Turner. Ruggles further stated that he had always been told that the committee would collectively pay for the libel case fees, but after a secret meeting to which he was not invited, the burden was suddenly placed on him. He explained at length negotiations over missing funds intended to pay for the libel suit from the committee's treasury and provided copies of the official audits made in previous years. Bell responded by telling the crowd that he had asked Ruggles earlier about the missing funds, which amounted to $17.50: "Ruggles! Where the Hell is that $17.50, which was pledged toward the 'Libel Suit.'" Ruggles, according to Bell, replied that he needed it to assist some runaways. "Hell and Damnation!" Bell responded, that money was to pay off the suit, and he told Ruggles that it was a "damned roguish trick to use the money for anything else." Johnson made a similar argument, in which he had asked Ruggles to listen to reason and not file a suit against the committee. Ruggles had the last word, beseeching the crowd to see him as "A Man and a Brother," a clear reference to himself as enslaved.[87]

Cornish responded with obvious contempt, describing Ruggles as a "notorious individual" who had written a "pamphlet filled with willful misrepresentations and base falsehoods."[88] Fortunately for Ruggles, members of the committee still considered him a friend. The venerable Samuel Hardenburgh headed a meeting held on September 9 at the home of Ransom F. Wake that Thomas Downing, Peter Vogelsang, and other prominent blacks attended. The committee was particularly upset at an article that appeared in the *Colored American* on July 27 referred to it as a "white-washing committee." The committee insisted that it originally had a private meeting with Ruggles and had no desire to "screen or hide anything" about his character. The *Colored American* accepted this explanation, except for the belief that they composed "Ruggles's committee." It then announced that it considered the matter closed.[89]

The biggest problem for the Committee of Vigilance was that its funds were severely depleted. It announced on September 19 that it had had to turn down requests for help from newly arrived fugitives. Members of the committee tried to distance themselves from the controversy by referring all questions to Ruggles's pamphlet, *A Man and A Brother*. The committee, having lost its most visible and contentious member, then turned its attention to kidnapping controversies in western New York. When the committee next made a report three years later, its tone was more subdued.[90]

On October 24, 1839, the Committee of Vigilance published a public notice in the *Colored American* that it was cutting ties with Ruggles over missing funds that amounted to $326.17. Angered, Ruggles sent a reply to the newspaper detailing his responses to the accusations. His letter was many pages in length and was filled with his customary use of extensive quotes from the works of his adversaries, followed by his rebuttals. The newspaper declined to print Ruggles's epistle, claiming that its mission was to fight slavery, not to intervene in private disputes. Privately, the executive committee of the American Anti-Slavery Society determined that, because Ruggles had not paid for the previous article, they would not "admit anything further into the *Emancipator* on the subject." Cut off from two of his main outlets for publication, Ruggles looked for new allies.[91]

Ruggles's unpublished response to the committee became known in the next months as the "Suppressed Letter." Cornish had refused to publish other lengthy screeds in the past, declining against much furor to print a speech by black porter Peter Paul Simon in 1837. As Leslie Harris has argued, there was more than a hint of snobbery in Cornish's decision. His attitude toward Ruggles, a struggling printer, was similar. Ruggles's letter would finally be published August 20, 1840, in the new Garrisonian newspaper, the *National Anti-Slavery Standard*. Publication occurred on the other side of a seismic separation within the antislavery movement and after a final rupture between Ruggles and his erstwhile allies. Ruggles opened his letter to George M. Tracy, George Barker, William P. Johnson, Theodore S. Wright, Samuel Eli Cornish, and other members of the executive committee of the New York Committee of Vigilance with volleys of sarcasm. He asked rhetorically how the committee could have the "temerity" to make a statement accusing him of embezzlement. Ruggles pushed the boundaries further by saying that he responded with reluctance because of his "pity for your imbecility and . . . treachery to the cause." He continued to lambaste the committee for publishing its contentions about missing funds, despite protestations of "kindness" toward the "late agent." Ruggles had nothing but contempt for this olive branch. The committee, he contended, used only malice and deceit in dealing with him; yet he could discern its evil intent because, quoting a proverb he translated from French, "The soul has no secret which the conduct does not reveal."[92]

Ruggles's next move revealed his remaining allies. He enclosed a letter from Thomas L. Jennings, Samuel Hardenburgh, and other notable black New Yorkers, which vouched that he had been "endangered, basely deserted in the Darg Case." The black community's inaction then required that Ruggles now deserved every expectation of innocence, indicating that the inaction of the black community to bail out Ruggles had antagonized him and his supporters. Having shown that he was not without friends, Ruggles then moved into the financial dispute. In the following pages, he reviewed the history of his salary negotiations with the committee, noting that he was promised four hundred dollars per year, while another official was paid six hundred dollars, a disparity that was a sore spot for Ruggles. The agent then contested the committee's facts over whether the three-hundred-odd dollars were missing and claimed to have made a full accounting of the funds he had received. All of this was done in quasi-legal terms salted with biblical quotations. He was understandably aggrieved that the committee had gone to the court of common pleas to collect the missing funds. Nor could he accept that, one year earlier, the committee had lauded him for his "ability with which he has accomplished his important duties as Secretary and Agent" of the organization and the next year alleged that he had incompetently handled cash and lost accounting books. Its actions, Ruggles showed with several more pages of argument, placed the committee next to the proslavery newspapers and judges in New York. He concluded by describing the *Colored American* as a "Dark Concern," presided over by a priest (Cornish) who had aspirations to be a giant but who really "personifies the Prince of Darkness." Ruggles further denounced Wright and the other black abolitionists for their desertion when he was jailed over the Darg case. The entire proceedings, he concluded, showed a "general, moral, and pecuniary bankruptcy prevailing in the Committee of Vigilance."[93]

Ruggles then took legal action. On October 19, 1839, he filed suit for back wages of $2,500 from the Committee of Vigilance, complaining that its members were attempting to defraud him. A week later, twenty-one men signed a statement in the *Emancipator*, which proclaimed that Ruggles had been badly injured in the Darg case and neglected by his friends in the antislavery movement. The statement's signers urged that "every man in the community who possesses the least sense of justice . . . to stand by Mr. Ruggles in these trying times." In the same issue, his former colleagues made public their suit against Ruggles and subsequent claim for $324 in lost donations.[94]

Why, after so many years of cooperation in the antislavery movement, was there such acrimony between Cornish and Ruggles, which then affected the rest of the committee and caused Ruggles to resign under fire? The amount of money mislaid was small; even the libel suit obligation was quickly satisfied. There was general recognition that Ruggles had done extraordinary service, faced down brutal slave catchers, and changed public and political attitudes about escaped enslaved people. Part of the reason, as Jane and William Pease have argued, has to do with personality. Ruggles and Cornish were proud, stubborn, arrogant men whose feelings, once pricked, turned angry. Yet there had to be a deeper reason. Perhaps Cornish and much of the committee had tired of Ruggles's confrontational style, felt endangered by his reckless publication of the Galvino letter, and wanted the institutions of antislavery to last, far more than they felt it necessary to protect its bravest soldier. Ruggles, though he had joined innumerable organizations, was essentially romantic and spontaneous in his approach, placing the needs of self-emancipated bond people far above any institution. Eventually, such an attitude forced him into a confrontation with a man such as Cornish, who believed in more cautious, slower approaches. Just as the Society of Friends would soon move to excommunicate Hopper and Corse for their abolitionist activities, the black antislavery movement regarded Ruggles as too hot to handle. The irony was that Ruggles's methods, anarchic as they might have been, had greater long-term effects than would Cornish's. In many ways, the split between Cornish and Ruggles and their respective supporters was similar to contemporary clashes among fledgling political reform movements in the city. Dependent on strong leaders, the groups fell apart over ideological and tactical reasons rather than valuing unity at any cost.[95]

The ideological differences between Ruggles and Cornish—indeed, most of the black antislavery authors active in New York City—are measured in their writing style. Cornish, as chief editorialist of the *Colored American*, could be harshly critical of his opponents but always wrote in a careful, analytic prose with rare examples of hyperbole. Ruggles, on the other hand, always wrote with guns blazing. Insults and sarcasm were his tools of trade.

Ruggles's extended influence can be found in the rapid spread of vigilance associations. As noted, Philadelphia blacks initiated their own within a year of the founding of the New York committee. Within a few years, other cities and towns established chapters with the intention of helping fugitive slaves secure their freedom and defend free blacks against kidnapping. Though Ruggles cannot be credited fully with the advance of this movement, his highly publicized activities in New York City undoubtedly raised consciousness about the abolition community nationally and made protection of black rights a critical part of the movement. Historians have concentrated recently on the formation of political parties among abolitionists in this period. Ruggles and the Committee of Vigilance accomplished something very important—crystallizing a movement that would eventually shake the nation: direct action to aid fugitive slaves and battle kidnappers, the movement known as the Underground Railroad.

Ruggles's actions make clearer the development of the Underground Railroad. Initially, Wilbur Siebert and other nineteenth-century historians described it as "a great system, and a chain of stations leading from the southern states to Canada." Most of those enabling fugitive slaves to safety were white farmers. More than a half century later, Larry Gara denied that the Underground Railroad was a system and decried white claims of involvement as romantic. Gara did argue for the importance of blacks working in urban vigilance societies as conveyors helping fugitive slaves to freedom. However, Gara argued even their efforts were hampered by the lack of a national organization and by lack of contact with actual fugitives. Gara further argued that many abolitionists were disconcerted by the energy spent transporting runaways to Canada.[96]

The example of David Ruggles and the Committee of Vigilance shows how blacks organized the Underground Railroad years before Siebert and Gara have recognized. The Committee of Vigilance was a genuine, long-term organization with officers, regular meetings with star speakers and heavy, enthusiastic attendance, extensive fundraising methods, and an office at the *Mirror of Liberty*. The Committee of Vigilance helped hundreds of fugitive slaves, made some into acolytes, and strived to employ their cases for legal battles using talented lawyers. Ruggles's magazine was perhaps the official journal of the movement, but there was ample, sympathetic support in the *Colored American*, the *Emancipator, Liberator, New York Evangelist*, and scores of newspapers across the country. The committee's philosophies of resistance were thereby publicized throughout the United States, even into the highly attuned slave South. Gara argued that the numbers of fugitives helped by the committee were small, but the publicity was immense. And it had lasting effect. By encouraging other organizers, Ruggles and the Committee of Vigilance had transformed the abolitionist movement. Ending slavery was still the main goal, but giving succor to fugitive slaves became a key method of abolitionists from the 1830s forward, with an increasing drumbeat of action into the 1850s. Such events bent the political democracy into passing the aggravating Fugitive Slave Act of 1850 that pushed many previously passive northerners into the antislavery movement. This became first apparent in mid-1830s New York City when angry actions of black and white northerners against kidnappers and slave catchers created a stronger crescendo against slavery. Ruggles was at the heart of this movement.

CHAPTER FIVE

Abolitionist and Physician

Forced from his position as secretary of the New York Committee of Vigilance, Ruggles seemed forsaken by erstwhile allies. Despite his departure from the Committee of Vigilance, Ruggles could find satisfaction from his accomplishments. He had, by his own count, enabled six hundred fugitives to gain freedom. One, Frederick Douglass, was beginning to attract attention in the movement, albeit as a lowly paid agent of the *Liberator*. Ruggles could see the effects of his efforts in mainstream politics. In 1841, New York State governor William Seward signed a bill ensuring the right of habeas corpus for escaped slaves, mandated that future governors provide legal assistance to freedom seekers, and guaranteed public education to all, including blacks. Seward intervened on behalf of free blacks kidnapped into slavery, declined to aid in the arrest of a fugitive slave charged with a crime in Louisiana, and refused to return alleged fugitives from justice in Virginia and Georgia. Ruggles's work in the Dixon and Darg cases pushed Seward into these actions. His associations made Ruggles a minor part of the national election later that year when a Democrat tried to tarnish the Whig candidate, contending that William Henry Harrison sought "the support of the Arthur Tappans and David Ruggles of the North."[1]

Ruggles received further vindication in early January 1840 when the charges against Hopper, Corse, and him stemming from the Darg case fourteen months before were finally dropped. Hopper stated at the hearing that he had already spent several thousand dollars in self-defense and that he intended to sue Darg for the money. He further argued that the entire affair was made up by Darg and his friends in an effort to bankrupt the three radicals. At a public meeting, several of his friends claimed that dismissal of the case in every way cleared Ruggles of any charges leveled against him in 1838. In other good news, Stephen Dickerson was released from slavery in Louisiana and returned home to his family in New York City. There was public acclaim for Ruggles's general contributions. In the first of many fundraisers, a committee, composed of Isaac Prince, John W. Hull, and Phineas Hudson, described Ruggles's health as much worse for the strain of the charges and asked for cash for his relief. Ruggles thanked them and Arthur Tappan and J. W. Higgins for their kindness while he was incarcerated. The committee's call for funds met with some success. In May, Ruggles published a list of contributors who gave a total of sixty-eight dollars for his maintenance and to help pay his legal expenses. Except for sums of ten dollars or more given by the Tappans and a relative of Hopper's, the rest of the donations were in small amounts of a few dollars or less.[2]

The Committee of Vigilance had righted itself and renewed its pledge to protect free blacks from kidnappers and enable fugitive slaves to secure their freedom. Helped by fresh donations, the committee thrived through the 1840s. It served as a model for other cities, including Boston, Worcester, Rochester, Cleveland, and Detroit, among others, that established their own committees. William Johnson estimated in 1843 that in the previous five and one-half years, 1,675 self-emancipated slaves "had passed through his hands from the slave states to Canada." He estimated that 5,000 slaves had attempted to escape, but "not a third of whom succeeded." The committee continued to struggle financially, though Gerrit Smith backed it, donating as much as five hundred dollars in 1849. While Ruggles's recent experience was bitter, he had to take satisfaction in the spread of local committees and the work of his former protégé, Frederick Douglass, who became a firm backer of the Committee of Vigilance's methods.[3]

Sometime in early 1840, Ruggles gave up his residence and reading room of several years on Lispenard Street and moved to 62 Leonard Street. He listed his occupation in the city directory as editor.[4] Nearby was the fanciest brothel in New York City as well as a member of the local police department. Apparently, Ruggles had to abandon the plan to travel to Paris to seek a cure for his blindness and devoted himself to publications and fundraising for himself and the abolitionist movement. His finances remained precarious, and he had to go on the road to solicit contributions from his friends outside New York City to help defray costs of the third issue of the *Mirror of Liberty*. He canvassed churches and meeting halls for funds for the prospective issue. On May 18 he addressed a public meeting at the "colored Congregational Church" in Hartford, led by Reverend James W. C. Pennington. Ruggles obtained a number of new subscriptions at the meeting. Also encouraging was its resolution that "the re-appearance of the *Mirror of Liberty*, by Mr. D. Ruggles, an uncompromising advocate of freedom, is an omen of brighter prospects to our cause."

The meeting also promoted a renewed national convention of colored people, an idea that Pennington had promoted for two years and which Ruggles now endorsed. A reporter at the meeting was James Mars, whom Ruggles had helped on his way to freedom a few years before. The *Emancipator* applauded the appeal on behalf of Ruggles, noting that whatever controversies had arisen about his behavior, he was a "useful servant of the cause," and common humanity required that he get help to restore his sight.[5]

While Ruggles was striving to revive his career, a major fracture occurred within the antislavery movement. Three issues divided the Garrison faction, located largely in Boston, and its opponents, many from New York and including the Tappans. The most nagging problem was the question of female participation in the national society. Beginning at regional gatherings in 1838 and then culminating at the 1840 meeting, delegates disagreed irreconcilably over women in the movement. The second issue was the increasingly anticlerical stances Garrison took, thereby alienating many supporters. The third was the desire of many in the movement to join in electoral politics. Garrison, who later would describe the American Constitution as a "covenant with death," derided any contaminating participation in politics. The issue of greater female involvement in movement politics dominated the 1840 meeting in New York City. Acrimony split the sides into two organizations, the Garrisonian American Anti-Slavery Society and the Tappanite American and Foreign Antislavery Society (A&F). The A&F allowed for separate female societies that would have male delegates representing them at conventions. Having thereby "solved" the woman question, the A&F pushed to form a political party to represent the movement. Though most black New Yorkers sided with the A&F because of their lack of sympathy with female advocates and likely for patronage reasons, Ruggles kept his ties with the Garrisonians. The American Anti-Slavery Society inaugurated a newspaper, the *National Anti-Slavery Standard* on June 11, 1840, that printed many of his letters.[6]

Seeking funds and friendship, Ruggles toured New England, receiving further acclaim, especially from younger, more radical blacks, who felt inspired by his devotion and courage. A few weeks after the Hartford meeting, a host of important black radicals in Boston hailed the *Mirror of Liberty* and Ruggles

with "heart-felt joy, and bid welcome to our beloved city, the consistent, devoted, self-sacrificing, uncompromising, and indefatigable friend of the slave
and universal freedom, David Ruggles." In addition to calling for subscriptions
to the *Mirror of Liberty*, the meeting also demanded publication of the suppressed letter about Ruggles's actions in New York, which the *Colored American* had refused to print. Signing the resolutions were the most prominent
black activists, including J. G. Barbadoes, William Cooper Nell, and John T.
Hilton. A third meeting in Worcester, Massachusetts, praised him. Worcester
was the home of a number of former fugitives who had made good and who
revered what Ruggles had done. His prominent friends in New York City
may have abandoned him, but Ruggles was still immensely popular in New
England. Samuel J. May later recalled that during this period of poor health,
New England friends of Ruggles cheerfully assisted him, though dependence
was irksome to him.[7]

Ruggles found genuine fellowship among black Bostonians and among
abolitionists in the rest of Massachusetts. Young black activists in Boston
admired Ruggles intensely, as he epitomized their affirmation of manhood.
While they revered William Lloyd Garrison, black abolitionists refused to dis-
avow violence as a tool for attacking slavery. Ruggles, though he had backed
Garrison in the organizational split in New York City, was on record for not
ruling out armed response. Young black Bostonians knew that he favored and
practiced direct confrontation and showed genuine leadership in dealing with
even the most powerful white abolitionists, a problem that they felt acutely.
They could agree with Garrison and with Ruggles about the importance of
including women in the movement. Boston black abolitionists had acted to
protect fugitive slaves in the 1830s, though not in the numbers that Ruggles
had done.

Ruggles's popularity stemmed from his courage. As a sign of his utter contempt for racist authority, later that month he issued a strong attack in the
Emancipator on Benjamin Onderdonk, the bishop of the Episcopal Diocese of
New York State, who defended slavery from his pulpit. Onderdonk, who had
publicly humiliated the saintly Peter Williams Jr. after the riots of July 1834,
was a powerful figure, and it took courage to go against him. Later that year,
Williams died. John Jay II, among others, sarcastically described the funeral
at which Onderdonk preached the sermon. Other racist Episcopalians who
had joined in hampering Williams's career took part in the ponderous ceremony. Many months before Jay's devastating public letter, which initiated the
downfall of Onderdonk, Ruggles had led the charge.[8]

The barrage against Onderdonk was one of many irons Ruggles had in the fire. He drummed up support for his magazine and himself on his tour. At each stop he raised the importance of a national meeting of black activists to rally support for "the press and the cause of freedom." His intentions became clearer when he returned to New York in June. At a meeting of an organization named the New-York Reform Society on June 9, Ruggles, as president of the society, took over the chair and pushed through a number of motions promoting the plan of a national convention to be held in New Haven. He argued that sentiments expressed in Hartford, Boston, and Worcester indicated that a number of black activists were dissatisfied with the current efforts to battle the colonization movement, slavery, and repression. Helped by black outrage over the patronizing attitude of the white abolitionist movement, which counseled patience about needed reforms, the movement picked up steam with support from a meeting of sympathizers in Pittsburgh, Pennsylvania.[9]

The planned convention soon became controversial because it would include only blacks and would compete with another convention scheduled for Albany at the same time. That convention attracted black abolitionist luminaries, many of whom would offer luster to Ruggles's plans, except that the Albany convention emphasized political party alliances with whites. The split in the national antislavery movement had convinced many blacks that independent efforts were necessary. The questions were where, when, and who would be invited. Ruggles favored an all-black convention in New Haven. William Whipper and Robert Purvis of Philadelphia complained to Ruggles that racially exclusive conventions were errors that only helped enemies of black people. James McCune Smith of New York contended that the New Haven convention should be abandoned as it was not based on sound principles of racial integration. Disagreeing with Smith and Whipper was Henry Highland Garnet, who argued that blacks had separate schools, literary and debating societies, and churches and so a racially exclusive convention would do no harm. Ruggles made a broader, if largely rhetorical appeal. History showed, he observed, that any oppressed group had to act on its own behalf as long as it was not wholly emancipated. Race was a factor, a "badge to our condition as *disenfranchised* and *enslaved* Americans." Indeed, slavery had reduced blacks in the eyes of the whites: "We have no right to hope to be emancipated from thralldom until we honestly resolve to be free. We must remember that while our fellow countrymen of the south are slaves to individuals, we of the north are slaves to the community, and ever will be so, until we rise, and by the help of Him who governs the destiny of nations, go forward, and like the reformed inebriates, ourselves strike for reform, individual, general, and radical reform, in every ramification of society."[10]

Amazingly for a man who was thoroughly condemned in New York City just months before and was now nearly disabled, Ruggles's call initially met with extraordinary success. More than one hundred black activists from all over the eastern United States signed an announcement for the convention to be held on the first Monday of September 1840 in New Haven. The signers were principally from New York City but included sizable numbers from Boston, Worcester, and Hartford, as well as from various cities in New Jersey and Pennsylvania, and as far west as Pittsburgh and Cincinnati. Among the signers from Boston were John T. Hilton, William Cooper Nell, and J. G. Barbadoes. James W. C. Pennington endorsed the call on behalf of Connecticut blacks. The name of David Ruggles still aroused considerable loyalty and support.[11]

Ruggles responded to Robert Purvis, the Philadelphia activist, who criticized the all-black format by contending that the oppressed had to free themselves if their liberty was to be genuine. He referred back to the American Revolution for guidance: "What would have been the condition of American Liberty, 'the great principle of man's equality,' as taught by the Revolutionary Fathers of our country in their Declaration of Independence, had they hesitated to convene as oppressed Americans to consider and act in reference to the burdens under which they groaned? Their Convention was 'exclusive in its character,' because they met as Americans, oppressed Americans."[12]

Despite his references to the American Revolution, Ruggles's motives for calling the convention are not entirely clear. There can be no denying that after the disastrous events in New York, he had to expand his base of support and to regain the leadership the scandal had cost him. He found backing from younger blacks, most of whom were not from New York City and were not tied to Lewis Tappan or to Samuel Eli Cornish. The rationale for an all-black convention might have been to help black activists sort out their next moves in the light of the split in the white abolitionist movement.

Other problems soon loomed about the proposed convention. A letter in the *Colored American* in August noted the importance of Ruggles's contribution but worried how hasty were the preparations for the convention. The *National Anti-Slavery Standard* published the "suppressed letter" in its issue of August 20, 1840, and thereby showed support for Ruggles, but reaffirmed its opposition to the proposed convention. Lewis Woodson of Pittsburgh published a reasoned letter in the *Colored American* two weeks later that repeated this warning and stated that New York City rather than New Haven was a better place for the convention. Ruggles dismissed this suggestion as coming from "emissaries from New York," rather than from the people of New Haven. Next, a trusted ally, James W. C. Pennington, retracted his support. Undaunted, Ruggles repeated his call for the convention in the same issue of the newspaper. Perhaps the final blow was a statement from New Haven abolitionists that they, not "emissaries from New York," had raised objections to the timing and reasons for the meeting. The signers declared that Ruggles could not be trusted and had maligned the people of New York and New Haven.[13]

The meeting drew only five delegates and twenty observers. Despite the poor turnout, it did succeed in creating a new organization, the American Reform Board of Disenfranchised Commissioners. Along with Ruggles, who served on the business committee, the new society included Samuel Hardenburgh of New York, a Ruggles stalwart, as president, and newcomer William Cooper Nell of Boston as secretary. The group passed motions strongly supporting the American Anti-Slavery Society and opposing the colonization movement, sought to help slaves and disenfranchised free blacks, and made a statement fervently upholding the power of the press. Ruggles exhorted the group by explaining that, "in our cause," words were not enough. "Rise, brethren, rise," he urged the audience and to slaves far away, he declared: "Strike for freedom or die slaves!"[14]

Further attempts to resuscitate Ruggles's reputation occurred in August 1840, when the next issue of the *Mirror of Liberty* finally appeared. A meeting of "colored citizens" in Boston on August 10, 1840, saluted the new issue of the *Mirror of Liberty* and resolved that Ruggles was a martyr to the cause. It called upon the leading antislavery newspapers to print the suppressed letter of the previous year. The power of Ruggles's appeal continued unabated in the late fall of 1840. William Cooper Nell, a rising star among black abolitionists, organized another testimonial for Ruggles in Boston on December 18, celebrating the *Mirror of Liberty* and Ruggles's career. The organizers invited William Lloyd Garrison to attend the meeting.[15]

The third issue of the *Mirror of Liberty* included full statements of the new laws in New York State that extended the right to trial by jury to self-emancipated enslaved people, along with an act to protect black citizens of the state from being kidnapped. These important pieces of legislation, pushed through by Governor William Seward to co-opt the rising power of abolitionism in the state, are testament to the importance of the actions of Ruggles and the Committee of Vigilance. His publication of these statements indicates that he saw them as a personal victory. However self-inflated that may be, there is no question that the activities of the Committee of Vigilance had drawn underground attention to the fugitive slave conundrum and radicalized much of the state's population toward slave catchers, inspired multiple committees of vigilance, and set the stage for community rebuffs of attempts to return fugitives to the South in the future. New York City may have seen continued skirmishes over the return to fugitive slaves and authorities often collaborated with agents of slave masters, but they could no longer do so uncontested. Ruggles had enhanced earlier Quaker efforts and added considerably to black radical responses to such events.[16]

Ruggles published the last issue of the *Mirror of Liberty* in May 1841. Enabled by a $250 gift in February and largely filled with the complete version of the "Suppressed Letter," the journal showed the debilitating effects of his blindness and other diseases. Production of the last issue had left him virtually penniless. "That persecuted, but indefatigable man, David Ruggles," is how the *National Anti-Slavery Standard* hailed the publisher of that issue. It also reported that a soiree was held in his honor in Boston. A similar event occurred in New York City on May 17, 1841. At the Boston gathering, Ruggles spoke of his career as secretary of the Committee of Vigilance without bitterness:

> I have had the pleasure of helping six hundred persons in their flight from bonds. In this, I have tried to do my duty, and mean still to persevere, until the last fetter shall be broken, and the last sigh heard from the lips of a slave. But give praise to Him who sustains us all, who holds up the heart of a laborer in the rice swamp, cheers him when, by the twinkling of the North Star, he finds his way to liberty. Six hundred in three years I have saved; had it been in one year, I should have been nearer my duty, nearer the duty of every American, when he reflects that it was the blood of colored men, as well as whites, which crimsoned the battle-fields of Bunker Hill and the rest, in the struggle to sustain the principles embodied in our Declaration of Independence.[17]

In this remarkable statement Ruggles fused together his Congregational spirituality, emphasizing the requirement that a person actively attempt to right a sinful world, with the emerging belief that radical abolitionism was one with the valiant warriors for the American Revolution and with the tenets of the Declaration of Independence.

In a fundraising prospectus for the *Mirror of Liberty* in the spring of 1841, Ruggles sought an endowment of five hundred dollars and called for agents to canvass for subscriptions in Pennsylvania, Ohio, Indiana, Michigan, Illinois, and Upper Canada. Those ambitious goals were merely his obligation because, as he wrote in verse, "Up, then, in Freedom's manly part / From

William Cooper Nell. A promising young abolitionist in his own right, Nell was an enthusiastic supporter of Ruggles during a difficult period in the early 1840s. Courtesy of the Massachusetts Historical Society.

grey-beard eld to fiery youth / and on the nation's naked heart / Scatter the living coals of truth."[18]

Ruggles maintained his ties with New York City and hoped to revive the *Mirror of Liberty*. His advertisement for the magazine listed his address in New York City, but he was on the road much of the time. Ruggles also worked hard to circulate the journal, sending fifty copies off to William Cooper Nell in Boston. Nell labored hard for Ruggles in Boston and even arranged additional fundraisers. Ruggles asked Nell to give a copy to William Lloyd Garrison and requested that the editor of the *Liberator* publish the proceedings of the New Haven meeting in his newspaper.[19]

David Ruggles's influence on the young radical William Cooper Nell and his cohorts can be seen in the formation of the Boston Committee of Vigilance in June 1841. Presided over by Charles Torrey, the organizational meeting adopted a constitution that endorsed the actions of its New York counterpart in opposing the return of fugitive slaves and, perhaps gesturing toward Ruggles's legacy, invited "the friends of liberty in all those seaport towns, especially those with commercial intercourse with slaveholding states and countries, to cooperate with us," and sent explanatory articles to all the "various antislavery papers which circulate in New England." What Nell, Torrey, and their counterparts were doing was to advance the crusade by methods that Ruggles and Hopper had perfected in New York years before.[20]

Ruggles shuttled between meetings in Boston and New Bedford in June 1841, seeking support for a revival of the *Mirror of Liberty*. Boston black radicals John T. Hilton, Joshua B. Smith, and Nell headed a committee of twelve, which also included three women, that promised to raise money to support and publish the magazine. Their efforts indicate general backing for Ruggles's brand of radical abolitionism. Boston was not the only source of support. On June 30 in New Bedford, Ruggles addressed a "very large and highly respectable concourse of the friends of freedom." After he spoke, Frederick Douglass read passages from the *Mirror of Liberty* and then introduced a successful measure to pledge fifty dollars in support of the magazine. Douglass became the New Bedford agent for the *Mirror of Liberty* at this meeting. In one of his first published letters, Douglass reported the meeting's support for Ruggles in the *New Bedford Morning Register*; the article then appeared in the abolitionist media. Two months before Garrison encountered Douglass, the young activist was still learning antislavery methods from David Ruggles.[21]

After his problems in New York City, Ruggles benefited from the adulation he received in New England. Boston's black community boasted an established militant leadership with younger, even more radical black activists who admired Ruggles's combination of intellectual and physical confrontation. In New Bedford, where the Society of Friends and a strong black community had long made the city hospitable for self-emancipated blacks, a new generation epitomized by Frederick Douglass was propelling black abolitionism and challenging the paternalism of the white leadership. Again, Ruggles was the example of what these younger men admired. Historians have described Ruggles as beaten and impoverished at this time, but the events in Boston and New Bedford make plain the exalted position he held among black activists.[22]

An example of how much Douglass and even veteran activists learned from Ruggles came in the early summer of 1841. During these trips around New England, Ruggles showed his old grit in two incidents involving segregated seating. On June 12 Ruggles was evicted from the regular railroad car after he refused to move to the seats reserved for people of color, a clear example of civil disobedience. A week later, he was rebuffed on a steamboat from New Bedford to Nantucket. Ruggles arrived at the ticket booth of the steamboat *Telegraph* on June 19 and attempted to buy a two-dollar general ticket rather than a cheaper ticket restricted to the front deck. The captain refused to accept his money. The white conductor ejected Ruggles from his seat over the protests of Reverend John Spear. Ruggles described the fracas in the *Liberator*. His initial dispute came over the purchase price of a ticket. Ruggles insisted upon paying a higher fare to avoid sitting in the windy forward deck; his grounds were that he had the right to sit where he pleased as long as he paid the appropriate fare. Ruggles declared, "While I advocate the principles of equal liberty, it is my duty to practice what I preach, and claim my rights at all times." No American Revolutionary could have said it better.

Burdened by and yet defiant of such discriminatory behavior, Ruggles was brought lower a few days later when his father, David Sr., died in Norwich at the age of sixty-six. The death of a father forces a man to confront his own meaning, and Ruggles could find his in the virtue of resistance. He could no longer tolerate the insulting behavior of boorish conductors. Two weeks later, Ruggles again confronted keepers of segregated public transport. While traveling from New Bedford to Boston on the New Bedford and Taunton branch railroad on July 6, Ruggles refused the orders of the conductor to move to the car where blacks were assigned seating areas. After an argument, the railroad superintendent and several other white men dragged Ruggles from the white car and threw him off the train, damaging his clothing. Ruggles also lost his traveling bag that included checks and subscriptions for the *Mirror of Liberty*. Angrily, Ruggles brought suit against his assailants for assault and battery. Judge Henry Crapo of New Bedford, a stockholder in the railroad, heard testimony in the trial, which was held on July 19 and 20. The company contended that regulations posted by its agent, William A. Crocker, on January 1, 1841, stated that passengers on the train should take seats as assigned by the conductor and that Ruggles was shown the regulations during the incident. Judge Crapo ruled that, as a private concern, the company had the right to regulate seating for the welfare and comfort of its passengers. He also ruled that the superintendent and his men had not used undue force than would normally be necessary to subdue an unruly passenger. Across the country, newspapers applauded the decision, concluding that the railroad had the right to expel Ruggles.[23]

The abolitionist movement disagreed and took more direct action. Ruggles led the charge against the decision by describing it in an article entitled "Lynching in New-Bedford." His report and the decision galvanized the antislavery movement in New Bedford and around New England. There had been reports of incidents over segregated seating for years, including ones involving Ruggles in 1834 and in 1838 and another recent incident involving Thomas Jennings of Boston. A Massachusetts representative had voted against an extension of wharf use sought by the Eastern Railroad in the spring of 1841 because of the company's Jim Crow policies. But it was Ruggles who aroused public opinion. The *National Anti-Slavery Standard* ripped the railroad for its "shameful behavior." The *Boston Times* demanded that the judge have his ears cropped. Ruggles headed a mass meeting on July 12 in New Bedford in which he presented his version of the attack. William Lloyd Garrison offered a resolution. Frederick Douglass led a procession of speakers at the Meeting of Colored Citizens to protest the actions of the captain. Soon, railroad ride-ins became a frequent method of protest by demanding equal rights to public conveyances. Not all the protests were planned. Frederick Douglass learned firsthand of the segregated policies of the railroads when he was beaten by a "whole 'posse' consisting of brakemen, baggage men, and &ct," for refusing to sit in the "Jim Crow Car." In early 1842, a riot occurred when two young black abolitionists were told to get out of the main car. When one of them, Shadrach Howard, was attacked, he drew a knife. Another abolitionist wrenched it out of his hand. Howard and the conductor, a man named Bird, had an angry exchange. When the train arrived in Taunton, Howard went to search for a sheriff to arrest Bird. During that time, a mob formed, shouted racial epithets, and threatened to beat Howard. He barely escaped with his skin.[24]

The abolitionist community got another taste of steamship segregation policies en route to a series of meetings on Nantucket in August. Douglass and Ruggles accompanied William Lloyd Garrison and about forty other abolitionists for what promised to be a comfortable sail from New Bedford to Nantucket. After buying their tickets, the group was informed that the black members had either to go to the upper cabin or to get off the vessel before it would depart. The captain explained that he would refund any fares and that the policies were not his decision but those of the directors of the company. A compromise was soon reached by which white and black abolitionists sat together on the upper deck. The journey was so pleasant that all the passengers joined them, including a slaveholder from Louisiana. Upon reaching the island, the abolitionists held a series of meetings. At one, Douglass gave an extraordinary speech. The reporter noted how "Flinty hearts were pierced, and cold ones melted by his eloquence. Mr. Garrison said his speech would have done honor to Patrick Henry." Douglass made a second speech later the same day, which was "listened to by a multitude with mingled conditions of admiration, pity, and horror." Significantly, Douglass's first assignment was to raise money for the defense of a fugitive slave George Latimer, whom the city of Boston authorities were trying to remand to his owner in the South. Douglass spoke often and eloquently about the unfairness of Latimer's treatment, echoing themes about the rights of fugitive slaves that Ruggles had taught him years before.[25]

The furor over the railroad's mistreatment of Ruggles continued unabated. At a meeting of the Bristol Antislavery Society in New Bedford on August 9, Garrison offered a resolution condemning the railroad's actions against "our unflinching and unfaltering coadjutor, David Ruggles." As Carleton Mabee has noted, Garrison's speech impressed Douglass, but the subject was Ruggles. Other activists followed Ruggles's example. In late September, Mrs. Mary Newhall Green, the secretary of the Lynn (Massachusetts) Anti-Slavery Society, a light-skinned black woman, who had previously ridden the railroad without incident, was dragged out of the whites-only car with a baby in her arms. The child was badly injured, as was Green's husband, who tried to help her. The same day, several white men were evicted from a railroad along with a black man who had accompanied them. Charges against the company were dismissed in both cases.[26]

The power of the movement did not abate because of adverse judicial opinions. Over the next two years, petitions to the legislature attacking the railroads' segregated policies finally influenced the legislature. Though the state lawmakers did not take any real action, threats of regulation meant that gradually the railroads dropped their policies. Because of David Ruggles's courageous example, blacks in Massachusetts could, by late 1843, sit where they pleased on such common carriers.[27]

Ruggles continued to urge the creation of a national black congress. In August 1841 he called for a second meeting of the American Reform Board of Disenfranchised Commissioners, to be held in New York City in September. Ruggles argued in Garrison's newspaper, the *Liberator*, for issues that were specifically related to the conditions of free black people in the North. He asked delegates to collect materials on the conditions of black people in their locales, seeking information on the number of children in schools, mechanics employed in distinct trades, how many people of color were working on chain gangs, and how many churches and clergy were in the area. Ruggles proclaimed that "IMMEDIATE EMANCIPATION," was meaningless without "full ENFRANCHISEMENT." Without civil rights, blacks could never be or act as equals of whites. To obtain those rights, they had to act on their own.[28]

The congress met at the Wesleyan Methodist Episcopal Zion Church in New York City on September 10, 1841. Forty-one people attended. Samuel

Eli Cornish editorialized that notice of the meeting was necessary only "to say that we have no faith in the movement." He noted caustically that the men associated with the convention were, "with one exception," unexceptionable men, and "that is the ground of our objection." In short, except for Ruggles, the group was composed of nobodies. In fact, that was not true; Samuel Hardenburgh was present, and William Cooper Nell gave a speech. Cornish also pointed out the small numbers attending the convention, the fees required to vote, and the little that was accomplished. Indeed, not much occurred. Those present denounced the American Colonization Society, endorsed abolitionist magazines including the *Mirror of Liberty*, and voted to salute Governor Seward for the legislation securing for fugitives the right to a trial by jury. Characteristically, Ruggles, ever the purist, angrily condemned this motion as the statute "acknowledged the right of man to hold property in man" and thereby disgraced the legal code. The convention then adjourned for the year. In contrast, the *Colored American* chronicled the high-powered list of conventioneers who had recently met in Troy, New York, a group that included other members of the Committee of Vigilance and leading pastors such as Theodore S. Wright, Christopher Rush, and Charles B. Ray. That convention was only a state meeting, not a national one, yet by focusing on the struggle to restore the vote to black citizens, it did more than the New York convention would have done, even if its numbers were greater.[29]

Meanwhile, Ruggles's eyesight continued to deteriorate. He now needed an editorial assistant to help him read and write. By the fall of 1841, Ruggles's blindness forced him to suspend publication of the *Mirror of Liberty*. Back in New York City and living at 251 Elizabeth Street, Ruggles pledged that either he would resume publication or it would be "conducted by a competent brother." He planned to have an operation that might restore his sight; if the procedure did not work, he promised to return the "$913.88" in pledges, donations, and subscriptions. The operation apparently did not work. Ruggles then went to New Rochelle, New York, to stay with Joseph and Margaret Carpenter, two close friends of his. At their home, Ruggles then underwent a treatment using a lotion on his eyes. He rejoiced in January 1842, proclaiming that the lotion had removed the cataracts from his eyes and that he could once again "use my pen to urge this guilty nation to immediate emancipation."[30]

The treatment apparently lasted but a short while, because Ruggles was again blind by mid-1842. He persisted in trying to pay off old debts. In the early fall, Ruggles tried to settle accounts with the Committee of Vigilance by listing all the contributors to the funds to assist him during the Darg affair.

The total was $344.47, which a committee of his friends declared would be raised privately to pay off the blind activist's debts.[31]

David Ruggles finally found a refuge in the storm when he arrived in November 1842 at the Northampton Association of Education and Industry (NAEI), located in Bensonville, a village just outside of Northampton, Massachusetts. Its admissions board, in a special meeting, invited Ruggles "to come amongst us as a member, without being admitted until better acquainted." Final approval never occurred, but Ruggles lived with the NAEI until its dissolution four years later and stayed in Northampton for the rest of his life.[32]

The NAEI, founded the year before, enjoyed a reputation for liberalism. Its members encouraged liberty of thought but presumed that members were antislavery, antiwar, and temperate. Dependent for income on a silk thread factory, the community practiced frugality, especially in diet. Ruggles could rejoice in the community's educational methods. The Northampton community had its own boarding school. Ruggles called it the best in the country and urged other blacks to send their children to it. Directed by William Adam, a former Harvard professor, the school forbade corporal punishment and emphasized study and labor. Its pupils worked in the community silk farms, learned biology and botany, and studied geography using a hands-on approach. Ruggles could find new life in such a place. Moreover, antislavery agents had worked diligently to make Northampton a staunch abolitionist stronghold. Blacks could prosper there. William Howard Day, sent by his parents in New York City to apprentice with Northampton ink manufacturer J. P. Williston, learned printing skills and was about to enter Oberlin College. Residents were prepared to take abolitionism into the political arena. The local Congregationalist Society notably determined to pursue this agenda. Known as the Free Congregational Society of Florence, its membership included Ruggles and many others in the NAEI.[33]

The agents had only partially succeeded in making the area an antislavery stronghold. Northampton did have a small antislavery society, but in general the town remained conservative, even among the ranks of the antislavery adherents. The city's churches used the "negro pew." Denominational attitudes were conciliatory about slavery. Lydia Maria Child wrote to her friend Abby Kelley that "the abolitionists here, with very few exceptions, exist for awhile without Righteousness for its foundation let there be peace in the church— peace in the neighborhood is the burden of this song." Child explained a church supported a minister who took hundreds of dollars from a rich slave auctioneer. Child proclaimed: "In gratitude for the slaver's support, the minister preaches against all reforms . . . and the slave-auctioneer is the deacon

Lydia Maria Child. One of the most famous children's book writers in America, Child made a bold choice to become an abolitionist. As first editor of the *National Anti-Slavery Standard*, she published Ruggles's letters and helped him find succor in Northampton, Massachusetts. Courtesy of the Library of Congress.

and teaches in his Sunday school class that the Africans are the descendants of Ham, fore-ordained to perpetual slavery. Therefore his profits come from the decrees of God." She concluded the abolitionists in the church do not raise their voices, "so highly do they value 'The Peace of the Church.'"[34]

Several people were likely responsible for the warm welcome that Ruggles received. The Williston family, long financial supporters of the Committee of Vigilance and the *Mirror of Liberty*, undoubtedly underwrote his arrival. Lydia Maria and David Lee Child had many contacts there. Ruggles found fellow radicals in the Northampton Association of Education and Industry. The organization was founded as a communitarian enterprise in 1841 on a substantial property acquired from the bankrupt Northampton Silk Company in Broughton's Meadow (renamed Florence in 1852) located in the western part of Northampton. The association combined, as its foremost scholar, Christopher Clark, noted, industrialism in a rural setting, without the class barriers already evident in manufacturing towns near Boston. Most of its

Abolitionist and Physician

David Lee Child. Lydia's husband, David, succeeded her as editor of the *National Anti-Slavery Standard* and was a frequent publisher of Ruggles's journalism. Courtesy of the historical collections the Beaman Memorial Public Library, West Boylston, Massachusetts.

leaders were from Connecticut, it proclaimed racial and sexual equality, and was resolutely antislavery. Ruggles found succor among the women of the community. Dolly Witter Stetson became a reader for Ruggles.[35]

Radical abolitionists founded the Northampton Association. George W. Benson, its leading figure, was from Brooklyn in Windham County, Connecticut, north of Norwich. He was the local agent for the *Liberator*, was prominent in the local antislavery society, and, from 1837 on was the Connecticut agent for the American Anti-Slavery Society. Benson was the brother-in-law of William Lloyd Garrison. He and Samuel J. May were the legal defense team for Prudence Crandall when racist mobs destroyed her schoolhouse for black girls in Canterbury, Connecticut, in March 1833. After business setbacks in Connecticut, Benson moved to Northampton in 1841 and started gathering potential business partners in silk manufacturing. Joining Benson were Theodore Scarborough, an abolitionist farmer, and Samuel L. Hill and Hiram Wells, both artisans and antislavery activists. Hill was rapidly becoming one of the most important financial figures in Florence. Though

Abolitionist and Physician

few Northampton residents were enthusiastic about the association, its numbers swelled with new arrivals. It attracted the attention of David Mack, a Cambridge, Massachusetts, schoolteacher and social reformer. Mack was born near Northampton, was educated at Yale, and later became preceptor of a Quaker school in New Bedford and joined the New Bedford Young Men's Anti-Slavery Society. After his marriage to another teacher, Maria Braswell, Mack moved to Cambridge, Massachusetts, where the couple started a school for girls. They nearly joined the Brook Farm community in February 1842 but, wary of rumors about the dictatorial style of that association's founder, George Ripley, veered away and moved to Northampton instead. Doubtless the idea that Northampton's group had no single leader, but rather a set of elected officers, attracted Mack. In time he would become president of the association and later serve as secretary and director of education. He nearly convinced his close friend Nathaniel Hawthorne to join the association, but the famous author declined.[36]

Ruggles also found support from David and Lydia Maria Child. The couple was widely known and respected in abolitionist circles, and Mrs. Child was among the most famous female writers in America. She had recently become the editor of the *National Anti-Slavery Standard* and had moved to New York in April 1841 from their home in Northampton, becoming the first female editor of a newspaper. Maria Child (she disliked her first name and rarely used it) had a sizable reputation among blacks because of such publications as *An Appeal in Favor of That Class of Americans Called Africans*, first published in 1833. She was a longtime associate of Isaac T. Hopper and later wrote his biography. After her arrival to work in New York in 1841, she became involved romantically with John Hopper. Such associations brought her into fairly continual contact with Ruggles. When Mrs. Child realized the extent of his ailments, she recommended that Ruggles join the Northampton Association of Education and Industry, and there regain his strength. Although David and Lydia had owned a beet farm in the community, they were not members of the Northampton Association. Yet they were well known to its founding members. David Lee Child remained in Northampton until taking over as editor of the *National Anti-Slavery Standard* in May 1843 after Maria resigned. Introduced by their supportive recommendation, Ruggles joined the association on November 30, 1842, and was "welcomed and treated as an honored friend."[37]

Ruggles found new hope for improvement in his health in Northampton. Hope was required. In January 1843 Ruggles was desperate. His blindness had returned and he now suffered from liver ailments. He complained to William Lloyd Garrison that he longed to "be with you on duty" but could not because of problems with his diaphragm. By Ruggles's own account, he had seen many of the most eminent physicians. He had been "repeatedly bled, leached, cupped, plastered, blistered, salivated, doused with arsenic, nuxvomica, iodine, strychnine and a variety of other poisonous drugs." Following these treatments, Ruggles suffered by his own account from an "enlarged liver, the worst kind of dyspepsia, irritation of the lungs, chronic inflammation of the bowels, costiveness [constipation], piles, nervousness and mental debility, and numb or palsied state of the skin, which rendered me insensitive to the prick of a pin or extreme heat." His physicians told him "my life was limited to a few weeks." As a last resort, Ruggles decided to try a new medical cure called hydrotherapy, or the water cure.[38]

Ruggles may have learned about hydrotherapy from David Lee Child, who became interested in the subject in 1842. As he related a few years later, in January 1843, Ruggles heard of a new method of the water cure, "as practiced by Vincent Priessnitz, a self-taught peasant physician from Switzerland." Soon after Priessnitz established his water-cure method, his fame and remedy spread to the United States, where adherents tied the Swiss doctor's theories to more familiar ideas of healthy living espoused by the Grahamites, homeopaths, and Thomsonians, mixed with millennial urgencies to reform individuals and society. Weary and in great pain, Ruggles determined to try a private course of water treatment.[39]

Desperate but determined, Ruggles "commenced an indifferent application of water as a remedy," until he understood that "water, as an agent, was powerful for evil as well as good, and that unless it was understandably applied, my hopes for relief were chimerical." Fortunately, Ruggles learned of Dr. Robert Wesselhoeft, of Cambridge, Massachusetts. A native of Saxony, a law graduate of the University of Jena, Wesselhoeft had spent seven years in prison for "free thinking on political questions." Later he abandoned his legal career. Suffering from a "bilious and rheumatic fever," he received treatment from Priessnitz. After migrating to the United States, he settled in Cambridge, Massachusetts, opened a homeopathic clinic, and, along with his brother, Wilhelm, became a family doctor to such luminous families as the Hawthorns, Longfellows, Peabodys, and Channings. Soon, he opened a famous clinic for the water cure in Brattleboro, Vermont.[40]

Ruggles initially corresponded with Wesselhoeft and then, after a few months of "salutary advice," visited him in Cambridge. According to Ruggles, the doctor found a "liver so much enlarged, and my sight, and other symptoms so precarious, that he was not sanguine of success." He advised Ruggles to build a douche bath, in which he could fully immerse his body. Ruggles

Abolitionist and Physician

strived to achieve better health but went through crisis after crisis, which, by his own account, made him gloomy and suspicious that the treatment would ever work. The "crisis" toward which treatment aimed was the moment when the symptoms indicated either the incurability of the condition or the beginning of the patient's progress toward recovery. Manifestations could be boils, diarrhea, or feverishness. Patients with liver ailments, such as Ruggles suffered, were encouraged to pursue a crisis. As Christopher Clark has indicated, the crisis took on moral as well as physical significance, comparable to a religious conversion experience. Given that it maximized the symptoms of disease, the climax of a treatment itself took exceptional courage to endure. The rigors of hydropathical methods included endless baths, full body wraps in cold sheets, and bandaging, all of which demanded substantial inner strength and endurance. Successful completion of a course of hydropathical treatment, Clark relates, indicated moral as well as physical fitness.[41]

Ruggles and the doctor decided to continue the treatment, which had to be long-distance. He undoubtedly received help from association members interested in the water cure. Over the next eighteen months, Ruggles was packed in wet sheets once or twice a day, then plunged into a shallow bath, followed by washing of his hip, eyes, and feet. Although initially this routine had the effect of causing a fever and some hallucinations, gradually the fever dissipated and his eyes were restored to limited sight. His sense of feeling became acute, allowing him to recognize people by touch and "detect shades of difference in very minute objects." His years of misery did not seem to have destroyed Ruggles's physical appearance, except for his blindness. An associate of the time described him as "of ordinary size, with an athletic form and dark complexion."[42]

By his own and William Lloyd Garrison's account, written later as part of the black abolitionist's obituary, Ruggles went through crisis after crisis by himself. Wesselhoeft advised Ruggles to undertake a milder treatment, "until new symptoms required a more rigorous course." Despite the initial help he received from association members, Ruggles's solitary ordeal raises questions about the vaunted racial egalitarianism of the Northampton community and of Wesselhoeft's treatment. Ruggles was not the only community member going through the water cure. Early in 1843, angry local responses to reports of men and boys bathing naked in the Mill River that flowed by the community prompted construction of a bathhouse. The bathhouse may have been racially restricted because Ruggles apparently found his own supply of pure water in the wilderness nearby and douched himself. George R. Stetson, a son of a prominent family in the association, recalled that one of his childhood duties was to lead Ruggles out to his bath. The boy's altruistic behavior ran contrary to water-cure protocol. One of the tenets of the water cure was that it should take place within an institutional framework. Eventually, Ruggles would develop his own clinic and prescribe and carry out the treatment of many white patients. Yet, by all accounts, Ruggles underwent much of his initial treatment alone.

By 1844 Wesselhoeft had purchased buildings and the following year opened a soon-to-be famous water-cure hospital in Brattleboro, Vermont, a short train ride from Northampton. Wesselhoeft used his extensive social contacts in Boston to attract a glittering clientele. Catherine Beecher and Harriet Beecher Stowe were patients. Wesselhoeft used national magazines extensively to gain more customers, despite the hefty fees that started at more than ten dollars per week. Wesselhoeft succeeded in garnering national patronage, including a number of southerners. Wesselhoeft did not charge Ruggles for consultations, for which the black man was understandably grateful. Neither did he invite him up to Brattleboro for the treatment, although long-term residence was deemed necessary for successful treatment. In Northampton and surely in Brattleboro, the prospect of a naked black man amid white fellows unquestionably would raise an uproar, something the socially connected doctor and the residents at Northampton wanted to avoid. Their liberality with Ruggles ended with his clothed body. Later, as with southern slave masters, they could accept ministrations on their own naked bodies but not the other way around.[43]

Ruggles's solitary self-treatments are testaments to the powerful inner strength he derived from his family and Congregational Church upbringing and to the fruits of his accomplishments during the abolitionist movement. Despite his travails and rejections in New York, Ruggles had to know that many former enslaved people attributed their freedoms to his guidance and courage. Many younger people in the abolitionist movement deeply admired him. He had put his life on the line in New York and, now, though broken in body, his spirit became refreshed in the cool, pure waters of rural Massachusetts. Gradually, his body returned to a semblance of health.

In the course of his treatment, Ruggles befriended David Mack, one of the early leaders of the Northampton Association and by now a proponent of the water cure, though more, as Christopher Clark relates, as a writer than as a practitioner. Mack left the association in 1845 and moved his family to Brattleboro, where he and his wife, Maria, underwent treatment from Wesselhoeft. As Maria's treatment took eighteen months, Mack edited a monthly journal, the *Green Mountain Spring*, which publicized Wesselhoeft and hydropathy in general. Mack and Ruggles stayed friends and eventually Mack would aid and defend the physician-abolitionist.[44]

Despite the arm's-length treatment of his condition, Ruggles was content in Northampton. In a letter to the black abolitionist Stephen A. Myers of Albany, New York, Ruggles happily spoke of the restorative powers of rural New England. Doubtless thinking of his younger days on Bean Hill in Norwich, Ruggles described the "music of the fresh mountain breezes . . . of the sonorous peals of thunder succeeding the warm spring showers." He listened to the bluebirds, sparrows, larks and other minstrels whose "mellifluous strains can be heard from every tree," of chattering squirrels, of sheep and lambs, and, best of all, the boys and girls, men and women, who "conspire to a harmony in exciting wonder and admiration . . . in this Home for Humanity." Here, Ruggles said, he would stay for a while in "quiet neutrality," to refresh his battered body. Ruggles could not see and his description highlights hearing as well as smell and touch.[45]

Notwithstanding indications of racial skittishness about having hydrotherapy treatments with him, Ruggles found succor in the Northampton community. Acceptance came particularly from young women, who regarded Ruggles as a wise man. Almira Stetson, one of the girls in the association, referred in a letter to her father in January 1843 how Mr. Ruggles, commenting on her growth, said "I should be so smart that I should jump over the meeting house by spring and do not know but that I could lift it too." Dolly Stetson, her mother, mentioned reading to David Ruggles about a temperance jubilee which he said was "rich." Sarah Stetson, writing to her father, James, reported that "Mr. Ruggles sends his love and best respects to you." Ruggles became a key informant, advising the Stetsons not to trust one man as a servant. He also helped prepare food. Dolly Stetson wrote, "After breakfast David Ruggles gets in the wood, shells peas, string beans, or prepares potatoes as the case may be." He advised younger members on financial matters. Dolly Stetson informed her husband about "pumping Mr. Ruggles about a land deal." Ruggles, present but a few months, was already comfortable in enforcing morality and at times on more emotional matters. On one occasion, for example, he took an unmarried, but cohabiting couple aside and beseeched them to consider the community's reputation and legalize their love. When they refused, he advised them "that they could never be admitted here as members and they had better go where the weather was warm." Ruggles apparently was speaking on behest of other community members who were shocked by the couple's open liaison and who worried that the association might be tarnished by accusations of hosting illicit relationships. As Paul Gaffney has insightfully concluded, Ruggles's advice went far beyond the boundaries of known racial codes of color and sexuality. The incident attests to Ruggles's staunch self-confidence and wisdom. The couple did not leave immediately because of an illness the woman suffered.[46]

In the outside world, his supporters continued to seek help for Ruggles and his projects. "H.W.H" penned a poem that appeared in the *Liberator* in the summer of 1844. It began with a plea:

Ho! Brothers, to the rescue
A brother calls for aid
Shall succor too much needed
Be longer yet delayed?
Save him from want and sorrow —
Save from the eroding care
Which throws o'er all life's radiance
From Cruel Hands and Strong

The poem went on to remind readers of

The eyes that blessed the hopeless
Are now with blindness dim
He brought sight to others
Who will be sight to him?[47]

Despite such support, Ruggles's health continued to decline. His blindness had become permanent, and he needed a scribe and reader for communications. He reported to the readers of the *Liberator* in August 1844 that although he was grateful to William Cooper Nell and other Boston abolitionists who held a dinner on August 12, 1844, to garner support for his water cure, that he would be unable to come to Boston. He reported that he was progressing through a six-month water cure consisting of an "uninterrupted series of swathing, fomenting and bathing, by showering, plunging, and dashing" all of which made travel impossible. He asked Frederick Douglass, who was then on tour for the antislavery cause, to tell his listeners of Ruggles's whereabouts. Ruggles had apparently already constructed a water-cure house, from which he could "obtain a douche from a spring of pure water," in hopes of regaining his sight.[48]

Inclement weather hampered attendance of the Boston dinner. Still, black antislavery activists John T. Hilton, who chaired the event, William Cooper Nell, and others recognized Ruggles for the sacrifices and persecutions he had suffered for his efforts on behalf of American enslaved people. The meeting recalled Ruggles's brave actions in 1841 against railroad discrimination. Wendell Phillips augmented the donations made on site with a generous grant. Nell, who wrote the report, was not the only young black activist to call for support for Ruggles. At the meeting of the New-England Antislavery Convention the following June, Frederick Douglass sought a resolution calling for every abolitionist to help Ruggles.[49]

Ruggles began to administer the water cure to others, even if he did not receive credit. In one instance at the Northampton community in April 1844, a young man fell off a roof. Although able to partially break his fall, still he dropped forty or more feet. A doctor on the scene recommended bleeding and leeching the young man. Ruggles objected and, once it was determined that no bones were broken, had the victim wrapped in a cold, wet sheet and then gave him a lengthy bath. Ruggles used a standard water-cure method. The young man recovered sufficiently that afternoon to walk on his own. The *Northampton Democrat* described the event in an article soon after without identifying Ruggles. Despite this failure of public recognition, Ruggles continued to treat community members. Samuel L. Hill wrote a creditor of the association in December 1845 that David Ruggles was using the water cure to treat his wife, who suffered from a lung infection and a cough, and his daughter, Mary. After just two years of membership in the association, Ruggles was now helping local people and sickly association members back to health.[50]

Hill, who was one of the leading local investors, was so grateful to Ruggles for his help that the next April he wrote a letter of introduction to C. E. Forbes, a local lawyer, asking Forbes to help Ruggles draw up a legal document that would protect all investors in a water-cure hospital. Hill volunteered to pay for the legal services. Other community members stepped forward to enable Ruggles to buy equipment for the water-cure business. Ruggles took up his bookselling once again, helped teach the community children, and became a key part of the association's leadership, as, for example, when he provided skilled opinions on cotton manufactures.[51]

Another of Ruggles's first patients was Sojourner Truth, who had arrived at the association in mid-1844. When she entered Ruggles's clinic in 1845, Truth, who was already gaining a major reputation as an orator, was seriously ill and close to becoming an invalid. Ruggles treated her for stomach and bowel problems, swollen and abscessed legs, and joint and muscle ailments. Truth was initially skeptical of the water cure and dismissed it as humbug. Gradually, Ruggles's treatments cured her first of dyspepsia. Constant wet-sheet packing and cold baths slowly provided relief from her leg problems. Ruggles's protocol enabled Truth to return to her work at the associa-

Sojourner Truth.
Ruggles and Truth may have
known each other in New York City
in the early 1830s when she was named
Isabella Van Wagenen. When she arrived in
Northampton beset with many illnesses,
Ruggles saved her with his water-cure protocol.
Courtesy of the American Antiquarian Society.

tion laundry room in about ten weeks. She praised his methods and became
a lifelong proponent of the water cure. Accounts of Truth's experience with
Ruggles indicate that he required his patients to use Sylvester Graham's diet
of wheat crackers. Graham lived in Northampton and argued that Americans had to forsake their fat-rich fried foods in favor of Graham bread mixed
with milk, soaked overnight and then eaten hot or cold. Ruggles and Graham
agreed that a cure must be holistic and approach mind, body, and spirit. Although Sojourner Truth occasionally resorted to pipe smoking, in general
she accepted the knowledge gained at Ruggles's establishment.[52]

Even as his business took up more of his time, Ruggles did not abandon
the antislavery movement. He kept up his thunderbolt letters. In one to
William Lloyd Garrison, he denounced the *Prigg v. Pennsylvania* decision that
reversed more than two decades of personal liberty laws in northern states,
denied the writ of habeas corpus to self-emancipated slaves, and opened up
the northern states to slave catchers. In this letter, which was published in
the *Liberator* on February 10, 1842, Ruggles argued that stigmatizing a man
"for wearing the skin he received from his Creator, or conceding to slavery

Abolitionist and Physician

the right to incarcerate humanity as a chattel personal," conflicted with his own understanding of the Declaration of Independence. Denying a jury trial to blacks, he argued, was at variance not only with the American Declaration of Independence but also with the laws of nature and of the living God. As Benjamin Quarles pointed out, Ruggles's statement was one of the most important among antebellum African Americans who indicated the contradictions between slavery and the Declaration.[53]

In April 1843 he wrote a forceful letter in the *National Anti-Slavery Standard*, castigated the proposed Hay-Ashburton Treaty, which, he argued, would make Canada as much of a hunting ground for slave catchers as the Fugitive Slave Act of 1793 had made the northern states. After the *Anti-Slavery Standard* had published his comments, he admonished the paper for referring to him, however sympathetically, as an employee of the Northampton Association. He was not hired by his fellow members, he assured the newspaper, but lived in terms of perfect equality with them. The association was, he said, an "equal brotherhood — *the all embracing law of love* — so emphatically taught by *true* Christianity." Ruggles was apparently so happy with his place in the association that he was willing to overlook the discrimination he experienced from other practitioners of the water cure.[54]

Ruggles's sense of personal equality extended to William Lloyd Garrison. Ruggles wrote the *Liberator* after Garrison visited Northampton in the summer of 1843. In his own correspondence, Garrison had spoken well of Ruggles and emphasized his struggle with blindness. Ruggles saw larger troubles for the famed abolitionist. Ruggles grieved to observe Garrison attending "all the meetings and conventions he can hear of, within thirty miles around," despite a severe pain in his side, which all friends ascribed to overwork. Ruggles urged his friends at the newspaper to force Garrison to take a vacation from his antislavery activities lest "his present course will lay him in a premature grave." His physician should deter him from his suicidal course. Though Garrison ignored this plea, Ruggles clearly wrote as an equal. He kept up his correspondence, his blindness notwithstanding. Every month, his account total for postage was one of the largest at the Northampton Association.[55]

In a letter to Stephen A. Myers, Ruggles showed that his other connections with the antislavery movement were intact. Though he declined to become an agent for Myers's newspaper, the *Albany Northern Star*, he did suggest Stephen Christopher Rush, a former fugitive and now a protégé of Ruggles, as a replacement. Ruggles praised Myers and his Albany Committee of Vigilance as "the most efficient organization in the State of New-York, in the business of aiding the way-worn and weather-beaten refugee from slavery's shambles." Showing that he was a part of the abolitionist community, Ruggles suggested that Myers contact a number of others "to form a constellation of correspondents." Included in his list were William Whipper, Robert Purvis, Sarah Douglass, James McCune Smith, Patrick Reason, Sarah Forten Purvis, and Frederick Douglass. That he recommended these names indicates that Ruggles, who knew how to bear a grudge, was still in contact with and favored the abolitionists. Ruggles then asked Myers to take on the case of James D. Lane, who had been tricked by a New York City lawyer into following a sea captain into slavery in Virginia. Showing he kept up with the abolitionist news, Ruggles referred Myers to several articles that appeared in the *National Anti-Slavery Standard* earlier in 1844. He suggested that Myers consult laws instituted by Governor William Seward of New York in 1840 to protect state citizens from being kidnapped. If Myers could not do this himself, Ruggles urged him to contact any one of several New York lawyers including Hiram Ketchum, Theodore Sedgwick III, Alanson Nash, John Jay, and John Hopper, or to ask "that sage veteran and friend of human freedom, Isaac T. Hopper, who has more experience in such cases than any other man in America." Ruggles's instructive tone to the younger man — as well as his quick grasp and recall of laws and key abolitionist and legal figures — indicates that his illnesses had not sapped his energy or knowledge of current antislavery efforts and causes.[56]

Ruggles expected his friends in the abolitionist community to help him out during times of need. In August 1844 he sent a letter to the *Liberator* that included a general call for funds to help him through the water cure he had initiated in hopes of regaining his health. He noted that he had spent much of his money constructing a bathing house from which "I could obtain a douche from a spring of cold water." Ruggles asked specifically that Frederick Douglass during his antislavery lecture tour tell listeners of his whereabouts and that he needed one hundred dollars to regain his strength, after which he would return the money.[57]

Douglass visited Northampton and was impressed by what he saw. He wrote the famous abolitionist Abby Kelley, describing it as "a strange gathering. I never saw anything like it. It was what Br. Rogers says, 'disgraceful, mortifying, alarming, divided, united, glorious, and most effective meeting.'" Although he was skeptical about any agricultural success in such an unpromising site, Douglass was taken by the equality he found there. Even though there were numerous members from "the upper walks of life," he noted "There was no high, no low, no masters, no servants, no white, no black." Douglass was pleased to find his old benefactor, Ruggles, prospering in this

Advertisement for David Ruggles's Water-Cure Hospital, Florence, Massachusetts. The culmination of Ruggles's second career, this flourishing hospital helped numerous patients regain their health. Courtesy of the Mount Holyoke College Archives and Special Collections.

setting. Douglass knew that Ruggles had come to Northampton bereft, blind, and sickly. Douglass reviewed Ruggles's past achievements and his own deep obligation to the man. Now he observed that Ruggles had a "grateful heart. ... His whole theme to me was gratitude to these noble people." Ruggles told Douglass that the hydropathic treatments he was receiving at the community were helpful and that he was becoming well versed in this protocol. Douglass also encountered Sojourner Truth at Northampton. He described Truth as "that strange compound of wit and wisdom, of wild enthusiasm, and flint-like common sense." Douglass admitted that Truth delighted in tripping up his civilized airs and described her as "a genuine specimen of the uncultured negro." Ruggles and Truth had a closer, more equal relationship. Community store ledger accounts list an expensive shawl that Ruggles purchased for Truth's daughter, Elizabeth Gedney, who arrived slightly after her mother. There are speculations that this gift indicated a romance between the two, but affairs went no further. It is one of the only hints of interest that Ruggles had for the opposite sex, but proof of any real attachment remains elusive.[58]

Her treatment and the fleeting possibility of romance with a daughter aside, Ruggles had a major impact on Truth's developing abolitionism. Although her narrative does not mention Ruggles, the two lived in very close proximity for at least five years. The gift of a shawl indicates some warmth between them. Nell Painter conjectures that Ruggles would not have liked Sojourner Truth for class and stylistic reasons. She was not as sophisticated as Maria Stewart, Hester Lane, Henrietta Ray, or other educated black females that Ruggles worked with in New York City, but there is no indication that Ruggles discriminated on the basis of class or that he had biased feelings toward Sojourner Truth. His relations with the families of kidnapped children or with male and female blacks belie that notion. It is likely that he admired Truth for her determination to rescue a son sold illegally into slavery. He also knew her background. Ruggles had spent much time in the Hudson River valley where Sojourner Truth was raised and perhaps shared church membership with her in New York City. It seems uncharacteristic for Ruggles to have rejected a potential convert to antislavery.

Under Ruggles's mentoring, Truth expanded upon her abolitionist views and methods. While white feminists encouraged and informed Truth, Ruggles was a constant presence for her and a man well versed in abolitionist thought and politics. Ruggles was the right person of color to help Sojourner Truth. Frederick Douglass, despite his fame, was an outsider and his comments on Truth were condescending at best. Ruggles, on the other hand, had urged blacks to find freedom through print for many years and had very good relations with Garrison. Ruggles surely had to approve of Truth for white abolitionists to trust her. While he was a member of the association, she was an employee and his word carried much weight.[59]

Sojourner Truth was part of an abolitionist community Ruggles created in Northampton to match the ones he had left behind in New York City and Boston. Basil Dorsey, whom he had helped years before, moved back into the area in 1844 and was soon active in helping fugitive slaves. In the first years after Ruggles arrived, there were gatherings to welcome the escaped slave George Latimer and a large meeting on August 1, 1843, to commemorate the tenth anniversary of emancipation in the British Empire. The following year there were public lectures by Frederick Douglass in April 1844, accompanied by performances by the Hutchinson Family Singers, all of whom stayed at or visited the community. Douglass, the Hutchinsons, and Ruggles had a lively reunion. Frederick Douglass spoke for more than three hours, and doubtless the Hutchinsons sang the radical lyrics of "Get Off the Track," their new song that called for "Freedom's Car, Emancipation." The audience became so moved that, by song's end, the listeners were dancing and pounding their feet. Ironically, the singers had adapted the tune of "Old Dan Tucker," the racist melody that was the most popular song in America the year before. The Hutchinson Singers so enjoyed their performance that they were loath to leave. Their visit was marked by controversy when the *Boston Atlas* printed a story accusing the Northampton community of encouraging mixed-race love. The newspaper reported that the community "comprises all colors, from jet black to pure white," and that young Abby Hutchinson, one of the singers, "was gallanted to her hotel by one of the members, and he a huge *black man!*" The indication that the black man was a member best fit Ruggles, though it could have been Douglass or Stephen Christopher Rush, for whom we have no physical description. Still, these events are indications of Ruggles's growing influence upon the community.[60]

Ruggles organized meetings of black Americans in Northampton. The first was held in August 1844 and featured a debut by his friend Rush. In September, Ruggles chaired the meeting at which Sojourner Truth made her first public antislavery address on the practical workings of slavery in the North. Welcome at the meeting was Nathaniel Colver, whom many Garrisonians blamed for the splits of the late 1830s. As chair, Ruggles had significant say over who could speak, giving him a deserved leadership in Northampton. At the same time, the meetings are evidence that Ruggles viewed Northampton as a potential site for Underground Railroad transfers and other black abolitionist activities. As early as May 1843, association member Sophia Foord wrote her friend Robert Adams: "This place is becoming quite a depot for fugitives."[61]

In time, Ruggles's neighborhood coalesced into a tiny black community. What would become Nonotuck Street near the mill was the home to seven black and ten native Irish families. Ruggles was the attraction for several individuals. Basil Dorsey moved into the neighborhood in 1844 and built his own home in 1849. Nelson Askin, a black American from Pittsfield, Massachusetts, set up a livery stable on Nanotuck Street in 1844. By the mid-1840s Sojourner Truth and her three daughters, Stephen Rush, George Washington Sullivan, James Wilson, and Ruggles lived on the street. Hannah Randall, who worked for Ruggles at the water-cure hospital, lived nearby as did Lewis French and his family and Henry and Susan Freeman. Many of these people were former slaves who found comfort living near Ruggles. Bruce Laurie has observed that blacks in rural Massachusetts maintained a low profile because of their small numbers, poverty, and lack of leadership. Blacks in Northampton, therefore, benefited from the presence of one of most dynamic and well-respected black abolitionists in the nation. Ruggles's arrival gave an immediate boost to the town's black community. As Steven Hahn has argued, such a community, especially one so packed with radicals, constituted an antebellum vision of a maroon society in which blacks governed themselves.[62]

Ruggles also helped white abolitionists in the area. Another veteran of the antislavery wars was Erasmus Darwin Hudson, from Torrington, Connecticut. He was a trained physician and schoolteacher, was militantly protemperance and antislavery, had been mobbed in 1838, and wanted to make the Northampton community a sanctuary for self-emancipated bond people. In 1845 Hudson became enmeshed in legal proceedings when he attempted to help an enslaved woman, named Linda, escape from her master. She later denied that she wanted to leave slavery. Hudson was jailed twice and was excommunicated from his Congregational Church in Connecticut. Although Hudson was no longer part of the community, Ruggles testified on his behalf, appearing at the meeting with his namesake, David W. Ruggles of New Bedford. The seaport town was not always hospitable to the blind physician. In October 1845 he sought membership in the town Lyceum, only to be rebuffed. Even the privilege of purchasing tickets to events was revoked in order to keep blacks out of the meetings. Soon, an article appeared in the *Liberator* castigating the lecture forum for discrimination. Ruggles beseeched Ralph Waldo Emerson and Charles Sumner to decline lectureships at the Lyceum, using the shunning technique he had promoted before.[63]

Ruggles quickly counteracted any attempt to exclude him from public or private moments with whites. One newspaper story angrily denounced the practice at the Northampton Association of allowing blacks to eat at the communal table. Ruggles responded angrily to the report of a "disgusting male negro" dining openly with other members of the association. In a letter to David Lee Child, he responded sarcastically to reports published about integrated dinners in Northampton that the "male negro" had, in years past, dined with numerous editors of major New York newspapers and with some of the principal merchants of that city. Ruggles said that his former dinner companions would have been sickened by the "false and scurrilous" reports in the *Journal of Commerce*. Ruggles could also have mentioned that the local children delighted in having him test the development of their muscles. One girl recalled later her great satisfaction that "my muscle always stood well in his estimation."[64]

Ruggles was fit enough by March 1845 to travel to New Bedford, Massachusetts, to chair an antislavery convention featuring some of the biggest names in the movement. Among the speakers who lectured to a sizable crowd at a local church were William Lloyd Garrison, Wendell Phillips, Edmund Quincy, and Frederick Douglass, whose narrative had been recently released and had become a best seller. Douglass had also been very active on the lecture circuit and polished his narrative on the stump. Ruggles and Douglass had a fond reunion. Ruggles described Douglass as a "Toussiant in eloquence and philanthropy, yet without his dependence on the sword for the defence of his rights." Douglass, whom Ruggles noted was but "five or six years from his master's plantation," was "living refutation to those who doubted the intelligence of the enslaved." It is noteworthy that Douglass thanked Ruggles by name in his autobiography for his "vigilance, kindness and perseverance [that] I will never forget." Douglass famously declined to identify those who helped him flee from Maryland and kept his escape methods secret until publication of his third autobiography in 1882. In 1845 Douglass was still enslaved and remained so until English benefactors donated his purchase price, paid his old master off, and then manumitted him. This purchased freedom infuriated many of Douglass's abolitionist supporters, who regarded the act as cooperation with slave masters. Despite the outcry, the narrative sold thousands of copies in the next few years. In 1845, publication of Ruggles's identity in a best-selling narrative and mention in numerous public forums opened him to federal and state charges of harboring a fugitive slave. It is very likely that Ruggles, in frequent contact with Douglass, gave permission for his identity to be made public.[65]

In addition to the water cure and abolitionist activities, Ruggles revived his efforts to make life uncomfortable for slave owners visiting the North. As in New York, he soon found white allies who supported his efforts. He quickly attacked the practice of southern slaveholders who brought their chattel to Northampton while enjoying summer holidays. As he had done in New York, Ruggles forced local authorities to acknowledge that once a slave was brought into a free state, liberty was guaranteed. In one case, a slave girl, when notified of her rights, refused to leave her master.[66]

Ruggles maintained public support for radical abolitionists. He apparently became a salesman for Frederick Douglass's narrative and ordered the best seller by the boxful. He spoke strongly in favor of Charles Torrey, a Congregationalist minister who worked on behalf of self-emancipated slaves and suffered from imprisonment so much that he feared for his own life and sanity. Ruggles spoke firmly in favor of Torrey, saying "Some soi-disant friends of Mr. Torrey have said that he was rash and impractical. This charge is always made against the faithful and true in the cause of humanity." Ruggles believed, argues Stanley Harrold, that Torrey was simply braver than other abolitionists. Also speaking at the meeting was "Sojourner of Northampton," who lectured on the "practical workings of slavery in the north." When, in fact, Torrey did die after being imprisoned in the Maryland Penitentiary on May 9, 1846, Ruggles mourned him as a Good Samaritan and, the following year, contributed a dollar to funds to support Torrey's family. Recognizing that Ruggles had sacrificed his health to the movement, Gerrit Smith hailed Ruggles and Torrey at the Liberty Party convention in 1848, citing them both as "hearty, whole-souled, glorious slave-stealer[s]." Torrey and Ruggles, Smith argued, were worth more than more timid men who asked the party to obey slavery laws.[67]

Meanwhile, Ruggles's medical practice prospered and he began to expand his operation. The records of the Northampton Association reveal that by early 1845 Ruggles was supervising the renovation of a building to use as a water-cure establishment. Bills for nails, screws, linseed oil paint, lumber, and carpeting all attest to his new ambition, to operate his own hospital. Ruggles gave very precise measurements for some window blinds that should be "4 ft 4½ inches long by 2 ft 6 inches in width provided that they can be obtained for 2 dollars or less." James A. Stetson was instructed that the blinds were made of small splints of wood woven like the rush curtains and could be purchased at woodenware stores or furnishing stores. Ruggles purchased personal items as well. Through Dolly Stetson, he ordered a new dark-colored sack suit. He reminded James A. Stetson, who would get the suit, that he was "4 inches taller than yourself and just about your size in the chest but smaller at the bottom of the waist." Such minutiae indicate that Ruggles, though sightless himself, was very aware of personal and home fashion.[68]

By mid-1846, the water-cure establishment was in operation on a limited basis. The *National Anti-Slavery Standard* wished him all the best and strongly recommended patronage of his new business. Ruggles and the Northampton Association had put a sizable sum into a new facility. Construction costs were about two thousand dollars for the building, which measured about fifty by thirty-six feet. By Ruggles's calculations, the building could house thirty or forty patients. A local newspaper reported that Ruggles had already turned down fifty applications for admission since the beginning of the year.[69]

Ruggles developed a special diagnostic method he called "cutaneous electricity." He believed that his blindness allowed him to judge the state of a person's health by touching their skin. He described how he could "feel in every healthy person, an incessant, regular, and energetic emission of electricity from every pore. This I call vitality or power." In sick people, however, Ruggles judged that sensation was feeble and irregular. He further detailed the treatment of a neuralgic, seventy-year-old man. First Ruggles ordered his patient to be robed in a wet sheet at seventy-five degrees Fahrenheit for ten minutes, twice a day for three days, along with copious amounts of water. This technique produced a feeble electric action in the patient, who previously had been coping with pain only through liberal doses of opium. After the first three days, the man was packed in a woolen blanket for two hours a day for a week. He also took warm baths accompanied by cold water poured down his back. Within two weeks, the patient was walking five to six miles a day, to the amazement of his family. Within a few months, Ruggles was treating patients with a huge variety of ailments. Among the diseases he had treated were liver complaint, jaundice, dyspepsia, lung disease, skin problems, bronchitis, paralysis, and addiction to alcohol and tobacco. His terms were not cheap. Ruggles charged $5.50 per week, and there were extra costs for nursing and heat. Ruggles also expected every patient to supply his own linen. Still, his fees were well under the standard rates of medical care.[70]

Ruggles tried to use rigorous standards for admission. He asked every applicant to send a description of symptoms. Because of his use of cutaneous electricity to diagnose patients' problems, a method that made it impossible to determine the illnesses of any sick person who lived far from Northampton, Ruggles used the testimony of successful treatments to determine whether or not his practice would work. His conservative method was necessary, he declared, because exaggerated claims were hurting the reputation of hydrotherapy. Ruggles's fame began to grow nationally and other doctors consulted him about their patients. He advertised his hospital in abolitionist and other newspapers. Despite his glowing claims, Ruggles's establishment was not financially strong. In November 1846 he wrote Wendell Phillips to ask for a $400 donation to keep his business afloat.[71]

Ruggles was also able to borrow from his extensive network of friends and supporters. Between 1846 and 1849, more than fifty individuals extended credit to Ruggles and his water-cure establishment. Some of the amounts due were quite small store debts, such as one to Ebenezer Wood, whom Ruggles owed $1.75, and White, Potter & Wright, to whom he was indebted for $4.50. Others may have been for work, such as the $24.82 that Ruggles owed to Basil Dorsey. But there were also sizable debts, such as the $547.00 owed to Frederick B. Coleman and the $288.74 for which he was indebted to W. A. Arnold. In all, Ruggles had outstanding loans amounting to more than $3,000.00.[72]

Ruggles was not wasting this money. Rather, he was investing it in land and buildings. His first purchase was the Barrett House. Ruggles used the house as his home and for an office where he met his first patients. Ruggles paid $1,000 to Benjamin Barrett for the building under an unusual arrangement of a bond first and then a deed in 1846, due in 1851. This property was right next to the association, which was breaking up and selling its property. As the Barrett House was large enough for only six patients, Ruggles needed to expand. In September 1846 Ruggles bought seven acres of land just across the Mill River on Spring Street from Nathaniel Clark for $134. The following year, Ruggles made three more acquisitions totaling thirty-five acres of land within close proximity of the Barrett House and the Clark Land. His final known purchase, on March 4, 1849, was of two lots of about an acre each, bought from Samuel L. Hill, a Florence-based financier active in developing local manufacturing. Within three years of starting his water-cure business, Ruggles owned, even if encumbered by mortgages, nearly forty acres of land just outside of Northampton and along the Mill River. His transactions attest to his astute business dealings and the willingness of his friends and supporters to put their money in his hands. Hill, who in 1850 had financial shares in the local post office, general store, a silk mill, a button and daguerreotype-case factory, and other businesses, is an example of a local industrialist who had confidence in Ruggles. He seemed to be a good investment.[73]

One of Ruggles's clients was William Lloyd Garrison. On December 8, 1847, Ruggles invited Garrison, exhausted by the rigors of his antislavery career and suffering from a swelling on his left side near the diaphragm and from fevers, to undertake a five or six week course at the water-cure hospital.

David Ruggles's home in Florence, Massachusetts. Steve Strimer's careful investigations have established this house as Ruggles's home. Photograph courtesy of Steve Strimer and the David Ruggles Center, Florence, Massachusetts.

Ruggles added that "it would afford me the highest gratification, to put you through, free of charge, as I have at present, but few patients, and can give you the best attention." Though grateful for this offer, Garrison declined, but admitted that he got little sleep because of the pain of the swelling.[74]

Garrison's ailments persisted in the next summer, nourished by his proclivity for an irregular diet and overwork. By July 1848, suffering additionally from a nasty cough and urged on by friends and children, Garrison prepared to submit to the rigors of the water cure. He informed his *Liberator* readership that he would take a three-to-four month leave to seek help from Ruggles at the water-cure clinic. Garrison provided in letters to his friends (sneaked out during his treatment to the dismay of Ruggles) a good description of an initial diagnosis and the daily treatment at the clinic. Upon Garrison's arrival in the evening of July 17, Ruggles wanted to give his friend a "half-bath" (which Garrison soon learned was equivalent to a bath and a half), but the tired abolitionist put it off until the morning. Garrison struggled with sleep on the narrow, straw bed and awoke at three o'clock in the morning to the sounds of "packers" preparing to wrap other patients. Garrison's turn did not come until six o'clock, during which time he dreamed that he had already received his bath. He found it refreshing and enjoyed the rubdown with a wet sheet that followed. He was served a breakfast of wheat and rye bread, cracked wheat boiled like hominy, stewed prunes, milk and cold water. Other baths followed throughout the day, including footbaths, a sitz, a shallow bath, and a spray baptism. The intention was to bring on a "crisis" after which Garrison was "packed, plunged and drenched and douched." His initial assessment was that he was "decidedly improved in health."

Garrison was forced to take long walks in the beautiful countryside and forbidden to read or write letters. Ruggles complained, however, that Garrison was "engaged on a suicidal course" by his constant tours and lectures, which distracted him from the water-cure treatment.[75] Ruggles found Garrison corresponding with his friends one day and scolded him: "Now, this will never do — you might as well be in Boston as here, if you mean to use your pen — the water cure can do you no good, if you do not abstain from mental exertion, but will rather do you harm." Garrison admitted that, despite the application of cold water, his hotheadedness never lapsed, and, though acknowledging that he should stay a year, he lasted only four months. He added his name to the many testimonials Ruggles received for his cures. After his treatment, Garrison returned to Boston and on October 3, 1848, wrote his friend Elizabeth Pease, "You will be glad to learn that for the last twelve weeks, under the care of Dr. Ruggles at Northampton, I have been packed, and plunged, and drenched, and douched — had two or three flattering crises — and am decidedly improved in health. I ought to continue the treatment for at least a year; but circumstance forbid. I shall pursue it at home, however, as far as practicable. My aversion to cold water has been fairly completed. I am now its ardent advocate."[76]

Garrison also spoke of the harmony achieved at the hospital. There was little controversy over the gender of the clients. He counted twenty-three patients in all, "of whom, thirteen are ladies, with one exception, *young* ladies, though several of them are married, and therefore not in the market; luckily neither am I." Hydrotherapy, as its scholars have emphasized, enabled patients to take control of their lives and ailments. In particular, women found hydrotherapy attractive because, as Susan Cayleff noted, it helped them "redefine their physiological process, control their medical care and, ultimately, expand their social roles and opportunities." Just as he had done in New York while helping self-emancipated slaves and protecting free blacks, Ruggles's practical methods offered succor and empowerment to women. It is remarkable that Ruggles instilled such trust in his female clientele. In an age in which Frederick Douglass was stoned for walking arm in arm with a white woman through the streets of New York City, unmarried young women accepted medical help from Ruggles. While it is likely that either Sojourner Truth and her daughters or other local girls did the actual bathing of the female patients, Ruggles was able to create an atmosphere of general racial and gender harmony.

Garrison noted that both sexes seem very amiable and "as there is not a single, dogmatic, controversial spirit among us, it is not only impossible to get up a breeze, it is difficult even to raise a zephyr, on any subject." Within the walls of the hospital, society's ills were set aside. Garrison acknowledged that there was no medicine like cold water and wondered at his "alarmingly good appetite" for the simple fare. Ruggles, Garrison observed, had a remarkable touch, with "much physiological knowledge at his finger tips." Garrison commented on Ruggles's blindness, not realizing that the doctor's tactile powers stemmed in large part from his loss of sight. The following year, when Garrison's health declined again, Ruggles wrote Garrison that "I regret to learn that you have had a relapse," and he offered a new round of treatment free of charge.[77]

Ruggles sense of gratitude and concern for William Lloyd Garrison did not translate into unbending loyalty. When his erstwhile protégé Frederick Douglass announced plans for a new, independent abolitionist newspaper, the *North Star*, Garrison was irritated and denounced his former protégé for creating unnecessary competition. Ruggles, however, quickly wrote a letter of congratulation and support to Douglass and Martin R. Delany. Soon, he served as an agent for the fledgling newspaper. Ruggles displayed a deft handling of a delicate situation by praising Douglass and Garrison because both were engaged in the freeing of all enslaved people.[78]

Ruggles became a Free Soil Party member in 1848, a move that could not have pleased Garrison but which Frederick Douglass surely endorsed. The Free Soil Party emerged from the Liberty Party of the 1840s and caught the enthusiasm of many of Ruggles's Northampton friends and supporters, including Samuel L. Hill, Basil Dorsey, and Benjamin Barrett. Numerous black abolitionists — including Charles B. Ray, Samuel Ringgold Ward, James W. C. Pennington, and Douglass — supported the party. Garrison's influence had faded in Massachusetts recently. Ruggles, perhaps not as rigid about political compromise, joined the local movement. The Free Soil Party did quite well in Massachusetts in the election of 1848, polling 28.3 percent of the vote in the state and receiving nearly 1,800 votes in Northampton. As blacks could vote in Massachusetts, Ruggles may have cast a ballot. It would have been a bitter pill to vote for a ticket headed by Martin Van Buren, but Ruggles could console himself with the knowledge that the Free Soil Party created political power for blacks and that many members, black and white, were active participants in the Underground Railroad. They shared many of his values and beliefs. His participation in the party indicates that he was willing to grow with the times and did not feel tied to Garrison.[79]

Garrison was at least an old friend. Absconders occasionally cheated Ruggles (as happened to any small businessman). William Wilcox of Princeton, Illinois, underwent treatment for several weeks for "bronchitis, liver complaint, and dyspepsia." He continually put off payment, arguing that a long overdue check would soon arrive. In October 1848 Wilcox, as Ruggles stated in several newspaper notices, suddenly disappeared without paying, leaving behind only a small trunk with some valueless clothing. Fast developing competition hurt Ruggles more. Northampton was a well-known retreat, and his was not the only hydrotherapy institute in the area. By the end of 1846, there were at least two others within a few miles of Ruggles's establishment, both of which were well-appointed resorts providing not only water but also "drugs and high living."[80]

Despite his financial problems, Ruggles persevered. He raised his weekly rents to six dollars for the lower floors of his establishment, with the third floor costing fifty cents less. Standard fees for nursing and single rooms rose to eight dollars a week. Ruggles's hospital now included nature walks where patients could range freely "without being exposed to public gaze."[81] His successes brought favorable publicity. The highly respected Reverend Payson Williston of Easthampton told readers of the National Era how Ruggles's treatment had helped him overcome seven years of lameness and, later, gangrene. Henry Richards Crummell lauded Ruggles's work in a lengthy article in the National Anti-Slavery Standard in 1846. Ruggles also gained recognition outside of the abolitionist community. In a significant speech, Dr. A. Means spoke before the Medical College of Georgia, praising the work and methods of "cutaneous electricity" practiced by Ruggles. This praise was important because other water-cure physicians did not generally know Ruggles's method of determining the cause of disease.[82]

While he built this water-cure practice, Ruggles did not neglect his antislavery activities. He made "living support" contributions to the Liberator. At the same time, he was one of several agents for Frederick Douglass's newspaper, the North Star. Ruggles made clear in a letter in early 1848 that he fully supported Douglass, despite the anger of friend Garrison. He wrote the North Star that it was "a beacon light of liberty, to illuminate the pathway of the bleeding, hunted fugitive of the South."[83] Douglass visited Ruggles in the autumn of 1848 for the first time since his return from England. Douglass remembered how just a decade earlier Ruggles was the first to "welcome me from the land of whips and chains and to place me beyond the reach of my blood-hounded pursuers." The famed abolitionist noted with approval how, despite his blindness, Ruggles's whole heart was in his new profession. The water-cure hospital now had fourteen patients, with prospects for more. Further showing his appreciation, Douglass often gave Ruggles free advertising space in his newspaper, a perquisite that Ruggles used frequently. Only in one instance did he pay Douglass for space in the newspaper.[84]

By 1849 Ruggles had amassed a sizable estate, though it was primarily composed of land and personal property. He had little cash on hand. Still, a walk through his property revealed a prosperous, if not ostentatious business. There were six buildings: the old Barrett house where Ruggles and many patients lived, the water cure house, a boardinghouse, washhouse, wood storage building, and a gymnasium, valued at more than five thousand dollars. Additionally, he owned a pasture, a douche spring lot, and a barn with twelve acres, all worth about a thousand dollars. Combined with personal items, he had an estate of more than seven thousand dollars, though much of it was encumbered by mortgages.

A look inside the water-cure house reveals a spare but comfortable existence. Inside the door of the ladies' parlor was the most valuable piece of furniture, a pianoforte worth $175. The room had an airtight stove, straw carpet, more than a dozen cane chairs, a settee on casters, two lamps, and a cracked looking glass. There were curtains on the window. It is easy to imagine Ruggles, his patients, and friends gathered around the piano during evenings, singing abolitionist songs.

The gentlemen's parlor boasted a secretary, another settee, numerous chairs, a stove, a center table, an intact mirror, straw carpet, and curtains. The hall in between was sparsely furnished with an umbrella stand, a hall lantern, and some cloth carpet. Cleaning equipment, including brooms, brushes, and pans, and a wood table were stored there. Room number 1 apparently was used for medical purposes, as it housed a mahogany desk and table, and a plethora of medical equipment including thermometers, sheets for wrapping patients, wicks, and a large supply of sewing materials. The next few rooms were sleeping rooms for patients, with two to three beds in each, bureaus, mirrors, and wardrobes. A gentlemen's dressing room included a wardrobe, a wood clock, numerous chairs, and, for medical purposes, arm and leg baths for partial immersion. Spittoons were supplied. The ladies' dressing room was much the same, though it had its own stove. Rooms beyond were reserved for the cures. A bathing room included twenty-two "dip tubs," along with footbaths and other containers to soak various parts of the body. There were six more dormitories upstairs with beds, bureaus, tables, wardrobes, an occasional bookstand, mirrors, and stoves. Ruggles apparently lived part time in room number 12. Other utility rooms and the attic were for cleaning supplies, spare tubs, chairs, and assorted items. The general dining room was in the next building, which also housed more fully equipped sleeping and bathing rooms. The dining room could seat at least forty-eight people at five tables, which required substantial size. The dining room was equipped with formal dining ware, while the pantry was filled with plates, bowls, cups, saucers, creamers, and more than 150 knives, forks, and spoons, along with specialized cutlery.[85]

William Cooper Nell reported favorable visits to Ruggles's water-cure establishment on two occasions, in April 1848 and in July 1849. Nell marveled over the physical beauty of the setting along the Mill River in Bensonville and advised his readers that Ruggles was a man of immense medical talents who had cured himself and many others with his cold-water treatments. Nell told his readers that Ruggles's invitation was "come wash and be healed." Nell later wrote a laudatory article linking Ruggles with Isaac T. Hopper and the martyred Charles Torrey.[86]

The fall of 1849 promised to be another successful season at the water-cure hospital. One of Ruggles's patients was Mary Ann Day Brown, wife of the abolitionist and future martyr, John Brown. Friends strived to round up other patients. Catherine Beecher wrote a Mrs. William B. Bannister of Newburyport, Massachusetts, to urge her to take sessions at Ruggles's water cure to curb her "unnatural excitement." Catherine Beecher described Ruggles as "a most remarkably sagacious common sense man & is very careful and cautious."[87]

Ruggles spent the last few months of his life in his room in the main water-cure building, so that he could receive treatment there rather than walk to his home nearby. He left few personal items at the Barrett House and appears to have moved into the main building of the hospital. Always dapper, Ruggles purchased in his last months some new clothes. In the bedroom were a fine coat costing fourteen dollars, a new velvet vest valued at five dollars, linen socks, shirts, expensive pants and suspenders, and a summer hat and coat. Most of his other possessions were books, for which he had a personal reader. For self-diagnosis, there were copies of *Wilson's Anatomy*, a book on the *Elements of Physiology*, and a title on consumption (tuberculosis). For spiritual assistance, Ruggles had handy a Bible, a copy of Bunyan's *Pilgrim's Progress*, and temperance documents. Augmenting his historical acumen were Macauley's *History of England* in two volumes; a history of the Mexican War; the biography of abolitionist Abel Brown, a martyr from the Underground Railroad days in New York State; and the *Prison Life and Reflections of George Thompson*, an Illinois college student imprisoned in Missouri for attempting to help enslaved people gain liberty. To help with writing, Ruggles kept a "Worcester Dictionary," and a book of anecdotes.[88]

Sadly, Ruggles was in fact struggling to save his own life. His physical condition worsened over the next few months. Early in September Ruggles suffered from a severe pain and inflammation in his left eye. Convinced by the pain that something had lodged in his eye, Ruggles first consulted Dr. Walker of Northampton and then went to a Dr. Dix of Boston, who agreed that the problem was a serious inflammation of the optic nerve. Both physicians recommended that Ruggles take a rest cure. With a house packed with patients, some of them very ill and all dependent on him for daily advice and attention, Ruggles accepted medical advice by refusing any new patients, but his health continued to fail. By late November he suffered from a severe inflammation of his bowels. Despite the intervention of Dr. Charles Walker and Dr. Wesselhoeft of Brattleboro, and the temporary relief of the inflammation, Ruggles could not shake his illness. He suffered a relapse of an old problem, indurations of the bowels, which worsened his situation. By the beginning of December, Ruggles became delirious from the pain at times, while worrying about his patients and arranging renovation of the hospital and the grounds. At times he could converse cogently with his friends and then would lapse back into delirium. His mother and sister came to Northampton to care for him, but to no avail. Ruggles died on December 16, 1849, at the age of thirty-nine. He was interred in the Ruggles family plot in Yantic Cemetery in Norwich, Connecticut.[89]

William Cooper Nell was among the first to learn of Ruggles's death. The Boston abolitionist wrote Amy Kirby Post on the evening of December 18 that, "by all accounts from Northampton, we learn that David Ruggles is probably not alive. . . . He is now prostrated having overtaxed his powers." A few days later, Nell wrote Post again, "The death of Dr. Ruggles has filled our hearts with sadness for this has been made a blank not easily filled." Others shared Nell's sorrow. Newspaper coverage was quick and respectful. William Lloyd Garrison wrote a lengthy review of Ruggles's career and punctuated the obituary by proclaiming, "We were not at all prepared for his dissolution. He deserves to be ranked among the benefactors of his race. His biography remains to be written." Laments of Ruggles's demise rose as far west as Mil-

Ruggles Family Grave Site, Yantic Cemetery, Norwich, Connecticut.
David is buried on this site near his mother, Nancy. Photograph by the author.

waukee, Wisconsin, where a journalist described him as "a warm-hearted, able man and an untiring friend of his own (the colored) race."[90]

At the close of his short, powerful life, David Ruggles had a key role in the transformation of American abolitionism by emphasizing an aggressive, confrontational style. Broken in body by the struggle, he reinvented himself as a hydropathical physician while maintaining the battle against slavery. He had met a deep test of character and health to carve out a respected career while pushing for equality and freedom. His deep investment in hydropathy demonstrates how Ruggles had fused his abolitionist life with yet another reform. As he had done with the Free Produce movement and with temperance and education in New York City, Ruggles combined antislavery with the communitarian and water-cure movements. Many of these reforms are regarded as peopled by whites only, but Ruggles's sizable presence shows how blacks broadened the sociology of antebellum reform. Just as he garnered praise for his hard work in the Northampton Association, friendships there enabled construction of his water-cure hospital. In the last decade of his life, after suffering from debilitating disease and his costly battles with other black abolitionists in New York City, Ruggles still had a vibrant presence in radical abolitionism across the northern states. He had many protégés across the northeast, most notably Frederick Douglass, who would ensure that David Ruggles would not be forgotten.

Abolitionist and Physician

David Ruggles did not live to see the enactment of the Compromise of 1850. Its portion known as the Fugitive Slave Act, which opened the northern states to slave catchers and kidnappers, mandated that white citizens help them and drove sizable percentages of black citizens into exile in Canada. There were immediate consequences. On September 26, 1850, Alexander Gardiner, the local commissioner to the law, ordered the arrest of James Hamlet, at the request of Mary Brown, a Maryland slaveholder, as the first case of the new Fugitive Slave Law. Hamlet, who had lived in New York City for several years and now worked as a porter in a store and had a wife and children, denied that he was a slave. Despite his protests, Hamlet was handcuffed, forced into a carriage, and then "hurried to a steamboat and taken to Baltimore," where he was imprisoned until Mrs. Brown could make a favorable deal and sell him to the Deep South.

Outraged by this kidnapping, more than fifteen hundred sympathetic black New Yorkers rallied at the Zion Church to hear a new group, the Committee of Thirteen, protest Hamlet's seizure and the pernicious effects of the new law. The committee included Philip A. Bell, George Downing, James McCune Smith, and others who had worked with Ruggles in the 1830s. Speakers used strong language to blast the city authorities. One member of the committee, Jeremiah Powers, argued that the only reasonable response to the Fugitive Slave Act was the "bowie knife and the revolver." Earlier, a group of black New Yorkers vowed to meet slaveholders with "death-dealing weapons in their hands." A more practical approach was to raise eight hundred dollars to redeem Hamlet and secure his return to New York City. Five thousand New Yorkers gathered in City Hall Park to welcome his return.

Surely, Ruggles would have joined the leaders of the ten Northampton blacks who called for a meeting in October 1850 to denounce the act. Henry Anthony and Basil Dorsey were key signers of the petition that spawned a contentious gathering. Local Free Soil advocates strived to assure local blacks that they had little to worry about, while they and white supporters such as local editor Henry S. Gere demanded sharper resistance. The memory of David Ruggles energized such sentiments, which were part of the general outrage that spread across the northern states in opposition to the law.[1]

Memorials for David Ruggles continued into the early months of 1850. Frederick Douglass penned a full account of Ruggles's last struggles against his fatal illnesses. The abolitionist blamed overwork for Ruggles's passing: "He has literally worn himself out in humanity's struggle." Douglass sorrowfully commented: "To the cause of Hydrotherapy, the Antislavery movement, and to the cause of humanity in general, his loss is irreparable. — We look in vain for another to fill his place." Speaking before the Massachusetts Antislavery Society, William Lloyd Garrison concurred, stating that the death of David Ruggles was a public loss. Ruggles's career, the abolitionist argued, "proves the power of individual intellect and energy in making their way under the most trying disadvantages of race and position, and of personal infirmity and ill health." Garrison concluded that all should imitate Ruggles in both conduct and character. Nor was his second career ignored. Speaking to the Young Men's Christian Association in Glasgow, Scotland, James W. C. Pennington cited Ruggles as an example of a black American doctor. Dr. S. Rogers wrote a moving obituary in the *Water-Cure Journal* that cited Ruggles's "degree of skill, prudence, and admirable penetration which brought him patients from all over the Union."[2]

In death, Ruggles left several legacies. One was his personal estate, which took several years to probate. His real estate property was heavily mortgaged but worth a substantial amount of money. The personal estate, composed chiefly of equipment and furniture for the water-cure institute, was modest but extensive. His water-cure establishment was abandoned for a short time, then purchased, reopened, and expanded by the Munde family of New York City. The Mundes, as potential purchasers of the property, described it as dilapidated, a term that must be discounted given their obvious self-interest. Borrowing money from the trustees of the Ruggles estate, Dr. Charles Munde redid the buildings and soon had a prosperous business catering almost entirely to southerners. By besmirching Ruggles's reputation as a businessman while building upon his achievements, the Munde family was able to erase his memory and make his water-cure establishment a refuge for slave masters seeking relief from hot southern weather and their ailments.[3]

One claimant rushed to assert his rights as a creditor of the estate. Alanson Nash, a lawyer, had represented Ruggles in the suit against the Committee of Vigilance in 1839. Apparently reading of Ruggles's demise in the newspapers, he stated a detailed claim for $146.50 against the abolitionist's estate.[4] In all, David Ruggles owed $3,662.53, an amount that tilted his estate into a deficit. One scholar has claimed that Ruggles was headed for bankruptcy when he died. Yet, of the $3,662.53, a significant sum was owed to Cyrus Bradley, a nurse, who cared for Ruggles without calling him into account while he was alive. Ruggles owed Bradley $750.00 for nursing care. He also owed Dr. Charles Walker $45.00 for assistance in the last months of his life. Ruggles's coffin cost $10.50, indicating that more than $800.00, exceeding 20 percent of his indebtedness, could be attributed to his illnesses, not to poor financial management or potential failure of the business. Many of his creditors were friends, such as John P. Williston, who was owed $15.00, and who revered Ruggles for helping him in time of sickness. Williston was also an important local investor who would likely put more money into Ruggles's ventures if needed. While creditors lined up after his death, there is little indication that they were hounding him before it. Even with the rise in competition, Ruggles had a flourishing health establishment of a type popular in antebellum America. At the time of his death, Northampton was a prosperous town with one of the most vigorous economies in western Massachusetts, so his property would likely appreciate in value over time. He was only thirty-nine and vigorous before his final illness, and was thereby someone in whom others could entrust their cash. He probably appeared to be a good credit risk, and, indeed, nearly all of his debts were paid off shortly after completion of probate.[5]

Ruggles's family did not benefit from any of this. His mother and siblings had stayed in Norwich but had left Bean Hill behind to move to cheaper dwellings downtown. Henry worked as a whitewasher and Richard as a laborer. Felix worked as a coachman and took care of his mother. By the mid-1870s, only Felix's widow remained in the directories. The achievements of the illustrious first brother did not translate into any upward mobility for his family.[6]

A second legacy was memory of his activities. During the 1850s and after the Civil War, recollections of Ruggles appeared in accounts of the Underground Railroad and of the abolitionist struggles. In his introduction to William Cooper Nell's *Colored Patriots of the American Revolution*, published in 1855, Wendell Phillips held up the memory of Ruggles as an abolitionist and as a doctor as "the example of one whose career deserves be often spoke of, as complete proof that a colored man can rise of the social respect and highest of employment and usefulness." Phillips added that Ruggles had overcome prejudice and crushing personal burdens of poverty, blindness, and debility to become a venerated doctor, whose skills were sought even by slaveholders.[7]

In Frederick Douglass's second autobiography, which was published in 1855, he wrote that Ruggles decided his destination as a fugitive after learning that he had caulking skills. Having just visited New Bedford, Massachusetts, in August 1838, Ruggles learned that there would be employment available to a man in his situation. Douglass also describes "Mr. Ruggles as the first officer of the under-ground railroad with whom I met after reaching the north, and, indeed, the first of whom I ever heard anything." Earlier in his recounting of the meeting, Douglass had described Ruggles as "a very active man in all the antislavery works." These two descriptions fuse antislavery and the Underground Railroad and suggest that Ruggles's name was on the lips of self-emancipated blacks headed for freedom in the North. In his 1869 book, *Recollections of our Antislavery Conflict*, Samuel J. May recalled Ruggles as "a most active, adventurous, and daring conductor on the Underground Railroad," indicating how veterans of the fugitive slave battles still revered Ruggles.[8]

Overall, memory of Ruggles faded during the turbulent events of the 1850s and the Civil War. Postwar histories of the abolitionist movement tended to emphasize Garrison's role, concentrated on national goals and aspirations, and limited much of the discussion of abolitionism and the Underground Railroad to the years just before the Civil War. After the war, Ruggles appeared less frequently in black histories of the antebellum period. He is not mentioned in George Washington Williams's histories of black life, or in William Still's history of the Underground Railroad, although Still owed his stylistic method of listing stories of fugitives to Ruggles. William J. Simmons's *Men of Mark*, a vast compendium of noteworthy nineteenth-century blacks, omits mention of Ruggles. W. E. B. Du Bois does not mention him in his list of heroes of color in *The Souls of Black Folk*.[9]

These lacunae make Frederick Douglass's recollections of his early days of freedom all the more important. Douglass completed his recollection of the saga of meeting Ruggles first in speeches and then in his last autobiography, which was published in 1882, and then reprinted in several subsequent editions. Douglass's biographers of the 1890s repeated his words, thereby ensuring that such memories appeared in William Siebert's massive history of the Underground Railroad. Using Douglass's narrative as a source for his three-volume history of the struggles against slavery, Henry Wilson described Ruggles as a "colored gentleman of much intelligence and worth, who by his positions (in the Committee of Vigilance) and executive ability did much for his people." Such comments established the foundation for twentieth-century studies by Dorothy Porter, Benjamin Quarles, and the many journalists who hailed Ruggles's achievements.[10]

Frederick Douglass's role in keeping the memory of David Ruggles alive is fitting. Ruggles was not the only black abolitionist of the antebellum period, but he was among the most militant, along with David Walker, Maria Stewart, and Henry Highland Garnet. His final legacy is apparent in the contours of the antebellum fight against slavery. Much attention has been given lately to political abolitionism, particularly in the Liberty Party. While blacks vied to take part in the movement and often supported it—Douglass most famously—they were not allowed to be leaders until much later. To find black commanders one must look to street-level organization. That is where Ruggles stood out.

In his writing and in his drive for black literacy, Ruggles created a dynamic fusion of education and radical abolitionism. His writings are difficult to enjoy now. With the exception of *The Abrogation of the Seventh Commandment*, which retains a powerful moral quality, his style comes across as strident and packed with anger. His pamphlets lack the artistry of Douglass or the powerful connections with American themes found in Walker's *Appeal*. They were not meant for the ages, but were tough, fierce journalism intended for immediate use. Ruggles should be credited as one of the first black journalists. His writing was deeply personal; Cornish and other critics were not wrong in identifying egocentrism as a mark of Ruggles's writing. Yet, his work matched the anger of the times. In the pieces written about kidnappers, the slave trade, and the ACS, Ruggles reflected the anger of the black masses. In other articles, he hit upon themes of immortal struggle.

His interpretation of education, enunciated in his four essays published in early 1835, combined literacy with resistance against southern slavery and northern racism. For Ruggles, it was not enough for a black person to read; one had to use that knowledge to support and strengthen the abolitionist movement. His bookstore and reading room served the same purposes. As well, Ruggles pushed hard against the boundaries of contemporary antislavery. His courageous actions against the daily indignities of slavery and its infernal accomplice, northern racial prejudice, crystallized the methods of

Epilogue

the movement against them. Again, although he did not invent it, Ruggles raised assistance to fugitive slaves and confrontation against kidnappers and the illegal slave trade to a much higher public profile. For several years, he made New York City, once a safe harbor for slave masters who wanted to bring their enslaved domestics north, a very hazardous spot. Again, though Ruggles did not originate the notion of engaging in immediate battles against slave catchers, he elevated popular consciousness of the tactic in a series of bold strokes and influenced political attitudes about them. Unlike any activist before, Ruggles brought ordinary blacks into the struggle by empathizing with the plight of families damaged by kidnappers or by tapping into the anger of young blacks in the street. Eventually, even as the Free Soil Party's efforts became absorbed into the Whig and Republican parties, in the aftermath of the Fugitive Slave Law of 1850, local uprisings against slave catchers and kidnappers borrowed methods and names directly from Ruggles's activities in the 1830s.

Upstate New York became increasingly radicalized and was the scene of a number of slave rescue cases and a vigorous Underground Railroad. The Committee of Vigilance had revived in the late 1840s under the leadership of Isaac T. Hopper. After Hopper's death in 1852, Sydney Howard Gay led the organization, which enabled dozens of self-emancipated slaves to secure their freedom. Louis Napoleon, a local black activist, used Ruggles's confrontational methods in the sensational Lemmons case of 1852, in which he helped eight enslaved people gain freedom from a visiting Virginia slaveholder. When a court ruled that the enslaved people were free by virtue of being in New York City, Louis Napoleon led them out of the courthouse in triumph. Although city residents quickly gave Lemmons, the slave master, five thousand dollars as compensation for loss of his chattel, the state of Virginia promptly appealed the decision freeing the slaves. The dispute became one of the most important litigations over slavery in the 1850s. As the slave trade reappeared at this time, opponents could recall how Ruggles personally arrested three sea captains for slave trafficking.[11]

In his voluminous writings, Ruggles demonstrated a powerful sense of equality with whites, especially antagonistic ones. Demonstrating immense courage, Ruggles served as an example of black masculinity and was far in advance of other black abolitionists in his attention to women's rights. His life was brief, but his example of cogent intellectualism remains powerful to us today. Self-sacrifice and direct confrontation with evil made his short life worth living and emulating.

NOTES

INTRODUCTION

1 Blassingame et al., *Douglass Papers*, ser. 2: 1:75–76; Douglass, *Narrative* (1845), 75–76, 144; *New York Times*, March 11, 1873; McFeeley, *Frederick Douglass*, 72–73, 78 (for name change); Martin, *Mind of Frederick Douglass*, 20. Dixon's warning is curious, given that he was at the center of a lengthy court case regarding the rights of fugitive slaves to a jury trial, a dispute covered later in this book. On Pennington, see Blackett, *Beating against the Barriers*, 5–9, and Swift, *Black Prophets*, 204–44; on the letter, see Grover, *Fugitive's Gibraltar*, 144. Douglass described how Ruggles came to get him in the first American, Irish, and English versions of the narrative, adding the information about Jake and Stewart on the 1855 edition and expanding further in the 1881 autobiography. The early editions strongly suggest that Bailey knew of Ruggles as he planned his escape from Maryland and that Ruggles may even have expected his arrival. Murray's trip to New York may also have been planned in advance.

2 For an excellent review of biographies and other works on black abolitionism, see Manisha Sinha, "Coming of Age: The Historiography of Black Abolitionism," in McCarthy and Stauffer, *Prophets of Protest*, 23–40. For new style, see Richard Newman's "Protest in Black and White: The Formation and Transformation of an African American Political Community during the Early Republic," in Pasley et al., *Beyond the Founders*, 192.

3 In this light, Quarles's *Black Abolitionists* is perhaps the greatest work of contribution and cooperation. For comments on this tradition, see Rael, *African-American Activism*, 4–5.

4 Trouillot, *Silencing the Past*, 4–13. For works reconfiguring the history of abolitionism, see Newman, *Transformation of American Abolitionism*; Harris, *In the Shadows of Slavery*;

Wilder, *In the Company of Black Men*. For call for synthesis, see Timothy Patrick Mc-
Carthy and John Stauffer, introduction to McCarthy and Stauffer, *Prophets of Protest*.
See also Rael, *African-American Activism*, 2–3. Stauffer's two books, *The Black Hearts of
Men* and *Giants* are significant achievements in this direction.

5 Harris, *In the Shadow of Slavery*, 188–90. See also Newman, *Transformation of American
Abolitionism*, 86–107; Stewart, *Abolitionist Politics*, 3–57; Goodman, *Of One Blood*, 45–65;
and Perry, "Black Abolitionists and the Origins of Civil Disobedience," in Halttunen
and Perry, *Moral Problems in American Life*, 103–22.

6 For a concise description of the evolution of radical abolitionism, see Stewart, *Abolitionist Politics*, 3–35.

7 Bordewich, *Bound for Canaan*; Mitchell, *The Under-Ground Railroad*; W. Still, *Underground Rail Road*; Siebert, *The Underground Railroad from Slavery to Freedom*; Gara, *Liberty Line*, 165–94. For early suspicion of the motives of white participants in the Underground Railroad, see Douglass, *Narrative* (1845).

8 For an important exception to this neglect, see Bordewich, *Bound for Canaan*, chap. 9.
For upstate New York generally, see Sernett, *North Star Country*, and Milton C. Ser-
nett, "Reading Freedom's Memory Book: Recovering the Story of the Underground
Railroad in Upstate New York," in Blight, *Passages to Freedom*, 261–79.

9 [Ruggles, ed.], *First Annual Report of the New York Committee of Vigilance*, as quoted in
Hahn, *The Political Worlds of Slavery and Freedom*, 36–37.

10 Quote in Quarles, *Black Abolitionists*, 152–53.

11 Friedman, *Gregarious Saints*, and Pease and Pease, *They Who Would Be Free*. See also the
fine discussion in Rael, *African-American Activism*.

12 Wilder, *In the Company of Black Men*; Harris, *In the Shadow of Slavery*; and Alexander,
African or American.

13 See the useful discussion in Luckett, "Protest, Advancement and Identity," 35–36, and
Harris, *In the Shadow of Slavery*, 181.

14 See, in particular, Rael, *African-American Activism*, 13, and Harris, *In the Shadow of
Slavery*, 3–6, 119–21, 133, 172–73, 218–19.

15 For the relative poverty of black women in New York City, see Dabel, *A Respectable
Woman*. See also Curry, *Free Black in Urban America*, 28–29, 266. Here I am influenced
by the comments on class in Goodman, *Of One Blood*, 138. For characteristics of the
black elite, see, most recently, Rael, *Black Identity*, and Carla Peterson, "Black Life in
Freedom: Creating an Elite Culture," in Berlin and Harris, *Slavery in New York*, 181–
215.

16 James Oliver Horton and Lois E. Horton, "The Affirmation of Manhood: Black Garrisonians in Antebellum Boston," in Jacobs, *Courage and Conscience*. See also Dorsey,
Reforming Men and Women, 190–91.

17 Stewart, *Abolitionist Politics*, 203–26. For recent works that limit religious discussion,
see Newman, *Transformation of American Abolitionism*, 2, and Rael, *Black Identity*.

18 Newman, *Transformation of American Abolitionism*.

19 For David Ruggles of Poughkeepsie, see Orcutt, *History of New Milford and Bridgewater,
Connecticut*, 758, and New York City Supreme Court Law Judgments, LJ 1815, S-96,
1820, B 57, 1827, B-130, 1817, B-130, 1831, H-45, for representative examples of some
thirty items. I am grateful to Bruce Abrams of the Division of Old Records, County

Clerk of the Supreme Court, City of New York, for this information. For David W. Ruggles, see Grover, *Fugitive's Gibraltar*, 314n.

CHAPTER ONE

1 Porter, "David Ruggles, an Apostle of Human Rights," 23–24; Perkins, *Old Houses*, 598–600; Records of the First Congregational Church, Norwich, Connecticut, 74.
2 For Ruggles's testimony about his birthplace, see *New York Daily Express*, September 7, 1838. For Norwich, see Caulkins, *History of Norwich*, 26–27, 60–62, 561–62.
3 Caulkins, *History of Norwich*, 520.
4 See the comments on blacksmiths in Rucker, *The River Flows On*, 136–37, 239n50. For Patrick Lyon and other blacksmiths, see Bernard F. Reilly Jr., "The Art of the Anti-slavery Movement," in Jacobs, *Courage and Conscience*, 52, 69–70.
5 Description taken with apologies, from Dickens, *Martin Chuzzlewit*.
6 Statement and Map of A. B. Sherman.
7 Porter, "David Ruggles, an Apostle of Human Rights." Dates of birth are approximate as later federal census reports show variations.
8 Hyde, "Reminiscences of Bean Hill, Norwich," 300; Statement and Map of A. B. Sherman. For comments on abolitionists and parents, see Stewart, *Holy Warriors*, 38–39.
9 Caulkins, *History of Norwich*, 510–12; Perkins, *Old Houses*, 24; Sigourney, *Letters of Life*, 97–120, 149–49.
10 Caulkins, *History of Norwich*, 510–12; Perkins, *Old Houses*, 80, 94, 122–23; Clarke, *Methodist Episcopal Churches of Norwich*, 15, 23–26; [Winslow], *A Memoir*, 53–55. For national trends, see Andrews, *The Methodists and Revolutionary America*, 127–32, and Wigger, *Taking Heaven by Storm*, 139–43.
11 Caulkins, *History of Norwich*, 511–15.
12 Ibid., 513–14, 602–3; Sigourney, *Letters of Life*, 100–101.
13 For letters, see *Courier*, January 6, October 6, 1808.
14 Caulkins, *History of Norwich*, 520–21, 556.
15 Swift, *Black Prophets of Justice*, 8–9.
16 Ruggles, *Extinguisher*, 14. For discussion of Cowper's poem and its reception in America, see Gellman, *Emancipating New York*, 119.
17 Ruggles, *Extinguisher*; Porter, "David Ruggles, an Apostle of Human Rights," 27; Caulkins, *History of Norwich*, 556; Sigourney, *Letters of Life*, 200, 234; and [Winslow], *A Memoir*, 50–55. For development of such schools, see Boylan, *Sunday School*, 23–30.
18 Ruggles, *Extinguisher*, 14.
19 *Confessions of the Two Malefactors*. For several harsh penalties for petty crimes, see Yang, "From Slavery to Emancipation," 146–47, and *The Life and Confession of Minor Babcock*. For punishment of horse thieves in New England, see Greene, *The Negro in Colonial New England*, 150.
20 For the most recent discussion of the rise of racism in New England, see Sweet, *Bodies Politic*, 271–312.
21 Greene, *The Negro in Colonial New England*, 74–75, 107, 345. Another large slaveholder, Colonel William Brown owned a sizable farm in Lyme, Connecticut, where Nancy Ruggles was born. Ibid., 107. For numbers in New London County, see Yang, "From Slavery to Emancipation," 278.

22 Zilversmit, *The First Emancipation*, 122–23; W. Jordan, *White over Black*, 296–97, 307–8.

23 For blacks in New York and New Jersey, see Hodges, *Root and Branch*, chap. 5. Quotations are from McManus, *Black Bondage*, 171. For blacks in the navy, see Bolster, *Black Jacks*, 153, and for soldiers, see Quarles, *Negro in the American Revolution*, 8–9, 12, 17. For Haynes, see Saillant, *Black Puritan*.

24 Zilversmit, *The First Emancipation*, 122–25; Melish, *Disowning Slavery*, 68–70.

25 Peter Hinks, "Timothy Dwight, Congregationalism and Early Antislavery," in Mintz and Stauffer, *The Problem of Evil*, 148–64. See also Scott, *From Office to Profession*, 76–94.

26 Zilversmit, *The First Emancipation*, 107–8; Melish, *Disowning Slavery*, 53–69.

27 Quoted in Robinson, *Slavery in the Structure of American Politics*, 210.

28 On conservative Connecticut, democracy, and slavery, see Wilentz, *The Rise of American Democracy*, 119–20, 125. For New Jersey, see Hodges, *Slavery and Freedom in the Rural North*.

29 Yang, "From Slavery to Freedom," 230–30; Strother, *Underground Railroad in Connecticut*, 20–21.

30 Strother, *Underground Railroad in Connecticut*, 14–20.

31 Bruce, *Origins of African American Literature*, 8, and Sweet, *Bodies Politic*, 125–26.

32 [Venture Smith], *A Narrative of the Life and Adventures of Venture*.

33 Statement of Grinning, a slave from Canterbury, Slavery Papers, Connecticut Historical Society.

34 Sigourney, *Letters of Life*, 220–21. For importance of domestics in Norwich, see Caulkins, *History of Norwich*, 108. For comments on historical amnesia and new understanding of importance of slavery in New England, see Melish, *Disowning Slavery*, 3, 6, 16–17.

35 Greene, *Negro in Colonial New England*, 201–4; D. White, *Connecticut's Black Soldiers*; and Sweet, *Bodies Politic*, 179–82. On Haynes, see Saillant, *Black Puritan*. For New York, see Hodges, *Root and Branch*. On penalties for mixed-race marriage, see Gellman, *Emancipating New York*, 49, and Harris, *In the Shadow of Slavery*, 58–59, 148, 171–72, 191–98.

36 Richards, *Slave Power*, 43–50, 71–75; Morris, *Free Men All*, 35–40, 219–22.

37 For Norwich practices, see Caulkins, *History of Norwich*, 331.

38 See the summary of this argument in Melish, *Disowning Slavery*, 46–47.

39 Greene, *Negro in Colonial New England*, 315.

40 Caulkins, *History of Norwich*, 393–94; Kramer, *Lafayette in Two Worlds*, 160–64, 190–92, 217–18.

41 *Longworth's American Almanac, New York Register and City Directory . . . for 1827*, 422. For African American seamen, see Bolster, *Black Jacks*, 235. On steamships and local trading in Norwich, see Caulkins, *History of Norwich*, 567. On reasons to leave home, see Gillis, *Youth and History*, 16–17.

42 Grover, *Fugitive's Gibraltar*, 67–118; on Quaker women, see Norling, *Captain Ahab Had a Wife*.

43 Grover, *Fugitive's Gibraltar*, 94–110.

44 Hodges, *Root and Branch*, 207; Curry, *Free Black in Urban America*, 260; Hodges, *Chains and Freedom*.

45 Cecelski, *The Waterman's Song*, 133–37.

1   Hodges, *Root and Branch*, 223–24; Wilder, *In the Company of Black Men*, 122–24. For oration, see Gilje and Rock, *Keepers of the Revolution*, 242–43; Ripley et al., *Black Abolitionist Papers*, 3:178–79. For Ruggles's 1825 arrival, see testimony of William P. Johnson in the Darg case of 1838, as reported in *New York Daily Express*, September 7, 1838. Johnson, a native New Yorker, noted that he had known Ruggles for thirteen years. For emphasis on divisions, see Harris, *In the Shadow of Slavery*, 122–28; Alexander, *African or American*, 53–58; and Kachun, *Festivals of Freedom*, 43–49.

2   For population of New York County, see Hodges, *Root and Branch*, 279. For establishment of African Free School, see Gellman, *Emancipating New York*, 58, 72–75, 155, 157, 197–98.

3   For full coverage of the disenfranchisement of blacks, see Gellman and Quigley, *Jim Crow New York*, 67–200.

4   Hodges, *Root and Branch*, chap. 7; Swift, *Black Prophets*, 22–24. For artisan antislavery, see Jentz, "Artisans, Evangelicals and the City," 51.

5   Franklin, *A Southern Odyssey*, 21–24, 89–107, 139–47, 173–81.

6   Howe, *What Hath God Wrought*, 50–61, 97–107.

7   *Freedom's Journal*, October 31, November 7, 14, 1828, as quoted in J. Bacon, *Freedom's Journal*, 237, 239, 246.

8   For 1826 incident, see S. White, *Stories of Freedom*, 25–30. For general study of kidnappers, see C. Wilson, *Freedom at Risk*. For early work of New York Manumission Society, see Gellman, *Emancipating New York*, 204–5.

9   Hodges, *Root and Branch*, chap. 7; Bruce, *Origins of African American Literature*, chaps. 3 and 4. For Bancroft and black historians, see Ernest, *Liberation Historiography*, 54–55, 98–99, 132; for public space, see DeLombard, *Slavery on Trial*.

10 Hodges, *Root and Branch*, 198–200. For residence, see *Longworth's American Almanac, New York Register and City Directory . . . 1828*, 507.

11 For Ruggles and Truth at African Methodist Episcopal Zion, see Walls, *African Methodist Episcopal Zion Church*, 48–50, 70–76, and Washington, *Sojourner Truth's America*, 89.

12 For Cornish, see Swift, *Black Prophets*, 20–28. For the best account of black Presbyterianism in this period, see Swift, *Black Prophets*, chaps. 1 and 2. For numbers of émigrés, see Burin, *Slavery and the Peculiar Institution*, 26.

13 See Timothy Patrick McCarthy, "'To Plead Our Own Cause': Black Print Culture and the Origins of American Abolitionism," in McCarthy and Stauffer, *Prophets of Protest*, 114–46; J. Bacon, *Freedom's Journal*, 71–96; McHenry, *Forgotten Readers*, 91–108; and Newman, *Transformation of American Abolitionism*, 90–93.

14 J. Bacon, *Freedom's Journal*, 46–48.

15 Walker quoted with comments in Horton and Horton, *In Hope of Liberty*, 172–73. For intellectual background of the *Appeal* and on Walker generally, see Hinks, *To Awaken My Afflicted Brethren*, esp. 173–96, and Bruce, *Origins of African American Literature*, 179–87. See also Newman, *Transformation of American Abolitionism*, 97–99, and Goodman, *Of One Blood*, 26–32. For *Freedom's Journal*, see J. Bacon, *Freedom's Journal*, 46–58, 63.

16 For good comments on Walker's impact, see Timothy Patrick McCarthy, "To Plead Our Own Cause," in McCarthy and Stauffer, *Prophets of Protest*, 135–43; Hinks, *To Awaken My Afflicted Brethren*, 237–61; and McHenry, *Forgotten Readers*, 25–42.

17 Hodges, *Root and Branch*, 244–45; Bruce, *Origins of African American Literature*, 183–84. For good comments on Young and his effect, see Finseth, *Shades of Green*, 265–68.

18 For meeting, see minutes in Porter, *Early Negro Writing*, 281–85. For Ruggles's participation and work as agent, see *Liberator*, August 20, 1831. For support, see Garrison, *Thoughts on African Colonization*; Wilder, *In the Company of Black Men*, 149; and Bruce, *Origins of African American Literature*, 194. See also Mayer, *All on Fire*, 65, 77, 93, 107–16; Mabee, *Black Freedom*, 10; Wyatt-Brown, *Lewis Tappan*, 98; Wiecek, *Sources of Antislavery Constitutionalism*, 161; Swift, *Black Prophets*, 71.

19 See the useful list in Luckett, "Protest, Advancement, Identity," 301–3. For sense of youth, see Quarles, *Black Abolitionists*, 15–27 (quote on 15), and Wilder, *In the Company of Black Men*, 125–41. For Ruggles quote, see *Emancipator*, February 3, 1835.

20 On moral suasion, see Stewart, *Holy Warriors*, 57–72. On question of resistance, see Perry, *Radical Abolitionism*, 233–39.

21 *Freedom's Journal*, April 8, May 9, 16, August 22, September 5, 25, October 10, 1828, and December 12, 1828–March 29, 1829. For grocers, see Hodges, *Slavery, Freedom and Culture*, 122–45. For address, see *Longworth's American Almanac, New York Register and City Directory . . . for 1829*, 489. This may have been a different entrance to the same building because Ruggles's address was now 3 Cortlandt. For the Free Produce movement, see Ripley et al., *Black Abolitionist Papers*, 3:55, 81n, 189–94, 201; Nuermberger, *The Free Produce Movement*; Jeffrey, *The Great Silent Army*, 20–23; Salerno, *Sister Societies*, 12–16; and Mabee, *Black Freedom*, 184–204.

22 Headley, *History of Orange County*, 193. Goshen, Connecticut, which was north of Norwich, was also famed for the high quality of its butter.

23 *Rights of All*, October 7, 1829; Wesley, "The Negroes of New York in the Emancipation Movement," 71–72; Pease and Pease, *They Who Would Be Free*, 124; Swift, *Black Prophets*, 31. For a new look at Russwurm, see Sandra Sandiford Young, "John Russwurm's Dilemma: Citizenship or Emigration," in McCarthy and Stauffer, *Prophets of Protest*, 90–113. For the temperance movement and for Humphrey, see Abzug, *Cosmos Crumbling*, 82, 95.

24 *The Humorist: A Collection of Entertaining Tales*. On prostitutes, see Gilfoyle, *City of Eros*, 41–43, 47–48, 50–51, 53. On the Five Points, see Burrows and Wallace, *Gotham*, 391–92, 478–80.

25 The principal scholar of this group is Shane White. See his *Stories of Freedom in Black New York* and (with Graham White) *Stylin'* in particular. See also Hodges, *Root and Branch*, 203–5, 236. I am borrowing the term "petty urbanites" from modern Chinese historiography, which describes urban residents who attended dramatic performances, teahouses, and street events with little interest in politics. For the most recent word on petty urbanites, see Yeh, *Shanghai Splendor*, 129–33.

26 *New York Spectator*, December 18, 1829. My reading of this incident differs from the emphasis placed in White, *Stories of Freedom*, 33, where Ruggles's "conciliating manners" suggest deferential behavior. For David and Elizabeth Bliss, see Bliss, *Genealogy*, and Perkins, *Old Houses*, 31–35. For their ownership of New York property, see Record of Assessments, City of New-York, 1827, 3rd Ward, reel 13. They continued to own the property at least through 1832. See Record of Assessments, 3rd Ward, reel 13.

27 Ward, *Autobiography*, 30.

28 Kraditor, *Means and Ends*, 8–9.

29 Ibid., 8; Wiecek, *Sources of Antislavery Constitutionalism*, 154–56; Stewart, *Holy Warriors*, 47; Wyatt-Brown, *Lewis Tappan*, 81–85.

30 David Blight, "William Lloyd Garrison at Two Hundred: His Radicalism and His Legacy for Our Time," in Stewart, *William Lloyd Garrison*, 1–13; Kraditor, *Means and Ends*, 5–8. Discussion of the formation of the American Anti-Slavery Society can be followed in Barnes and Dumond, *Letters of Theodore Dwight Weld*, 2:115–24.

31 [Garrison], *Address Delivered*, 5, 11, 13.

32 Mabee, *Black Freedom*, 17–20; Wyatt-Brown, *Lewis Tappan*, 103; Wiecek, *Sources of Antislavery Constitutionalism*, 154, 171; *Address of the New York City Anti-Slavery Society*, 3–4, 16. See Myers, "The Agency System," 368–71, for detailed listing of Arthur Tappan's contributions.

33 For the fullest account of the Manumission Society, see in general Gellman, *Emancipating New York*. See also Wiecek, *Sources of Antislavery Constitutionalism*, 159–62; Morris, *Free Men All*, 53–57. For Corse, see Barrett, *Old Merchants of New York*, 1:254–55. For Isabella Van Wagenen, see Papers of the New York Manumission Society, January 10, 1827, and Washington, *Sojourner Truth's America*, 65–68.

34 *Emancipator*, March 23, 1833; Porter, "Organized Educational Activities of Literary Societies," 568–69; McHenry, *Forgotten Readers*, 50–53.

35 For the convention movement, see Bell, *Minutes of the Proceedings of the Third Annual Conference . . . for 1837*; Pease and Pease, *They Who Would Be Free*, 119–23; Rael, *Black Identity*, 31–32, 60–61, 133, 178–79. For New York society, see *Abolitionist* 1, no. 2 (February 1833): 28–29.

36 Franklin and Schweninger, *Runaway Slaves*, 160.

37 Stewart, *Holy Warriors*, 30–31; Wiecek, *Sources of Antislavery Constitutionalism*, 127. For the fullest account of the 1817 northern black shift against the ACS, see Newman, *Freedom's Prophet*, 204–7. On connection between ACS and Indian removal, see *Liberator*, November 5, 1831, and July 13, 1833.

38 For early organization, see *First Report of the New-York Colonization Society* and Seifman, "A History of the New-York State Colonization Society," 50–77. For later actions, see Carter, "Black American or African," 233–34; Dick, *Black Protest*, 12–15. For quote on Indian removal, see *Liberator*, November 5, 1831, and July 13, 1833. For abolitionist connections, see Zaeske, *Signatures of Citizenship*, 27.

39 *Emancipator*, June 20, July 20, 1833. Ruggles was in Philadelphia as an agent for the *Emancipator* the previous month. See *Anti-Slavery Reporter* 1, no. 1 (June 1833). For Sepulcher, see *Emancipator*, May 20, 1834.

40 On debt, see Seifman, "A History of the New-York Colonization Society," 88–92. For anxieties, see Joshua N. Danforth to Ralph Gurley and Board of Managers, January 17, 1834; Washington W. David to Gurley, January 14, 1834, and April 23, 1834; Ralph Gurley to Joseph Gates, April 1, 17, 21, 30, 1834, in American Colonization Society Papers, series 1, vol. 56, part 2.

41 American Anti-Slavery Society Agency Committee Minutes.

42 See Myers, "The Agency System," for the fullest discussion.

43 I am adapting the fine work of Newman, *Transformation of American Abolitionism*, 166–

68, about white activists to cover Ruggles's efforts. For shared interests, see Rael, *Black Identity*, 45–48.

44 *Liberator*, May 11, 1833; *Emancipator*, June 1, July 13, 20, August 31, December 28, 1833; *Anti-Slavery Reporter* 1, no. 1 (June 1833). See also *Emancipator*, May 5, 1834.

45 Newman, *Transformation of American Abolitionism*, 155–60, 188–90.

46 Ruggles, *Extinguisher*, 45–46.

47 Bay, *White Image in the Black Mind*, 37; Mabee, *Black Freedom*, 107.

48 On sensitivity, see Rael, *Black Identity*, 120–24, 140.

49 *Emancipator*, January 28, 1834.

50 Bell, *Minutes of the Proceedings of the Third Annual Convention . . . for 1833*, 7, 10, 14–15, 18–19, 22–23, 29, for Ruggles's participation. For boardinghouse, see *Liberator*, June 22, 1833. On former slaves, see Rael, *Black Identity*, 28–30.

51 Rael, *Black Identity*, 31–33, quote on 32.

52 Ibid., 39–42.

53 On Blount, see *Liberator*, August 8, 1831, March 24, 1832, October 5, 1833, June 1, 1839.

54 *Liberator*, May 31, 1834.

55 *Emancipator*, April 8, May 24, 1834; for Stewart, see [Stewart], *Productions of Mrs. Maria W. Stewart*, 84. For other skills, see *Emancipator*, July 22, 1834. On the neighborhood, see Scherzer, *The Unbounded Community*, 148.

56 On Stewart, see Harris, *In the Shadow of Slavery*, 178–79; Wilder, *In the Company of Black Men*, 128; James Oliver Horton and Lois E. Horton, "The Affirmation of Manhood: Black Garrisonians in Antebellum Boston," in Jacobs, *Courage and Conscience*, 134; and Richardson, *Maria W. Stewart*.

57 For discussion of gangs and their methods, see C. Wilson, *Freedom at Risk*, 18–35.

58 Wright, *Quarterly Anti-Slavery Magazine*; Goodheart, "The Chronicles of Kidnapping."

59 *Emancipator*, March 25, 1834.

60 *Emancipator*, May 6, 13, 1834.

CHAPTER THREE

1 Lemire, *"Miscegenation,"* 59–66; for newspaper quotes, see Zaeske, *Signatures of Citizenship*, 49.

2 Gilje, *Road to Mobocracy*, 156–60, 162–70, Riker quote on p. 169; Tappan, *Life of Arthur Tappan*, 206–13; and de Beaumont, *Marie*, 123–29, 242–53. For frequency of interracial sex, see Hodges, *Slavery, Freedom and Culture*, chap. 10. For list of black homes targeted by whites, see 1834 Riot Folder, Manuscripts, New-York Historical Society. For a new look at the riots, see Townsend, *Faith in Their Own Color*, 44–51.

3 *African Repository* 10 (1835): 190. For replies, see *Emancipator*, July 22, August 6, 12, 1834. For Ruggles, see *Extinguisher*, 18.

4 For Cincinnati, see Taylor, *Frontiers of Freedom*. For anxieties about Cincinnati among black New Yorkers, see Alexander, *African or American*, 77.

5 For comments, see Pease and Pease, *They Who Would Be Free*, 71–72, and Harris, *In the Shadow of Slavery*, 199–200. On splits in churches, see McKivigan, *The War against Proslavery Religion*, 46–47, 58–59, 62–63. For Williams's nuanced reply, see Townsend, *Faith in Their Own Color*, 57–59. For further humiliation via a racist letter contending

that Williams was incapable of writing such a letter, see Alexander, *African or American*, 87–88.

6 For this view, see Pease and Pease, *They Who Would Be Free*, 7–8; Harris, *In the Shadow of Slavery*, 197. For an important criticism of the class and race approach, see Wilder, *In the Company of Black Men*, 82–84.

7 Barnes and Dumond, *Letters of Theodore Wright Weld*, 1:275–76. For letter to mayor, see *Emancipator*, July 22, 1834.

8 For Hopper, see Mabee, *Black Freedom*, 29–30; Child, *Isaac Hopper*; Newman, *Transformation of American Abolitionism*, 31, 71, 74, 75. For conservatism of Society of Friends, see R. Jordan, *Slavery and the Meetinghouse*, 31–34.

9 Henderson, "History of the New York Anti-Slavery Society," 23–27. For Goodell, see Ripley et al., *Black Abolitionist Papers*, 3:267.

10 For announcements of bookstore and circulating library, see *Liberator*, May 24, October 11, 1834.

11 On Dickinson's sermon, see *Liberator*, December 19, 1835.

12 On Dickinson, see Caulkins, *History of Norwich*, 552, 592. On Bacon, see Grimsted, *American Mobbing*, 42–44.

13 *Emancipator* July 22, August 12, October 11, 1834, December 2, 1834. On Congregationalists, see McKivigan, *The War against Proslavery Religion*, 38–39. On Dickinson, see his *Genealogies of the Lymans* and *Middlesex Gazette*, September 20, 1826; *Connecticut Courant*, August 19, 1831; *Religious Messenger*, February 11, March 24, 1832; *Pittsfield Sun*, August 30, 1835. He died in 1884. See *New York Times*, July 24, 1884. For Presbyterian minister, see Strother, *Underground Railroad in Connecticut*, 35. For Thompson, see Grimsted, *American Mobbing*, 26, and for women's antislavery society, see Jeffrey, *The Great Silent Army*, 42.

14 *Emancipator*, September 21, 1833, April 18, 1834, May 27, 1834; Quarles, *Black Abolitionists*, 105–6; Wilder, *In the Company of Black Men*, 75, 87; Porter, "Organized Educational Activities of Literary Societies," 564–65.

15 *Liberator*, August 30, 1834. For importance, see Kerr-Ritchie, *Rites of August First*, 84, 94–98.

16 Wilder, *In the Company of Black Men*, 27, 136–41; Horton, *Free People of Color*, 80–98.

17 For the Magdalen Report and Reese's part, see Tappan, *Life of Arthur Tappan*, 116–17. For the exchange between Reese and abolitionists, see *Supplement to the Evangelist*, May 10, 1834. For Ruggles's bookstore, see *Emancipator*, August 12, 1834. For his argument, see [Ruggles], *A Brief Review*, 7–9. For a capsule biography of Reese, see Wilson and Fiske, *Appleton's Cyclopedia of American Biography*, 5:345; Duffy, *History of Public Health in New York City*, 1:309–11, 468–69, 481–84, 499–501; Carlisle, *An Account of Bellevue Hospital*, 42–43, 48, 53, 133–34; and *Portsmouth Journal of Literature and Politics*, December 10, 1825. For signature, see Jentz, "Artisans, Evangelicals, and the City," 367. For abolitionism, see Friedman, *Gregarious Saints*, 35, 37.

18 Friedman, *Gregarious Saints*, 14–19.

19 Ibid., 44.

20 Ruggles, *Extinguisher*. On difficulties of publishing, see Richard S. Newman, "A Chosen Generation," in McCarthy and Staufer, *Prophets of Protest*, 72. For study of black pamphleteering, see Newman et al., introduction to *Pamphlets of Protest*. For announce-

ment of Ruggles's pamphlet, see *Liberator*, October 11, 1834. For admission of a few errors, see *Emancipator*, October 7, 1834. For Tappans, see Wyatt-Brown, "Abolitionists Postal Campaign," and Richards, "*Gentlemen of Property and Standing*," 49–53. For iron hand presses, see Rumonds, *Printing on the Iron Handpress*. For Walker, see his *Appeal*, and for Allen and Jones, see [Allen], *The Doctrines and Discipline of the African Methodist Episcopal Church*.

21 On literary public space, see DeLombard, *Slavery on Trial*, 53. On the importance of tone in black abolitionist pamphlets, see Newman et al., *Pamphlets of Protest*, 20–21.

22 For comment on sarcastic rhetorical ploy, see Newman et al., introduction to *Pamphlets of Protest*, 19, and Loggins, *The Negro Author*, 81.

23 Ruggles, *Extinguisher*, 7–9; Pease and Pease, *They Who Would Be Free*, 101.

24 Ruggles, *Extinguisher*, 20–21.

25 Ibid., 24–28.

26 Ibid., 10–17; Pease and Pease, *They Who Would Be Free*, 105–6.

27 For art of persuasion, see Newman et al., introduction to *Pamphlets of Protest*, 19.

28 *Working Man's Advocate*, October 4, 1834; *Address Delivered before the General Trades' Union*; Sedgwick, *A Collection of the Political Writings of William Leggett*, 1:32–36; 2:58–59, 64–68. For Leggett and Sedgwick, see Earle, *Jacksonian Antislavery*, 21–24, 52–54, 219n9.

29 Budney, *William Jay*, 34–37.

30 Ibid., 38.

31 *A Brief Review of the First Annual Report of the American Anti-Slavery Society, by David M. Reese, M.D. of New York Dissected*. Identifying Ruggles as the author of *A Brief Review* by Martin Mar Quack is uncertain, although the Library Company of Philadelphia and the American Antiquarian Society credit Ruggles as the author. It is noteworthy that Ruggles advertised it in conjunction with his own *Abrogation of the Seventh Commandment* and his *Extinguisher*. See *Emancipator*, August 1835. For quote, see *Extinguisher*, 1.

32 *Emancipator*, January 13, 27, 1835.

33 *Emancipator*, February 3, 10, 1835. The full articles may be found in Porter, *Early Negro Writing*, 637–50.

34 [Ruggles], *Abrogation of the Seventh Commandment*; *Address of the New York City Anti-Slavery Society to the People of the city of New York*. For women's petitions at this stage, see Zaeske, *Signatures of Citizenship*, 34–44, 59–65.

35 On the Magdalene Society and the furor, see Wyatt-Brown, *Lewis Tappan*, 65–72. See also *First Annual Meeting of the Female Moral Reform Society of the City of New York*; Grimké, "Appeal to the Christian Women of the South," *Anti-Slavery Examiner*, September 1836, reprinted as *Slavery in America*, 32–34.

36 On Stewart, see, for example, McHenry, *Forgotten Readers*, 68–70. On Child and women's writing overall, my comments are drawn and adapted from the introduction of Newman et al., *Pamphlets of Protest*, 15, and Karcher's introduction to her edition of Child's *An Appeal in Favor of that Class of Americans Called Africans*, xxxiv–xxxviii.

37 Amy Swerdlow, "Abolition's Conservative Sisters: The Ladies' New York City Antislavery Societies, 1834–1840," in Yellin and Van Horne, *The Abolitionist Sisterhood*, 31–45. For female abolitionist indifference to black ideas, see Hansen, *Strained Sisterhood*,

16–17. On the Chatham Street Chapel, see Wyatt-Brown, *Lewis Tappan*, 70–72, and Tappan, *Arthur Tappan*, 169–76.

38 Boylan, *The Origins of Women's Activism*, 35–36, 129–30; Jeffrey, *The Great Silent Army of Abolition*, 2–4; Wilder, *In the Company of Black Men*, 127–28; Jones, *All Bound Up Together*, 70–72. For a good account of conservative black attitudes toward female activism, see Rael, *Black Identity*, 150–54.

39 On black females and work in New York City around this time, see Dabel, *A Respectable Woman*, 69–82, and Hodges, *Root and Branch*, 154, 159.

40 *Liberator*, September 26, 1835. For residence, see *Longworth's American Almanac, New York Register and City Directory . . . for 1835–1836*, 578.

41 *Emancipator*, September 15, October 6, November, n.d., 1835; Porter, "David Ruggles," 31. For racist satire, see *New York Star*, reprinted in *Western Argus*, December 9, 1835.

42 For description of the riot, see *Proceedings of the New York Anti-Slavery Convention held at Utica*. See also Richards, *"Gentlemen of Property and Standing,"* 85–90, and Stauffer, *Black Hearts of Men*, 99–101. For author, see Lemire, "Miscegenation," 68. For aftermath, see Magdol, "A Window on the Abolitionist Constituency: Antislavery Petitions, 1836–1839," 49. For Ruggles's attendance, see *The Enemies of the Constitution Discovered*, 181, and *Proceedings of the New York Anti-Slavery Convention held at Utica*, 45. For town and county list, see *Rochester Daily Democrat*, October 2, 1835. For Smith, see his *Speech of Gerrit Smith* and Frothingham, *Gerrit Smith: A Biography*, 163–65. Theodore S. Wright was the next black abolitionist to visit Utica three years later. See *Colored American*, October 6, 1838. For abolitionists' origins, see Sorin, *New York Abolitionists*, 109.

43 Strong, *Perfectionist Politics*, 6–7. For a good discussion of abolitionism and Presbygationalists, see Davis, *Joshua Leavitt*, 118–12.

44 For kidnapping and resistance since the early republic, see Gellman, *Emancipating New York*, 47, 67, 108, 179, 186, 204–5, 220, and nationally, see Obadele-Starks, *Freebooters and Smugglers*. For flagrant examples in New York City, see Hodges, *Chains and Freedom, Or, The Life and Adventures of Peter Wheeler*. For a good description of kidnapping in New York around this time, see Harris, *In the Shadow of Slavery*, 209, and Burrows and Wallace, *Gotham*, 560–65.

45 For economic ties between the city and the South, see Foner, *Business and Slavery*, 5, and David Quigley, "Southern Slavery in a Free City: Economy, Politics, and Culture," in Berlin and Harris, *Slavery in New York*, 263–89. For Corse, see Barrett, *The Old Merchants of New York City*, 1:248–49, 252–55, and for family intermarriage, see Pessen, *Riches, Class, and Power before the Civil War*, 64, 66, 93. For an example of his work against kidnappers, see *Baltimore Gazette and Daily Advertiser*, June 25, 1835. For Standing Committee, see Minutes of the New York Manumission Society, 1834–38, reel 2.

46 Hurd, *Law of Freedom and Bondage*, 2:53, 55, 56. For Bergen County, see Hodges, *Root and Branch*, 279.

47 *Emancipator*, November 2, 1836.

48 [Ruggles], preface to *First Annual Report of the New York Committee of Vigilance*. For informal weekly meetings, see *Liberator*, December 26, 1838.

49 Harris, *In the Shadow of Slavery*, 211–12; Alexander, *African or American*, 89.

50 Hahn, *The Political Worlds of Slavery and Freedom*, 29–40. While I differ from Hahn's

thoughts, I have benefited immensely from his fascinating recasting of black antebellum history.

51 For standard community studies of black New York, all of which emphasize degrees of nationalism, see Hodges, *Root and Branch*; Harris, *In the Shadow of Slavery*; Alexander, *African or American*; and Wilder, *In the Company of Black Men*.

52 For initial organization, see [Ruggles], *The First Annual Report of the New York Committee of Vigilance*; *Liberator*, December 26, 1835; Pease and Pease, *They Who Would Be Free*, 208–11; Harris, *In the Shadow of Slavery*, 210–13; Hodges, *Root and Branch*, 245–48; Wilder, *In the Company of Black Men*, 127–28, 135. The organizing documents and personal identifications may be found in Ripley et al., *The Black Abolitionist Papers*, 3:168–80. A few weeks later Ruggles and several of the same people formed the Providence Female Juvenile Anti-Slavery Society. See *Liberator*, December 26, 1835. For tactics, see Wilentz, *Rise of American Democracy*, 552. For Philadelphia organization, see M. Bacon, *Robert Purvis*, 78, 79.

53 [Ruggles], *The First Annual Report of the New York Committee of Vigilance*. For announcement, see *Emancipator*, February 22, 1837.

54 *First Annual Report*, 10–13, as quoted in J. Bacon, *Freedom's Journal*, 235.

55 *New York Evangelist*, November 14, 1835; *Liberator*, April 2, July 16, December 1, 1836. For nonpayment, see *Emancipator*, February 3, 17 1835. On Lewis, see Rael, *Black Identity*, 120–24. For Steward, see his *Twenty-two Years a Slave. Forty Years a Freeman*, ed. Hodges. For continued activities by Ruggles, see *Emancipator*, July 28, 1836. For eleven-year-old, see *Emancipator*, December 1, 1836.

56 *Emancipator*, June 1, 1837.

57 David Ruggles to Gerrit Smith, April 22, 1836, Gerrit Smith Papers; Mabee, *Black Education in New York*, 58; Pease and Pease, *They Who Would Be Free*, 132. For donation, see *Emancipator*, September 21, 1833. For evening school, see *Emancipator*, October 27, 1836. See also Samuel Cornish to Gerrit Smith, March 23, 1834, and Peter Williams to Gerrit Smith, April 22, 1834, Gerrit Smith Papers. For sixty students, see *Weekly Advocate*, January 14, 1837. For land purchase, see Mortgage Books, 91 and 94, New Haven City Clerk's Office. For Dimond, see Dimond, *The Genealogy of the Dimond or Dimon Family*, 58–61.

58 *Colored American*, July 13, 1839. For Catskill meeting, see *Friend of Man*, August 18, 1836, as quoted in Calarco, *Underground Railroad in the Adirondacks Region*, 187, and *Emancipator*, August 11, 1836, as quoted in Kerr-Ritchie, *Rites of August First*, 91.

59 *Emancipator*, July 28, 1836; *Philadelphia Enquirer*, August 3, 1836; *Liberator*, August 6, 1836.

60 *Zion's Watchman*, August 3, 1836. On Boudinot, see *Emancipator*, September 15, 1836.

61 *Emancipator*, October 6, 1836; *Friend: A Religious and Literary Journal*, October 22, 1836.

62 *Friend of Man*, December 22, 1836. See for another case, *Emancipator*, December 1, 1836.

63 *Emancipator*, December 15, 1836.

64 *Emancipator*, December 15, 1836; *Liberator*, December 24, 1836.

65 For initial announcement, see *New York Evening Post*, December 13, 1836; *Emancipator*, December 17, 1838. For succeeding events, see [Ruggles], *First Annual Report of the*

New York Committee of Vigilance, 33–46; *Emancipator*, January 19, 1837; *National Enquirer*, December 24, 1836; *Pennsylvania Freeman*, December 24, 1836. For identification of de Souza as a slave trader, see *Religious Messenger*, August 2, 1831.

66 [Ruggles], *First Annual Report of the New York Committee of Vigilance*, 44–47; *Friend of Man*, December 22, 1836.

67 *Eastern Argus*, January 3, 1837; *New-Hampshire Patriot*, January 2, 1833, both quoting the *New-York Gazette*. On self-defense, see Perry, "Black Abolitionists and Self-Defense," 114.

68 *Weekly Advocate*, January 14, 1837; *Zion's Watchman*, January 14, 1837. For reminder of the case, see *Colored American*, April 29, 1837. Pease and Pease, in *They Who Would Be Free*, 210, argue that Ruggles was arrested as part of the *Brilliante* case, but my reading is that the kidnapping gang was looking for any pretext to seize Ruggles.

69 [Ruggles], *First Annual Report of the New York Committee of Vigilance*, 58–60, and *American Anti-Slavery Almanac for 1839*, 19.

70 William Jay to Theodore Sedgwick, December 3, 1836, Sedgwick Papers; William Jay to David Ruggles, December 10, 1836, Jay Papers, Jay Family Heritage House. On Jay in this period, see Budney, *William Jay*, 37–40.

71 Tappan, *Arthur Tappan*, 181–82.

72 *Colored American*, December 9, 1837.

73 *Weekly Advocate*, January 14, 1837.

74 Quarles, *Black Abolitionists*, 150, as quoted in Carol Wilson, "Active Vigilance Is the Price of Liberty," 113, in McKivigan and Harrold, *Antislavery Violence*.

CHAPTER FOUR

1 For note on salary, see *Colored American*, July 22, 1837; for petition, see *Colored American*, August 5, 1837. For organization of *Colored American*, see Ray, *Sketch of the Life of Charles B. Ray*, 9–11. For change of title of newspaper, see *Colored American*, March 4, 1837.

2 Howe, *What Hath God Wrought*, 502–4.

3 *Colored American*, March 11, May 20, 1837; *Emancipator*, March 17, 1837; *Emancipator*, April 27, 1837. For Literary Society, see *Colored American*, July 21, 1838. For increase in kidnapping and Morgan incident, see *National Enquirer*, January 14, March 25. On effects of the Panic of 1837, see Howe, *What Hath God Wrought*, 502–5, and Stauffer, *Black Hearts of Men*, 96–97.

4 Luckett, "Protest, Advancement and Identity," 18, 301–4.

5 *Colored American*, May 6, 1837. For Hopper's account in which he states that Nash hoped to get his hands on Ruggles, see *Jamestown Journal*, May 10, 1837.

6 *Emancipator*, April 27, June 15, 1837; *Philanthropist*, June 9, 1837; *Colored American*, May 6, 1837; and Child, *Isaac Hopper*, 319–36.

7 *Colored American*, April 15, 22, 29, 1837; Pease and Pease, *They Who Would Be Free*, 210–11.

8 For discussion of Dixon's case, see Child, *Isaac Hopper*, 340–56; *Baltimore Gazette and Daily Advertiser*, April 17, 1837; *Friend of Man*, May 3, 1837; *Colored American*, July 8, 15, August 12, September 9, October 28, November 4, December 9, 1837, January 20, 1838; *Emancipator*, June 8, 30, 1837, January 18, 1838; *Zion's Watchman*, November 18, 1837.

For pledge, see *Emancipator*, November 16, 1837, and *Zion's Watchman*, November 18, 1837. For costs and other details, see Meaders, *Kidnappers in Philadelphia*, 375–81. Years later, Dixon, now free and owning a seaman's protection certificate, was arrested for attempted murder at sea in Norfolk, Virginia, in 1845. See *Easton Gazette*, February 15, 1845.

9 *Colored American*, July 8, 1837.

10 *Colored American*, May 27, 1837.

11 *Colored American*, July 15, 29, August 5, 1837; Kerr-Ritchie, *Rites of August First*, 111.

12 *Colored American*, August 19, 25, 1837. On amalgamation and transport, see *Colored American*, June 23, 1838. For Ruggles's piece, see *Colored American*, June 30, 1838.

13 *Colored American*, March 11, May 20, 27, July 8, 29, September 16, 1837; *Zion's Watchman*, August 12, 1837; *Liberator*, October 13, 1837. For Francis Maria Shields, see *Colored American*, May 20, 27, 1837. For number of cases, see Ruggles's statement in *Emancipator*, November 2, 1837. Within a few months, Ruggles added to that total with a recitation of new appeals. See *Emancipator*, March 1, 1838.

14 *Zion's Watchman*, August 12, 1837, and *Liberator*, October 13, 1837.

15 *Colored American*, September 9, 1837.

16 Ibid.

17 Chudacoff, *Age of the Batchelor*, 30–33; Gilfoyle, *City of Eros*, 92–106; Stott, *Workers in the Metropolis*, 166.

18 Harris, *In the Shadow of Slavery*, 86–88.

19 *Colored American*, September 30, 1837.

20 David Ruggles, Mortgage, October 16, 1837, Norwich, Connecticut, Town Hall.

21 *Colored American*, October 7, 1837; *Philanthropist*, October 24, 1837. For problems at Russell's tavern and boardinghouse, see Kaplan, "The World of the B'Hoys," 28–30.

22 *Colored American*, October 28, 1837. The case became a precedent for similar actions. Calling someone a kidnapper, which Ruggles did routinely, could be costly. In 1841, D. D. Nash, the New York City policeman whom Ruggles referred to as a kidnapper, won a $1,500 judgment against the *Abolition Almanac* for such a reference. See *Emancipator*, March 31, 1841, and *Connecticut Courant*, March 3, 1841.

23 *Colored American*, September 16, 1837.

24 *An Address to Free Colored Americans issued by an Anti-Slavery Convention of American Women*, 29. See also *First Annual Report of the Ladies' New-York City Anti-Slavery Society*.

25 On Lovejoy, see *Colored American*, November 25, 1837. For debate, see *Colored American*, December 9, 21, 1837; American Anti-Slavery Society Minutes, November 1837. See also Harris, *In the Shadow of Slavery*, 214. For Whipper, see *Colored American*, September 9, 1837.

26 *Colored American*, September 9, October 28, 1837; *Emancipator*, November 16, December 28, 1837, January 4, 16, 1838. At the end of 1838, committee interest in Dixon's case was still strong. See *Emancipator*, November 15, 1838. For suffrage drive, see *Colored American*, January 20, February 3, 1838. For lengthy appeal, see *Colored American*, January 20, 1838. For other meetings of the Committee, see *Emancipator*, December 28, 1837; January 18, 1838, August 9, 1838.

27 *Colored American*, June 16, September 8, 1838. On Pennsylvania, see Winch, *A Gentle-man of Color*, 293–301, and Nash, *Forging Freedom*, 278.

28 *Colored American*, January 20, 1838.

29 *Emancipator*, March 1, 29, 1838. On Boudinot, see Meaders, *Kidnappers in Philadelphia*, 247–51.

30 *Emancipator*, March, 1, 8, 15, 1838; *Colored American*, February 24, 1838, March 8, 15, 1838. For Philos, see *Colored American*, March 22, 1838. For Ruggles's new work, see *Emancipator*, March 15, 1838, and *Colored American*, March 15, April 12, 1838.

31 Seifman, "History of the New-York State Colonization Society," 105–13.

32 *Colored American*, March 15, 22, April 12, 1838; *Philanthropist*, January 29, 1839.

33 American Anti-Slavery Society Minutes, April 5, 1838.

34 [Ruggles], *An Antidote*, 20.

35 Ibid., 21.

36 Ibid.; Finkelman, "Protection of Black Rights." For New York State Conference, see *Pennsylvania Freeman*, June 14, 1838; *Emancipator*, June 14, 1838. For Ruggles's refusal to endorse Seward, see *Mirror of Liberty* 1, no. 2 (January 1839): 36. Later in the year, Philadelphia supporters asked Ruggles to compose a similar rebuttal to *Abolitionism Exposed by a Dr. Sleigh*. He declined, though he made a number of sharp comments about the piece in the first issue of the *Mirror of Liberty*.

37 *Colored American*, January 20, 1838; *Emancipator*, March 15, May 3, 24, 1838.

38 *Mirror of Liberty* 1, no. 1 (July 1838). For announcement, see *Emancipator*, July 5, 19, August 5, 9, 1838; *Colored American*, July 21, August 11, 1838; and *Advocate of Freedom*, September 27, 1838. See also Pease and Pease, *They Who Would Be Free*, 115. For praise, see *National Reformer*, October 1838.

39 Sherman, *Invisible Poets*, 26–32.

40 An earlier interim report appears in the *Emancipator*, March 1, 1838.

41 *Mirror of Liberty* 1, no. 1 (July 1838): 5, 8; Proceedings of the Board of Managers, New England Anti-Slavery Society, July 2, 1838.

42 *Colored American*, February 17, 1838.

43 *Colored American*, January 20, 1838.

44 *Colored American*, February 5, 1836.

45 [John Thompson], *Life of John Thompson*, 103; James L. Smith, *Autobiography of James L. Smith*, 50–51; Strother, *Underground Railroad in Connecticut*, 53–57; [William Green], *Narrative of the Events in the Life of William Green*, 21. For minister, see *Emancipator*, May 5, 1838. For the Underground Railroad in Maryland, see Whitman, *Changing Slavery in the Chesapeake*, 164–201.

46 For the Dorsey case, see *Pennsylvania Freeman*, August 3, 17, 1837; *Colored American*, September 2, 1837; Salvatore, *We All Got Freedom*, 13. See also the narrative of Basil Dorsey in *Hampshire Gazette*, April 2, 1867, and Bearse, *Reminiscences of Fugitive-Slave Laws*, 11, about Ruggles's assistance.

47 For a nice summary of such homes, see John Michael Vlach, "Above Ground on the Underground Railroad," in Blight, *Passages to Freedom*, 95–115. For Ruggles's home, see *Longworth's American Almanac, New York Register and City Directory . . . for the year 1838*, 567. Ruggles remained there until 1840.

48 *Emancipator*, May 3, 24, 1838; *Friend of Man*, May 31, 1837; and Henderson, "History of the New York State Anti-Slavery Society," 141–44.

49 On coastal route, see note 31 and Strother, *Underground Railroad in Connecticut*. On the Hudson River, see Calarco, *Underground Railroad in the Adirondack Region*, esp. 177–214. For a thorough and scrupulous discussion of upstate Underground Railroad sites, see Wellman, "Born a Slave, Lived a Freeman, Died in the Lord." On Rokeby, see Jane Williamson, "Telling It like It Was at Rokeby: The Evolution of an Underground Railroad Historic Site in Vermont," in Blight, *Passages to Freedom*, 249–61. On central New York, see Sernett, *North Star Country*, 166–94. For testimonials, see *Mirror of Liberty* 1, no. 2 (January 1839).

50 *Emancipator*, March 29, 1838.

51 The letters are reprinted in *Mirror of Liberty* 1, no. 2 (January 1839): 22. Article is found in *Colored American*, June 23, 1838.

52 "Condition of Recognizance of David Ruggles, August 25, 1838"; "Deposition of J. Dayton Wilson" September 5, 1838," both Court of Common Pleas, November 9–December 7, 1838, reel 25. The *New York Sun* of August 28 wrote approvingly of Wilson's behavior.

53 I am grateful to Stan Crouch, member of American Handwriting Analysis Foundation, board member of Graphological Society of San Francisco, and Web master of <http://www.handwriting.org/> for his insightful comments on Ruggles's handwriting.

54 For Roberts, see *Emancipator*, March 29, 1838. For appeal to churches, see *Colored American*, July 21, 1838. For arrest of Wilson and case of the three boys, see *Colored American*, June 23, July 7, 21, 28, August 11, 1838; *Emancipator*, July 26, 1838; *New York Evangelist*, June 23, 1838; and *New-Yorker*, August 25, 1838. For Ruggles's arrest of Wilson, see Court of Common Pleas, November 9, 1838–December 7, 1838, reel 183. The case was not heard for several months and Ruggles's deposition can be found in those papers. For dropping of charges, see *New-Yorker*, September 9, 1838. For handwriting, see Thornton, *Handwriting in America*, 131–32. For slave master/juror, see *Emancipator*, February 21, 1839.

55 For a stimulating discussion of the power of the meetings at the Broadway Tabernacle and Chatham Street Chapel, see Kilde, *When Church Became Theater*, 22–65. For Garrison meetings, see *Colored American*, July 14, 21, 28, August 11, 1838. The full talk was published in *Colored American*, September 8–22, 1838, and *Mirror of Liberty* 1, no. 1 (July 1838). For protest over "negro pews," see *Colored American*, August 19, 1837. For antislavery society, see *Proceedings of a meeting to form the Broadway Tabernacle Anti-Slavery Society*.

56 For letters to Call, see *Mirror of Liberty* 1, no. 2 (January 1839): 24. For arrest of Lewis, see *Colored American*, August 18, 1838, and *Emancipator*, August 16, 1838. See also *New York Daily Express*, August 14, 1836, and *Boston Daily Courier*, August 13, 1838. These newspapers were quite hostile to Ruggles, contending that his action was another case of kidnapping white people.

57 For discrimination on boat and rail, see *Emancipator*, August 23, 30, 1838; *Colored American*, August 25, 1838. For an earlier incident involving black people, see Chace, *Anti-Slavery Reminiscences*, 15–17.

58 *Colored American*, August 25, September 1, 8, 1838; *Emancipator*, August 30, 1838; *New York Daily Express*, August 23, 24, 1838.

59 Douglass, *Narrative* (1845), 109–10; Douglass, *My Bondage and My Freedom*, 341; and *Farmer's Cabinet*, April 9, 1873. For operation of reading room at this time, see *Union Herald*, September 9, 1838. For discussion of New Bedford, see Grover, *Fugitive's Gibraltar*, 143–44. For carefully painted self-portrait, see Walker, *Moral Choices*, 212. Walker (p. 242) points out that Douglass's biographers are so eager to get him to the abolitionist stage and Garrison that they rush through the formative events. For influential studies emphasizing Garrison's influence, see Martin, *The Mind of Frederick Douglass*, 4, 47; McFeeley, *Frederick Douglass*, 83–84; and Mayer, *All on Fire*, 248. On Smith, see Stauffer, *Black Hearts of Men*; on Lincoln, see Oakes, *The Radical and the Republican*. McFeeley passes over Ruggles in a few sentences as does Quarles, *Frederick Douglass*, 9. See Quarles, p. 15, for quote on education. On Douglass, alcohol, and temperance, see Crowley, "Slaves to the Bottle," 127–36. One oddity about Douglass's recollection of his entry into New York was the warning he received from William Dixon, or Allender's Jake. Dixon advised Douglass to keep moving from New York City and not to trust anyone, white or black. This message came from a man whom the abolitionist movement had sheltered for more than a year. Either Dixon was trying to push potential competition away or Douglass had his own reasons for the confusing memory. On Pennington, see Blackett, *Beating against the Barriers*, 57–58.

60 *Colored American*, June 16, 23, 1838; *Emancipator*, June 28, 1838. See also McHenry, *Forgotten Readers*, 105–6.

61 Douglass, *Narrative* (1841), 111; McFeeley, *Frederick Douglass*, 76–78.

62 The case may be followed in articles in the *New York Sun*, September 5, 7, 10, 1838; *New York Daily Express*, September 6, 7, 1838; *New York Journal of Commerce*, September 6, 7, 10, 12, 1838; *Boston Evening Gazette*, September 15, 1838; *New Bedford Mercury*, September 14, 1838; *Newport Mercury*, September 15, 1838; *Farmer's Cabinet*, October 26, 1838. For arrest, see "People of the State of New York versus Barney Corse," District Attorney Indictment Papers, September 13–October 16, 1838, reel 182. For conditions in the cell, see *Mirror of Liberty* 1, no. 2 (January 1839). See also [Hopper], *Exposition of the Proceedings of the John P. Darg*. For meeting, see *Colored American*, September 8, 1838. For amount of bail, see *New York Daily Express*, September 10, 1838. For discussion of the bail, see *Liberator*, October 5, 1838, and Ruggles's own acknowledgment in *Emancipator*, January 23, 1840.

63 On B'hoys, see Wilentz, *Chants Democratic*, 300–301. On black dandies and bobolition cartoons, see White and White, *Stylin'*, 108–24.

64 For testimony and Ruggles's participation, see *Friend's Intelligencer*, September 1838. For Douglass's presence, see *New York Times*, March 11, 1873.

65 *New York Daily Express*, September 6, 7, 10, 1838. For Higgins, see Ripley et al., *Black Abolitionist Papers*, 3:179n13, and *Anti-Slavery Record* (1836).

66 *New York Daily Express*, September 7, 1838. Arthur Tappan and Finney had quarreled bitterly about where blacks could sit at the Chatham Street Chapel and the Tabernacle. The evangelist preferred that blacks be restricted to the upper, remote galleries, whereas the merchant insisted they be seated on the main floor with the rest of the congregation. Tappan won the battle and the Tabernacle became the site of numer-

ous antislavery meetings. Its membership put its tangible faith behind Ruggles, who apparently came into the church via the Congregationalists at the Chatham Street Chapel. See Hardman, *Charles Grandison Finney*, 262, 274, 311–14; Wyatt-Brown, *Lewis Tappan*, 71, 116–19, 159.

67 For prosecution of Corse, see *Hudson River Chronicle*, January 15, 1839. For similar views, see *New York Courier*, October 22, 1838; *Barre Weekly Gazette*, October 26, 1838; *Rhode-Island Republican*, October 24, 1838; *Farmer's Cabinet*, October 26, 1838; and *Daily Picayune*, September 15, 1838.

68 *New York Daily Express*, September 26, 1838; *Emancipator*, November 29, 1838. Hughes's story may be found in Meaders, *Kidnappers in Philadelphia*, 101–4, 177–78, and in *Colored American*, June 12, 1841.

69 *Colored American*, September 15, 29, 1838.

70 *Colored American*, September 29, 1838, and *Emancipator*, October 4, 1838. For *Mirror of Liberty*, see *Colored American*, October 20, 1838. For Tappan, see *Zion's Watchman*, October 26, 1839. For subscriptions, see *Colored American*, November 10, 1838.

71 For reference to Dr. Swain, see *Emancipator*, December 27, 1849, and for his practice, see *Connecticut Courant*, May 27, 1833. For discussion of physiological responses to racism, see Michael L. Blakey, "Psychophysiological Stress and the Disorders of Industrial Society: A Critical Theoretical Formulation for Biocultural Research," in Forman, *Diagnosing America*, 149–93. Swain died in a steamboat accident in August of 1839. See *Philadelphia Inquirer*, August 9, 1839.

72 *Emancipator*, August 30, 1838; *Mirror of Liberty* 1, no. 2 (January 1839), 21.

73 On Wilson, see *New-Yorker*, September 22, 1838. For committee problems, see *Mirror of Liberty* 1, no. 2 (January 1839): 18–20. For Hanson, see Ripley et al., *Black Abolitionist Papers*, 3:286–87.

74 *Colored American*, October 20, 27, November 3, 10, 1838; *Emancipator*, March 1, October 25, November 8, 1838. For Russell's case, see "John Russell vs. David Ruggles, Philip A. Bell, Samuel E. Cornish & Robert Sears," Court of Common Pleas, October 23, 1838. For detail of legal costs, see *Colored American*, January 26, 1839.

75 Samuel Eli Cornish to William Jay, November 3, 5, 1838, Jay Family Papers, Columbia University. For Cornish statements and for contributions, see *Colored American*, November 3, 10, 1838, December 15, 29, 1838. For demand for money, see *Colored American*, January 19, 1839.

76 For account, see *Mirror of Liberty* 1, no. 2 (January 1839): 30–33, and *Emancipator*, January 10, 1839. For hostile articles, see *New York Journal of Commerce*, December 31, 1838; *Evening Star* January 4, 1839, and *Hudson River Chronicle*, January 15, 1839, for a notorious and impertinent meddler.

77 Incident quoted in Bordewich, *Bound for Canaan*, 175.

78 *Liberator*, November 16, 1838; *Emancipator*, November 8, 22, 29, December 20, 1838; *Colored American*, November 10, December 1, 8, 15, 1838; *Mirror of Liberty* 1, no. 2 (January 1839): 30; *New York Evangelist*, December 8, 1839. On Williston, see Ripley et al., *Black Abolitionist Papers*, 3:476, and Blackett, *Beating against the Barriers*, 290–93. For New York Eye Infirmary, see Duffy, *History of Public Health in New York City*, 1:219, 253.

79 *Colored American*, December 15, 1838.

80 *Colored American,* January 26, February 23, 1839.

81 *Colored American,* January 26, 1839.

82 *Emancipator,* January 11, 1840; *Colored American,* February 23, 1839. For address, *Long-worth's American Almanac, New York Register and City Directory . . . for 1839–1840,* 567.

83 For castigation of Ruggles, see *Colored American,* February 23, 1839. See also *National Reformer,* February, 1839. For Tappan, see Lewis Tappan to Gerrit Smith, January 4, 1839, Gerrit Smith Papers.

84 *Colored American,* March 2, 1839.

85 *Colored American,* July 27, August 31, 1839.

86 *Emancipator,* May 23, 1839.

87 Ruggles, *A Plea for "A Man and A Brother.*

88 *Colored American,* September 7, 1839.

89 *Colored American,* September 14, 1839.

90 *Emancipator,* September 19, 24, 1839; *Zion's Watchman,* October 26, 1839; *Colored American,* November 23, 1839. Money problems continued the next year. See *Emancipator,* August 19, 1840.

91 *Colored American,* November 23, 1839; *Emancipator,* November 21, 1839; *National Anti-Slavery Standard,* August 20, 1839; American Anti-Slavery Society Minutes, October 17, November 21, 1839.

92 *National Anti-Slavery Standard,* August 20, 1840. On Cornish, see Harris, *In the Shadow of Slavery,* 202–4.

93 *National Anti-Slavery Standard,* August 20, 1840.

94 *William Johnston, George Tracy, George B. Barber, James W. Higgins and Theodore S. Wright vs. David Ruggles,* October 19, 1839, New York County Clerk Records, Document 2187, 1839. For statement, see *Emancipator,* October 24, 1839.

95 Pease and Pease, *They Who Would Be Free,* 210–11, 293–95. On expulsions of Hopper and Corse, see Minutes of the New York Monthly Meeting of Society of Friends, 1827–1849, microfilm MR-78, and *National Anti-Slavery Standard,* August 19, 1841. For report, see *Fifth Annual Report of the New-York Committee of Vigilance.* On splits among white working-class reform movements, see Wilentz, *Chants Democratic,* 172–219. I am indebted to David Gellman for this insight.

96 For a fine contemporary description of the workings of the Underground Railroad, see Bordewich, *Bound for Canaan,* 4–5, though he underestimates the degree of organization in New York City in the 1830s. For a good review of the literature, see David Blight, "Why the Underground Railroad, and Why Now? A Long View," in Blight, *Passages to Freedom,* 233–47. See also Gara, *The Liberty Line,* esp. 86–89.

CHAPTER FIVE

1 Finkelman, "The Protection of Black Rights in Seward's New York," 212–13; *Colored American,* June 19, 1841. For Douglass, see Proceedings of the Board of Managers," New England Anti-Slavery Society, June 13, 1843, and Blassingame et al., *Frederick Douglass Papers,* ser. 1: 1:lxxxvii–xci. For slur against Harrison, see *New-Hampshire Patriot,* October 19, 1840.

2 *Emancipator,* December 9, 1839, January 9, 11, 14, 23, February 21, March 12, 1840; *Liberator,* February 7, 21, 1840; *New Bedford Mercury,* January 31, 1840; *Christian Reflector,*

January 22, 1840. For Dickerson, see *Colored American*, July 18, 1840, and *National Anti-Slavery Standard*, October 8, 1840.

3 *Colored American*, May 8, 10, 15, August 7, October 2, 1841; *North Star*, May 18, 19, June 22, 29, July 13, 1849 ($500 donation), October 31, 1850. For Johnson estimates, see *Non-Conformist*, June 21, 1843. For later discussion, see *Frederick Douglass Newspaper*, November 13, 1851, January 15, 22, March 18, October 1, 1852, November 10, 1854, January 26, 1855.

4 *Emancipator*, May 1, 9, 1840; *Colored American*, May 9, 1840. For residence, see *Longworth's American Almanac, New York Register and City Directory. . . . for 1840-1841*, 546.

5 *Liberator*, June 19, 1840; *Emancipator*, February 13, May 18, 1840.

6 On the split, see Kraditor, *Means and Ends*, 49-53; Pease and Pease, *They Who Would Be Free*, 176-77; Ripley et al., *Black Abolitionist Papers*, 3:329-31.

7 *Colored American*, June 13, 1840. For Boston meeting, see *National Anti-Slavery Standard*, June 11, 16, 1840; *Liberator*, May 29, June 19, 1840; for Worcester, *Colored American*, July 4, 1840. See also [May], *Some Recollections of the Antislavery Conflict*, 285. For Worcester fugitives, see their narratives in McCarthy and Doughton, *From Bondage to Belonging*.

8 *Emancipator*, January 9, May 29, 1840. On Jay, Williams, and Onderdonk, see Townsend, *Faith in Their Own Color*, 95-100.

9 *Liberator*, July 4, 10, 1840. For Pittsburgh meeting, see *Colored American*, July 18, 1840. For white condescension, see Pease and Pease, *They Who Would Be Free*, 177-78.

10 *National Anti-Slavery Standard*, October 1, 1840. See also Pease and Pease, "Black Power: The Debate in 1840." On Purvis, see M. Bacon, *Robert Purvis*, 52-53. On New York City convention, see *Colored American*, August 15, 16, September 12, 1840.

11 *Colored American*, July 25, 1840. For Pennington, see Blackett, *Beating against the Barriers*, 14. For Albany convention, see Foner and Walker, *Black State Conventions*, 1:5-23.

12 *National Anti-Slavery Standard*, August 1, 1840.

13 *Colored American*, July 25, August 1, 15, 29, September 5, 1840; *National Anti-Slavery Standard*, August 13, November 5, 12, 1840.

14 For Ruggles quote and commentary, see James Oliver Horton and Lois E. Horton, "The Affirmation of Manhood: Black Garrisonians in Antebellum Boston," in Jacobs, *Courage and Conscience*, 127-55. See also Horton and Horton, *Black Bostonians*, 81-114, and Laurie, *Beyond Garrison*, 106-8. For convention, see *Colored American*, September 19, 1840; *National Anti-Slavery Standard*, September 24, 1840.

15 *National Anti-Slavery Standard*, August 13, 20, 1840, January 28, May 6, July 18, 1841, October 15, 1841; Wesley and Uzelac, *William Cooper Nell*, 92; Joshua Smith, Benjamin Weeden, Thomas L. Jennings to William Lloyd Garrison, July 28, 1841, Anti-Slavery Letters.

16 *Mirror of Liberty* 1, no. 3 (August 1840); Finkelman, *An Imperfect Union*, 300-309.

17 *National Anti-Slavery Standard*, May 6, 1841, quoted in [Nell], *Colored Patriots of the American Revolution*, 143. See also *Colored American*, February 6, 1841.

18 *National Anti-Slavery Standard*, May 20, 1841.

19 *National Anti-Slavery Standard*, January 28, February, 4, May 6, 20, 27, July 8, 1841; David Ruggles to William Cooper Nell, June 26, 1841, Post Family Papers, Univer-

sity of Rochester. For fundraisers, see Wesley and Uzelac, *William Cooper Nell*, 98–99, 101–3.

20 Wesley and Uzelac, *William Cooper Nell*, 99–100; Harrold, "On the Borders of Slavery and Race."

21 *Mirror of Liberty Extra*, July 1841; *Colored American*, July 10, 1841; Foner, *Life and Writings of Frederick Douglass*, 1:26; Blassingame et al., *Frederick Douglass Papers*, ser. 1: 1:lixxvii; *New Bedford Morning Register*, reprinted in *Free American*, July 22, 1841.

22 On black activism in New Bedford, see Grover, *Fugitive's Gibraltar*, chap. 6, and Horton and Horton, *Black Bostonians*.

23 *Liberator*, July 9, 22, August 6, 1841; *National Anti-Slavery Standard*, July 29, 1841. For incident involving Jennings, see *Colored American*, June 19, 1841, and *Free American*, August 5, 1841. For discussion, see Ruchames, "Jim Crow Railroads"; Grover, *Fugitive's Gibraltar*, 173–74; and Mabee, *Black Freedom*, 114. For articles applauding the decision, see *Connecticut Courant*, August 31, 1841; *American Masonic Register and Literary Companion*, July 31, 1841; *Daily Atlas*, August 23, 1841; *Floridian*, August 8, 1841; *Philadelphia Inquirer*, July 26, 1841; and *Daily Missouri Republican*, August 6, 1841. For death of Ruggles's father, see *Connecticut Courant*, July 3, 1841.

24 *Liberator*, July 9, August 6, 1841; Pillsbury, *Acts of the Anti-Slavery Apostles*, 238; and Grover, *Fugitive's Gibraltar*, 174. For ear cropping, see *Boston Times* reprinted in the *New York Evangelist*, August 14, 1841. For Douglass, see *Liberator*, July 6, 1841; *Colored American*, July 10, 1841; and *National Anti-Slavery Standard*, July 15, 29, 1841. Quarles, *Frederick Douglass*, 12, and McFeeley, *Frederick Douglass*, 92–93, do not connect the Ruggles incident with Douglass's own experience on the railroad. Douglass was not the only person impressed by Ruggles's determination. A young would-be novelist, Herman Melville, read the story and later used it in his masterpiece, *Moby Dick*. For Melville, see Bernard, "The Question of Race in Moby Dick." For frequency of protest, see Mabee, *Black Freedom*, 112, and Pease and Pease, *They Who Would Be Free*, 164–66, and for bad conditions, see Laurie, *Beyond Garrison*, 113–14. For Douglass's own experiences, see *Colored American*, October 30, 1841. For Howard, see *Liberator*, February 18, 1841.

25 *National Anti-Slavery Standard*, August 26, 1841. For Douglass on Latimer, see *National Anti-Slavery Standard*, December 8, 1842.

26 For Garrison resolution, see *Liberator*, September 3, 1841, and Ruchames, "Jim Crow Railroads," 65–66. For Douglass, see Mabee, *Black Freedom*, 114.

27 Ruchames, "Jim Crow Railroads," 66–68, 73–75; Laurie, *Beyond Garrison*, 113–16.

28 *Liberator*, August 13, 1841; *National Anti-Slavery Standard*, October 1, 1841; Pease and Pease, *They Who Would Be Free*, 179–80.

29 For Troy conference, see *Colored American*, August 14, 28, September 11, 1841, and Foner and Walker, *Black State Conventions*, 1:27–30. For dismissal of Ruggles's convention, see *Colored American*, September 4, 18, 1841. For details of motions, see *National Anti-Slavery Standard*, September 23, 1841.

30 *National Anti-Slavery Standard*, September 9, October 7, 1841, February 10, 1842; *Liberator*, October 1, 1841.

31 *National Anti-Slavery Standard*, September 22, 1842.

32 Christopher Clark, *Communitarian Moment*, 74.

33 Mabee, *Black Freedom*, 83–84; Newman, *Transformation of American Abolitionism*, 188–90; Laurie, *Beyond Garrison*, 256. For Ruggles's encouragement of black students, see *National Anti-Slavery Standard*, May 11, 1843. For Congregational Society, see *Hampshire Gazette*, April 2, 1867. On Day, see Simmons, *Men of Mark*, 978–85.

34 For antislavery society, see *Abolitionist*, March 19, 1840. For town, see Gere, *Reminiscences*, 132; Lydia Marie Child to Abby Kelley, October 1, 1838, American Philosophical Society.

35 Christopher Clark, *Communitarian Moment*, 11–14. For Dolly Stetson, see Clark and Buckley, *Letters from an American Utopia*, 40.

36 Christopher Clark, *Communitarian Moment*, 20–25.

37 For membership, see Northampton Association of Education and Industry Papers, Records, 1836–1853, folio 1, p. 73, folio 2, p. 35; Sheffield, *History of Florence*, 104, 117 (honored friend). For the Childs, see Sheffield, *History of Florence*, 85; Karcher, *The First Woman of the Republic*, 296–302, 312–13, 370–73; and L. Child, *An Appeal*.

38 For letter to Garrison, see *Liberator*, February 10, 1843. For treatments and ailments, see *Water-Cure Journal and Teacher*, April 1848.

39 For water-cure, see Cayleff, *Wash and Be Healed*; Donegan, "*Hydropathic Highway to Health*"; Beveridge, "The Water-Cure Days," 34–36; Porter and Rozwenc, "The Water Cures." For Ruggles's first awareness of water cure, see *National Anti-Slavery Standard*, February 10, 1848.

40 *National Anti-Slavery Standard*, February 10, 1848; Beveridge, "The Water-Cure Days," 60–62; and *Water-Cure in America*, 72–115.

41 Christopher Clark, *Communitarian Moment*, 199–200; Ruggles in *National Anti-Slavery Standard*, February 10, 1848; and Trall, *The Hydropathic Encyclopedia*, 2:61–64.

42 Ruggles recalled this treatment in a lengthy statement in the *North Star*, February 4, 10, 14, 1848. See also Frederick Douglass, "What I Found at the Northampton Association," in Sheffield, *History of Florence*, 129, and Clark and Buckley, *Letters from an American Utopia*, 84. For physical description, see Porter, "David Ruggles, 1810–1849, Hydropathic Practitioner," 132.

43 On Wesselhoeft, see Beveridge, "The Water-Cure Days," 50–70, and for naked bodies, see Christopher Clark, *Communitarian Moment*, 196. For George Stetson, see Sheffield, *History of Florence*, 120.

44 Christopher Clark, *Communitarian Moment*, 198–99.

45 *Liberator*, May 24, 1844.

46 Clark and Buckley, *Letters from an American Utopia*, 23, 40, 48–49, 52, 85, 100, 114, 115, 118, 137, 180. For incident with couple, see Paul Gaffney, "Coloring Utopia," 327.

47 *Liberator*, June 14, 1844.

48 For the dinner, see *Liberator*, August 30, 1844. Ruggles was using a contemporary meaning of fomenting, which meant to bathe with warm or medicated liquid. See also Clark and Buckley, *Letters from an American Utopia*, 114.

49 *Liberator*, August 31, 1844; for Douglass, see *Liberator*, June 6, 1844.

50 *Trumpet and Universalist Magazine*, April 15, 1848; Samuel L. Hill to Abner Sanger, Dec. 4, 1845, Northampton Association of Education and Industry, 4:115. Ruggles also helped George Washington Sullivan, a local black man, recover from a fall from a church belfry. Ruggles later warned association members from trusting him. See

Clark and Buckley, *Letters from American Utopia*, 36, 39, 141. For method, see Trall, *The Hydropathic Encyclopedia*, 1:55.

51 Samuel L. Hill to Charles E. Forbes, Northampton, April 28, 1846, Charles E. Forbes Papers, letters 1846, Forbes Library.

52 Washington, *Sojourner Truth's America*, 175–78.

53 *Liberator*, February 10, 1842; Quarles, "Antebellum Blacks and the 'Spirit of 76.'"

54 For letters, see *National Anti-Slavery Standard*, April 6, May 1, 1843, and David Ruggles to David Lee Child, September 4, 1843, Anti-Slavery Letters.

55 *National Anti-Slavery Standard*, May 6, 11, 1843; Northampton Association of Education and Industry Day Book, 4:46, 62, 77, 91, 141, 164, 189, 241, 276, 304, 337, 252, 373, 384. On Garrison, see *National Anti-Slavery Standard*, July 20, 1843, and Merrill and Ruchames, *Letters of William Lloyd Garrison*, 3:192.

56 *Liberator*, May 24, 1844. For more on Myers and the *Northern Star*, see Calarco, *The Underground Railroad in the Adirondack Region*, 71–73.

57 *Liberator*, August 2, 1844.

58 Frederick Douglass to Abby Kelley, June 19, 1843, Abby Kelley Foster Papers, and Douglass, "What I Found at the Northampton Association," in Sheffield, *History of Florence*, 129–32. On Sojourner Truth and her daughter, see Painter, *Sojourner Truth*, 100.

59 Painter, *Sojourner Truth*, 70, 98–101, 111; Washington, *Sojourner Truth's America*, 168–73; Mabee, *Sojourner Truth*, 51–54. Truth does not mention Ruggles in her 1850 memoir or in the more extensive version published in 1875. See [Truth], *Narrative of Sojourner Truth* (1850) and expanded version in 1875. The only Northampton associate mentioned is George Benson.

60 On Dorsey, see McCarthy and Doughton, *From Bondage to Belonging*, 120–21. On the black community, see Christopher Clark, *The Communitarian Moment*, 95; Gaffney, "Coloring Utopia," 241–42; Washington, *Sojourner Truth's America*, 168–71. On the Hutchinson Family, see Hutchinson, *Story of the Hutchinsons*, 1:114–16; Brink, *Harps in the Wind*, 89; and Roberts, "Slavery Would Have Died of That Music," 348–50.

61 Christopher Clark, *The Communitarian Moment*, 88–89.

62 History of Nonotuck Street, 1835–1891: Early Multi-Culturalism in Florence, Massachusetts; Gaffney, "Coloring Utopia," 241–43. On rural blacks, see Laurie, *Beyond Garrison*, 254–55. On maroons, see Hahn, *Political Worlds of Slavery and Freedom*, 43–45.

63 Christopher Clark, *The Communitarian Moment*, 192–93; *Liberator*, September 12, 19, October 27, 1845.

64 [A Community Maiden], "When I Was a Girl," in Sheffield, *History of Florence*, 124.

65 *National Anti-Slavery Standard*, March 20, 1845; *Northern Journal*, June 17, 1845. For partial but extensive list of Douglass's speeches at this time, see Blassingame et al., *Frederick Douglass Papers*, ser. 1: 1:xc–xcv.

66 Joseph Marsh, "The Underground Railway," in Sheffield, *History of Florence*, 165–68.

67 On Douglass's narrative, see Clark and Buckley, *Letters from an American Utopia*, 118. Torrey quote and statement in Harrold, *The Abolitionists and the South*, 71–80, quote on p. 80. See also Harrold, "On the Borders of Slavery and Race," 290; for meeting, see *Liberator*, September 27, 1844; for fund, see *Emancipator*, January 1, 1847. For Smith, see *Proceedings of the National Liberty Party Convention*, 50.

68 Northampton Association of Education and Industry Day Book, 4:186, 194, 196, 197, 203, 205 276. For order, see Clark and Buckley, *Letters from an American Utopia*, 147.

69 *National Anti-Slavery Standard*, August 20, 1846; *Hampshire Gazette*, August 4, 1846.

70 *National Anti-Slavery Standard*, May 21, November 19, 1846; *Water-Cure Journal and Teacher*, November 15, 1846; *Green Mountain Spring* 1, no. 5 (May 1846); *Liberator*, September 24, 1847. For consultation by other doctors, see *National Era*, March 16, 1848, and *North Star*, September 29, 1848.

71 David Ruggles to Wendell Phillips, December 2, 1846, Papers of Wendell Phillips. For another letter requesting help, see Lewis Tappan to David Ruggles, November 13, 1847, Lewis Tappan Papers, Library of Congress. For advertisements, see *Liberator*, December 22, 1848.

72 David Ruggles Probate Records, March 1850, Hampshire County Probate and Family Court.

73 Northampton Deed Book, 115: 41–42, 401; 118: 392–93, Hampshire County Probate and Family Court. On Hill, see Christopher Clark, *Roots of Rural Capitalism*, 268.

74 Merrill and Ruchames, *Letters of William Lloyd Garrison*, 3:537–42.

75 *Hampshire Gazette*, October 27, 1846; *National Anti-Slavery Standard*, July 20, 1843. For patient leaving without paying, see *North Star*, November 3, 1848, and *Liberator*, December 15, 1848.

76 Merrill and Ruchames, *Letters of William Lloyd Garrison*, 3:564–66, 584–85, 592–93, and *North Star*, July 21, 1848. For leave, see *Liberator*, July 14, 1848.

77 William Lloyd Garrison to E. F. Merriam, August 9, 1848, Garrison Papers; David Ruggles to William Lloyd Garrison, December 6, 1847, Anti-Slavery Letters; Cayleff, *Wash and Be Healed*, 18; Donegan, "Hydropathic Highway to Health."

78 For work as agent, see *North Star*, December 3, 1848. For quote, see January 28, 1848. Washington, *Sojourner Truth's America*, 189, speculates that Truth worked in the hospital. On the conflict with Garrison, see McFeeley, *Frederick Douglass*, 151.

79 For Ruggles's involvement with Free-Soilers, see Gere, *Reminiscences of Old Northampton*, 61. For the Liberty Party's popularity among blacks, 1848 vote, and connections with the Underground Railroad, see Johnson, *Liberty Party*, 91–94, 242–64, 326–83. Appendix D of Johnson's book lists innumerable associates of Ruggles's as Liberty Party and Free Soil activists. For votes and activities in Northampton, see Blanchard, "The Politics of Abolition in Northampton."

80 *North Star*, November 3, 1848; *Liberator*, December 15, 1848. For competition, see Porter, "David Ruggles, 1810–1849, Hydropathic Practitioner," 132, and McBee, *From Utopia to Florence*, 71–72.

81 *North Star*, January 21, 1847; *Liberator*, September 24, 1847.

82 *National Era*, November 18, 1847; *Liberator*, December 22, 1848; *National Anti-Slavery Standard*, April 17, 1846. For Georgia speech, see *Trumpeter and Universalist Magazine*, April 15, 1848. For other testimonials, see *Water-Cure Journal and Teacher*, May 15, 1846, November 1, 1848; *North Star*, January 14, 28, 1848, February 23, 1849.

83 *North Star*, December 3, 1847, January 20, 1848. Another abolitionist, H. W. Foster, concurred with Ruggles's argument. See *North Star*, March 3, 1848.

84 *Liberator*, March 3, 1849; *North Star*, November 24, 1848, February 28, 1849. For single charge, see Frederick Douglass Ledger Book, 1847–1850.

85 Inventory of the Estate of David Ruggles, January 8, 1850, Hampshire County Probate and Family Court.

86 Wesley and Uzelac, *William Cooper Nell*, 232, and *North Star*, April 14, 1848, July 6, 1849.

87 F. B. Sanborn, *The Life and Letters of John Brown*, 73–74; Catherine Beecher to Mrs. Wm. B. Banister, ca. 1849, Catherine Beecher Papers.

88 Inventory of the Estate of David Ruggles, January 8, 1850, Hampshire County Probate and Family Court. On Abel Brown, see Calarco, *Abel Brown, Abolitionist*.

89 *North Star*, February 1, 1850. Cemetery records indicate that Nancy, Felix, and Frances are buried in the family plot, allowing for speculation over where David Sr. and Jr. are buried.

90 Porter, *William Cooper Nell*, 251–52; *Hampshire Gazette*, December 18, 1849; *Emancipator and Republican*, December 27, 1849; *National Courier*, December 18, 1849; *National Anti-Slavery Standard*, December 20, 1849; *Liberator*, December 21, 1849; *Northampton Democrat*, December 25, 1849; *Wisconsin Free Democrat*, January 9, 1850.

EPILOGUE

1 For the case, see *The Fugitive Slave Bill: Its History and Unconstitutionality with An Account of the Seizure and Enslavement of James Hamlet*. For Committee of Thirteen, see Manisha Sinha, "Black Abolitionism: The Assault on Southern Slavery and the Struggle for Racial Equality," in Berlin and Harris, *Slavery in New York*, 257–58. For outcry, see *Emancipator*, October 13, 1850; *North Star*, October 3, 1850; *National Era*, October 10, 1850. See also Alexander, *African or American*, 123–24, and Hodges, *Root and Branch*, 26. For local meeting, see Laurie, *Beyond Garrison*, 244–24, 256–58. Laurie's interpretation of the meeting differs from mine, though I am indebted to his scholarship.

2 *North Star*, February 1, 8, 1850; Pennington, *A Lecture*, 26; *Water-Cure Journal and Teacher*, February, 1850.

3 *North Star*, April 12, 1850; Paul A. Munde, "The Munde Water Cure," in Sheffield, *History of Florence*, 190–93; on southern visitors, see McBee, *From Utopia to Florence*, 72.

4 "Statement of Alanson Nash," September 6, 1850," in Inventory of the Estate of David Ruggles, January 8, 1850, Hampshire County Probate and Family Court.

5 For suggestion of bankruptcy, see McBee, *From Utopia to Florence*, 72, as quoted in Painter, *Sojourner Truth*, 100. For Northampton's prosperity, see Christopher Clark, *The Roots of Rural Capitalism*, 262, 268–69, and for Williston, 190–91, 213–14.

6 *The Norwich City Directory . . . 1857*, 50; *The Norwich City Directory . . . 1861*, 106; *The Norwich City Directory . . . 1863*, 100; *The Norwich City Directory . . . 1867*, 111; *The Norwich City Directory . . . 1873*, 232; *The Norwich City Directory . . . 1878*, 232.

7 Phillips, introduction to [Nell], *Colored Patriots*.

8 Douglass, *My Bondage and My Freedom*; [May], *Some Recollections*, 285–86.

9 *Elevator*, September 29, 1865; W. Still, *Underground Rail Road*; Williams, *Centennial of the American Negro*, 35. There is no mention of Ruggles in the section on black abolitionists in Williams, *History of the Negro Race*, 2:111–25, or in the brief history of black resistance in Du Bois, *Souls of Black Folk*, 46–49. For general histories, see Jeffrey, *Abolitionists Remember*, 31–40.

10 Siebert, *The Underground Railroad*, 35, 71n, 126; H. Wilson, *Rise and Fall of the Slave*

Power, 3:503; Porter, "David Ruggles, Apostle of Human Rights"; Quarles, *Black Aboli-tionists*. For representative newspaper articles, see *New York Amsterdam News*, February 6, 13, 1988; *Atlanta Daily World*, November 1, 1963.

11 For upstate New York, among many studies, see Sernett, *North Star Country*, 129–62. For New York City actions against slavery, see, for example, Bearse, *Reminiscences of Fugitive-Slave Law Days*. For Committee of Vigilance, see list in Sidney Howard Gay Papers, Columbia University. For revival of the slave trade, see Howard, *American Slavers and the Federal Law*, 49–52, 78–83, 155–78. For Louis Napoleon and the Lemmon Case, see Finkelman, *An Imperfect Union*, 296–312.

BIBLIOGRAPHY

MANUSCRIPT SOURCES

American Antiquarian Society, Worcester, Massachusetts
  Agar Family Papers
  Lydia Maria Child Papers
  Abby Kelley Foster Papers
  Northampton Association of Education and Industry Papers
American Philosophical Society, Philadelphia, Pennsylvania
  Lydia Maria Child Correspondence
Boston Public Library, Boston, Massachusetts
  American Anti-Slavery Society Agency Committee Minutes
  American Anti-Slavery Society Minutes
  Anti-Slavery Letters
  William Lloyd Garrison Papers
  Proceedings of the Board of Managers, New England
    Anti-Slavery Society
Columbia University, New York City
  Sidney Howard Gay Papers
  Jay Family Papers
Connecticut Historical Society, Hartford
  Hanover Church Records
  Records of the First Congregational Church, Norwich,
    Connecticut
  Lydia Huntley Sigourney Papers
  Slavery Papers
Forbes Library, Northampton, Massachusetts
  Charles E. Forbes Papers

Friends Historical Collection, Swarthmore College, Swarthmore, Pennsylvania
    Friend's Intelligencer
    Minutes of the New York Monthly Meeting of Society of Friends, 1827–1849
Hampshire County Probate and Family Court, Northampton, Massachusetts
    Probate Record of David Ruggles
Harvard University, Cambridge, Massachusetts
    Crawford Blagden Collection of the Papers of Wendell Phillips
Jay Family Heritage House, Rye, New York
    Papers of Jay Family
Kroch Rare Book and Manuscript Room, Olin Library, Cornell University, Ithaca, New York
    Lafayette Papers
    Samuel J. May Papers
    Slavery Collection
Library of Congress, Manuscript Division, Washington, D.C.
    American Colonization Society Papers, series 1, vol. 56, part 2
    Frederick Douglass Papers
    Lewis Tappan Papers
Massachusetts Historical Society, Boston
    Sedgwick Papers
Mount Holyoke College Archives and Special Collections, North Hadley, Massachusetts
    Catherine Beecher Papers
Municipal Archives and Records Center, New York City
    Court of Common Pleas, 1836–1839
    District Attorney Indictment Papers, 1833–1840
    Record of Assessments, 1827–32
New Haven City Clerk's Office, New Haven, Connecticut
    Mortgage Books
New York County Clerk's Office
    Court of General Sessions
New-York Historical Society, New York City
    1834 Riot Folder
    Papers of the New York Manumission Society
Norwich, Connecticut, Town Hall
    Deeds and Mortgages
    Statement and Map of A. B. Sherman
David Ruggles Center, Florence, Massachusetts
    History of Nonotuck Street, 1835–1891: Early Multi-Culturalism in Florence,
        Massachusetts
Rush Rees Library, University of Rochester, Rochester, New York
    Frederick Douglass Ledger Book, 1847–1850
    Post Family Papers
Syracuse University Manuscripts Library, Syracuse, New York
    Gerrit Smith Papers

Address Delivered before the General Trades' Union of the City of New York at the Chatham-street Chapel, Monday, December 2, 1833 by Ely Moore, President of the Union. New York: James Ormond, 1833.

Address of the New York City Anti-Slavery Society to the People of the City of New York. New York: West & Trow, 1833.

An Address to Free Colored Americans Issued by an Anti-Slavery Convention of American Women Held in the City of New-York, by adjournments from 9th to 12th, May 1837. New York: William S. Dorr, 1837.

[Allen, Richard]. *The Doctrines and Discipline of the African Methodist Episcopal Church.* Philadelphia: Richard Allen and Jacob Tapsico for the African Methodist Connection in the United States, 1817.

Armistead, Wilson. *A Tribute to the Negro Being a Vindication of the Moral, Intellectual, and Religious Capabilities of The Colored Portion of Mankind, with Particular Reference to the Colored Race.* Manchester, England: Printed and Published by Wm. Irvin, 1848.

Barnes, Gilbert H., and Dwight L. Dumond, eds. *Letters of Theodore Dwight Weld, Angelina Grimké and Sarah Grimké, 1822–1844.* 2 vols. New York: D. Appleton-Century Company for the American Historical Association, 1934.

Barrett, Walter. *The Old Merchants of New York City.* 5 vols. New York: Worthington Co., 1862.

Bearse, Austin. *Reminiscences of Fugitive-Slave Law Days in Boston.* Boston: Printed by Warren Richardson, 1880.

Bell, Howard Holman, ed. *Minutes of the Proceedings of the National Negro Conventions, 1830–1864.* New York: Arno Press, 1969.

Blassingame, John, et al. *The Frederick Douglass Papers. Series One: Speeches, Debates, and Interviews.* 5 vols. New Haven: Yale University Press, 1979–92.

———. *The Frederick Douglass Papers. Series Two: Autobiographical Writings.* Vol. 1: *Narrative.* New Haven: Yale University Press, 1999.

Bliss, John Honor. *Genealogy of the Bliss Family in America from about the Year 1550 to 1880.* Boston: Printed by the Author, 1881.

[Bourne, George]. *An Address to the Presbyterian Church Enforcing The Duty of Excluding All Slaveholders from the "Communion of Saints."* New York: n.p., 1833.

———. *The Book and Slavery Irreconcilable; with Animadversions on Dr. Smith's Philosophy.* Philadelphia: J. M. Sanderson & Co., 1816.

———. *George Bourne and The Book and Slavery Irreconcilable.* Edited by John W. Christie and Dwight L. Dumond. Baltimore: Printed by J. H. Furst for The Historical Society of Delaware, 1969.

———. *Man-Stealing and Slavery Denounced by the Presbyterian and Methodist Churches Together with An Address to All the Churches by Rev. George Bourne.* Boston: Published by Garrison and Knapp, 1834.

———. *Picture of Slavery in the United States.* Middletown, Conn.: Edwin Hunt, 1834.

———. *The Virtuous Woman.* Mt. Pleasant, Mass.: N.p., 1820.

[Bradford, Sarah H.]. *Scenes in the Life of Harriet Tubman by Sarah H. Bradford.* Auburn, N.Y.: W. J. Moses, Printer, 1869.

[Brown, William Wells]. *The Rising Son; Or, The Antecedents and Advancement of the Colored Race by Wm. Wells Brown, M.D.* Boston: A. G. Brown & Co. Booksellers, 1874.

Calarco, Tom, ed. *Abel Brown, Abolitionist by Catherin S. Brown.* Jefferson: McFarland, 2006.

Carlisle, Robert J., ed. *An Account of Bellevue Hospital with a Catalogue of the Medical and Surgical Staff from 1736 to 1894.* New York: Published by the Society of the Alumni of Bellevue Hospital, 1893.

Caulkins, Francis Manwaring. *History of Norwich, Connecticut from Its Possession by the Indians, to the Year 1866.* Hartford, Conn.: Published by the Author, 1866.

Chace, Elizabeth Buffum. *Anti-Slavery Reminiscences.* Central Falls, R.I.: R. L. Peterson & Sons, State Printers, 1891.

[Child, David Lee]. *The Despotism of Freedom; or the Tyranny and Cruelty of the American Republican Slave-Masters, Shown to be the Worst in the World in a Speech, Delivered at the Anniversary of the New England Anti-Slavery Society, 1833 by David Lee Child, Counselor At Law.* Boston: Published by the Boston Young Men's Anti-Slavery Association for the Diffusion of Truth, 1833.

Child, Lydia Maria. *Anti-Slavery Catechism.* Newburyport: Established by Charles Whipple, 1836.

———. *An Appeal in favor of that Class of Americans Called Africans.* Ed. Carolyn L. Karcher. 1833; reprint, Amherst: University of Massachusetts Press, 1996.

———. *Isaac T. Hopper: A True Life.* Boston: John P. Jewett, 1853.

Clark, Christopher, and Kerry W. Buckley. *Letters from an American Utopia: The Stetson Family and the Northampton Association, 1843–1847.* Amherst: University of Massachusetts Press, 2004.

Clarke, Reverend Edgar Hedrick. *The Methodist Episcopal Churches of Norwich, Connecticut.* Norwich: n.p., 1867.

Cockrell, Dale, ed. *Excelsior: Journals of the Hutchinson Family Singers, 1842–1846.* Sociology of Music Series No. 5. N.p.: Pendragon Press, 1989.

Confessions of the Two Malefactors, Teller & Reynolds, Who Were Executed at Hartford, Connecticut on the Sixth of September, 1833, for the Murder of Ezra Hoskins at the Connecticut State Prison, Containing an Account of Their Numerous Robberies, Burglaries, Etc. Hartford: Hamner and Comstock, Printers, 1833.

Cottrol, Robert J., ed. *From African to Yankee: Narratives of Slavery and Freedom in Antebellum New England.* Armonk, N.Y.: M. E. Sharpe, 1998.

de Beaumont, Gustave. *Marie or Slavery in the United States.* Translated by Barbara Chapman with an introduction by Alvis L. Tinnin. Stanford: Stanford University Press, 1958.

The Declaration of Sentiments and Constitution of the American Anti-Slavery Society. New York: Published for the American Anti-Slavery Society, 1835.

Dickens, Charles. *Life and Adventures of Martin Chuzzlewit.* London: Chapman and Hall, 1844.

[Dickinson, James T.]. *Genealogies of the Lymans of Middlefield, of the Dickinsons of Montreal, and the Partridges of Hatfield.* Boston: David Clapp & Son, 1865.

———. *A Sermon Delivered in the Second Congregational Church, Norwich on the Fourth of July, 1834 at the Request of the Anti-Slavery Society of Norwich & Vicinity by James T.*

Dickinson, *Pastor of the Second Congregational Church*. Norwich: Published by the Anti-Slavery Society, 1834.

Dimond, Capen. *The Genealogy of the Dimond or Dimon Family of Fairfield, Connecticut: Together with Records of the Dimon or Dymont Family of East Hampton, Long Island, and of the Dimond Family of New Hampshire*. Albany: Joel Munsell's Sons, 1891.

[Douglass, Frederick]. *The Antislavery Movement A Lecture by Frederick Douglass before the Rochester Ladies Anti-Slavery Society*. Rochester, N.Y.: Press of Lee Man & Co. Daily American Office, 1855.

———. *My Bondage and My Freedom by Frederick Douglass with an Introduction by Dr. James M'Cune Smith*. New York: Miller, Orton & Mulligan, 1855.

———. *Life and Times of Frederick Douglass*. Hartford: Park Publishing Co., 1882.

———. *Narrative of the Life of Frederick Douglass, an American Slave. Written by Himself*. Boston: Published at the Anti-Slavery Office, 1845.

———. *Narrative of the Life of Frederick Douglass, an American Slave. Written by Himself*. Dublin: Webb and Chapman, 1845.

———. *Narrative of the Life of Frederick Douglass, an American Slave. Written by Himself*. 3rd English ed. Wortley, near Leeds: Printed by Joseph Barker, 1846.

[Drayton, Daniel]. *Personal Memoir of Daniel Drayton, for four years and four months A Prisoner (for charity's sake) in Washington Jail including a Narrative of Voyage and Capture of the Schooner Pearl*. 2nd ed. Boston: Published by Bela Marsh, 1854.

Du Bois, W. E. B. *The Souls of Black Folk*. Chicago: A. C. McClurg, 1903.

[Easton, Rev. H.]. *A Treatise on the Intellectual Character and Civil and Political Condition of the Colored People of the United States and the Prejudice Exercised Against Them by Rev. H. Easton, a Colored Man*. Boston: Printed and Published by Isaac Knapp, 1837.

The Enemies of the Constitution Discovered or, An Inquiry into the Origin and Tendency into Popular Violence Containing A Complete and Circumstantial Account of the Unlawful Proceedings at the City of Utica, October 21st, 1835 The Dispersion of the State Anti-Slavery Convention by the Agitators The Destruction of a Democratic Press, and of the Causes Which Led Thereto Together with a Concise Treatise on the Practice of the Court of His Honor Judge Lynch, Accompanied with Numerous Highly Interesting and Important Documents by Defensor. New York: Leavitt, Lord, & Co., 1835.

Fifth Annual Report of the New-York Committee of Vigilance for the Year 1842. New York: G. Vale, Jr. Printer, 1842.

First Annual Meeting of the Female Moral Reform Society of the City of New York, presented, May 1835; with the constitution, list of officers, names of auxiliaries, &ct. New York: William Newell, 1835.

The First Annual Report of the Auxiliary Bible Society of Norwich and Vicinity, Presented August 12, 1829. Norwich, Conn.: Printed by J. Dunham, 1829.

First Annual Report of the Ladies' New-York City Anti-Slavery Society. New York: William S. Dorr, 1836.

The First Report of the New-York Colonization Society; read at the annual meeting, October 29, 1823. New York: Printed by J. Seymour, 1823.

Foner, Philip S., ed. *The Life and Writings of Frederick Douglass*. 5 vols. New York: International Publishers, 1950–75.

Foner, Philip S., and George E. Walker, eds. *Proceedings of the Black State Conventions, 1840–1865.* 2 vols. Philadelphia: Temple University Press, 1979.

The Fugitive Slave Bill: History and Unconstitionality with An Account of the Seizure and Enslavement of James Hamlet and his Subsequent Restoration to Liberty. New York: William Harned, 1850.

[Garrison, William Lloyd]. *Address Delivered in Boston, New-York and Philadelphia Before the Free People of Color in April, 1833 by William Lloyd Garrison.* Published by Request. New York: Printed for the Free People of Color, 1833.

———. *Thoughts on African Colonization or an Impartial Exhibition of the Doctrines, Principles and Purposes of the American Colonization Society together with the Resolutions, Addresses and Remonstrances of the Free People of Color by William Lloyd Garrison.* Boston: Printed and Published by Garrison and Knapp, 1832.

———, ed. *The Abolitionist.* Boston: New England Anti-Slavery Society, 1833.

Gellman, David N., and David Quigley, eds. *Jim Crow New York: A Documentary History of Race and Citizenship, 1777–1877.* New York: New York University Press, 2003.

Gere, Henry S. *Reminiscences of Old Northampton; Sketches of the Town as it Appeared from 1840 to 1850.* Northampton: Press of the Gazette Printing Company, 1902.

Gilje, Paul S., and Howard B. Rock, eds. *Keepers of the Revolution: New Yorkers at Work in the Early Republic.* Ithaca, N.Y.: Cornell University Press, 1992.

[Green, William]. *Narrative of Events in The Life of William Green.* Springfield: L. M. Guernsey, Book, Job, and Card Printer, 1853.

[Greene, Asa]. *A Glance at New York, Embracing the City Government, Theatres, Hotels, Churches, Mobs, Monopolies, Learned Professions, Newspapers, Rogues, Dandies, Fire and Firemen, Water and other Liquids. &c. &c.* New York: A. Greene, 1837.

Grimké, Angelina. "Appeal to the Christian Women of the South." *Anti-Slavery Examiner,* September 1836. Reprinted as *Slavery in America.* Edinburgh: William Oliphant and Son, 1837.

[Hines, William]. *An Address Delivered at the Methodist Chapel in Norwich, December 2, 1827, at the Request of the Norwich Falls Society for the Promotion of Temperance: by William Hines.* Norwich, Conn.: Printed at the Request of the Society by J. Durham, Printers, 1828.

Hodges, Graham Russell Gao, ed. *Chains and Freedom Or, the Life and Adventures of Peter Wheeler, A Colored Man Yet Living.* Tuscaloosa: University of Alabama Press, 2009.

[Hopper, Isaac]. *Exposition of the Proceedings of John P. Darg, Henry W. Merritt, and Others in relation to The Robbery of Darg, the Elopement of His Alleged Slave, and the Trial of Barney Corse, Who Was Unjustly Charged as an Accessory.* New York: Published by Isaac T. Hopper, 1840.

The Humorist: A Collection of Entertaining Tales, Anecdotes, Epigrams, Bon Mots, Six Lines from Pope, with Copperplate engravings. Baltimore: Published by C. V. Nickerson and Lucas and Deaver, 1829.

Hurd, John Codman. *The Law of Freedom and Bondage in the United States.* 2 vols. Boston: Little, Brown & Company, 1858.

Hutchinson, John Wallace. *Story of the Hutchinsons (Tribe of Jesse).* 2 vols. Boston: Lee and Shepard, 1896.

Jay, William. *Inquiry into the Character and Tendency of the American Colonization and the*

American Anti-Slavery Societies. 2nd ed. New York: Published by Leavitt, Lord and Co., 1835.

[Kite, Nathan]. *A Brief Statement of the Rise and Progress of the Testimony of the Religious Society of Friends against Slavery and the Slave Trade.* Philadelphia: Printed by Joseph and William Kite, 1843.

Lansing, Dirck. *New-York, October 25, 1833. Sir: Annexed is the form of a constitution, approved by a number of gentlemen of this city, and designed for adoption at the formation of a national society, for the purposes therein specified.* New York: n.p., 1833.

Levasseur, A. *Lafayette in America in 1824 and 1825, or, Journey of a Voyage to the United States.* Philadelphia: Carey and Lea, 1829.

The Life and Confession of Minor Babcock Who Was Executed at Norwich, Connecticut, June 5, 1816. For the Murder of London, a Black Man Taken By the County Gaoler, At His Request. New London, Conn.: Printed by Samuel Green for the Proprietor of the Copy-Right, 1816.

[Marriott, Charles]. *An Address to the Members of the Religious Society of Friends on the Duty of Declining the Use of The Products of Slave Labour By Charles Marriott.* New York: Isaac T. Hopper, Stationer, 386 Pearl Street, 1835.

Matlack, Lucius. *The History of American Slavery and Methodism from 1780 to 1849 and History of the Wesleyan Methodist Connection of America in Two Parts, with an Appendix.* New York: no. 5 Spruce Street, 1849.

[May, Samuel J.]. *Some Recollections of our Antislavery Conflict by Samuel J. May.* Boston: Fields, Osgood, & Co., 1869.

McCarthy, B. Eugene, and Thomas L. Doughton, eds. *From Bondage to Belonging: The Worcester Slave Narratives.* Amherst: University of Massachusetts Press, 2007.

Meaders, Daniel, ed. *Kidnappers in Philadelphia: Isaac Hopper's Tales of Oppression, 1780–1843.* New York: Garland, 1994.

Meltzer, Milton, and Patricia G. Holland, eds. *Lydia Maria Child Selected Letters, 1817–1880.* Amherst: University of Massachusetts Press, 1982.

Merrill, Walter M., and Louis Ruchames, eds. *The Letters of William Lloyd Garrison.* 6 vols. Cambridge, Mass.: Belknap Press of Harvard University Press, 1971–81.

[Nell, William Cooper]. *The Colored Patriots of the American Revolution with Sketches of Several Distinguished Colored Persons to Which is Added a Brief Survey of The Condition and Prospects of Colored Americans by Wm C. Nell with an Introduction by Harriet Beecher Stowe.* Boston: Published by Robert F. Wallcut, 1855.

Newman, Richard, Patrick Rael, and Philip Lapsansky. *Pamphlets of Protest: An Anthology of Early African-American Protest Literature, 1790–1860.* New York: Routledge, 2001.

Pennington, James W. C. *A lecture delivered before the Glasgow Young Men's Christian Association and also before The St. George's Biblical, Literary, & Scientific Institute, London.* [Edinburgh?]: n.p., 1850.

Perkins, Mary E. *Old Houses of the Antient Town of Norwich, 1660–1800.* Norwich, Conn.: Press of the Bulletin, 1895.

[Pettit, Eber]. *Sketches in the History of the Underground Railroad Comprising Many Thrilling Incidents of the Escape of Fugitives from Slavery, and the Perils of Those Who Aided Them by Eber M. Pettit for Many Years a Conductor on the U. G. R. R. from Slavery to Freedom with Introduction by W. McKinstry.* Fredonia, N.Y.: W. McKinstry & Sons, 1879.

Pickard, Mrs. Kate E. R. *The Kidnapped and the Ransomed being the Personal Recollections of Peter Still and His Wife "Vina," After Forty Years of Slavery*. Syracuse, N.Y.: William T. Hamilton, 1856.

Pillsbury, Parker. *Acts of the Anti-Slavery Apostles*. Concord, N.H.: Clague, Wegman, Schlicht, & Co., Printers, 1883.

[Plato, Ann]. *Essays including Biographies and Miscellaneous Pieces in Prose and Poetry by Ann Plato*. Hartford, Conn.: Printed for the Author, 1841.

Porter, Dorothy, ed. *Early Negro Writing, 1760–1837*. Boston: Beacon Press, 1971.

Proceedings of a meeting to form the Broadway Tabernacle Anti-Slavery Society with the Constitution, &c and Address to the Church. New York: William S. Dorr, 1838.

Proceedings of the National Liberty Convention, held at Buffalo, N.Y. June 14th and 15th, 1848, including the resolutions and addresses adopted by that body, and speeches of Beriah Green and Gerrit Smith on that occasion. Utica: S. W. Green, 1848.

Proceedings of the New York Anti-Slavery Convention Held at Utica, October 21, and the New York Anti-Slavery State Society, Held at Peterboro, October 22, 1835. Utica: Printed at the Standard and Democrat Office, 1835.

Proceedings of the Session of the Broadway Tabernacle Against Lewis Tappan with the Action of the Presbytery and General Assembly. New York: For Sale at no. 143 Nassau Street, 1839.

Ray, Charlotte Augusta Burrough. *Sketch of the life of the Rev. Charles B. Ray*. New York: Press of J. J. Little, 1887.

Reese, David Meredith, M.D. *A brief review of the "First annual report of the American Anti-Slavery Society, with the speeches delivered at the anniversary meeting, May 6th, 1834."* Addressed to the people of the United States. New York: Howe & Bates, 1834.

[————]. *Humbugs of New York being a Remonstrance against Popular Delusion Whether in Science, Philosophy, or Religion*. New York: John S. Taylor, 1838.

————. *Letters to the Hon. William Jay being a Reply to His Inquiry into the American Colonization and American Anti-Slavery Societies*. New York: Published by Leavitt, Lord & Co., 1835.

Ripley, C. Peter, et al. *The Black Abolitionist Papers*. 5 vols. Chapel Hill: University of North Carolina Press, 1985–92.

Ross, Alexander Milton. *Memoirs of a Reformer (1832–1892)*. Toronto: Hunter, Rose & Co., 1893.

[Ruggles, David]. *The Abrogation of the Seventh Commandment by the American Churches*, by a Puritan. New York: David Ruggles, 1835.

[————]. *An Antidote for a Poisonous Combination Recently Prepared by a "Citizen of New-York," Alias Dr. Reese, Entitled, "An Appeal to the Reason and Religion of American Christians," &c. Also, David Meredith Reese's "Humbugs" Dissected by David Ruggles, Author of "The Extinguisher Extinguished," &c.* New York: Published by William Stuart, 1838.

[————]. *A Brief Review of the First Annual Report of the American Anti-Slavery Society by David M. Reese, M.D. of New York Dissected by Martin Mar Quack, M.D. L.L.D. M.Q.L.H. S.O.S.M.F.M.P.S.&c.&c. of that Ilk*. Boston: Printed and Published by Calvin Knox, 1834. Attributed to Ruggles.

————. *The "Extinguisher" Extinguished! Or David M. Reese, M.D., "Used Up." by David Ruggles, a Man of Color, Together With Some Remarks Upon a Late Production Entitled "An Address on Slavery and Against Immediate Emancipation With a Plan of Their Being*

Gradually Emancipated and Colonized in Thirty-Two Years by Herman Howlett." New York: Published and Sold by D. Ruggles, Bookseller, 65 Lispenard Street, near Broadway, 1834.

[————]. *First Annual Report of the New York Committee of Vigilance, for the Year 1837 Together with Important Facts Relative to Their Proceedings.* New York: Piercy & Reed, 1837.

[————]. *A Plea for "A Man and A Brother," by David Ruggles, made on the 18th July, 1838, Before a Public Meeting Held at the Hall 245 Spring Street, Also Extracts from the Speeches of Messrs. Philip A. Bell and William P. Johnson with Notes and Remarks.* New York: Published at the Office of the Mirror of Liberty, 1839.

[————], ed. *Mirror of Liberty.* New York: Office of the Mirror of Liberty, 1838–41.

Sanborn, F. B., ed. *The Life and Letters of John Brown, Liberator of Kansas and Martyr of Virginia.* Boston: Roberts Brothers, 1891.

Sedgwick, Theodore, Jr., ed. *A Collection of the Political Writings of William Leggett.* 2 vols. New York: Taylor & Dodd, 1840.

Sigourney, Lydia Huntley. *Letters of Life.* New York: D. Appleton and Co., 1866.

Simmons, Reverend William J. D. D. *Men of Mark: Eminent, Progressive and Rising.* Cleveland: George M. Rewell and Company, 1887.

Smedley, R. C., M.D. *History of the Underground Railroad in Chester and the Neighboring Counties of Pennsylvania.* Lancaster, Pa.: Printed at the Office of the Journal, 1883.

[Smith, Gerrit]. *The Speech of Gerrit Smith, In the Meeting of the New-York Anti-Slavery Society, Held in Peterboro October 22d 1835.* N.p.: n.p., [1835].

Smith, James L. *Autobiography of James L. Smith.* 1881; reprint, New York: Negro Universities Press, 1969.

[Smith, Venture]. *A Narrative of the Life and Adventures of Venture. A Native of Africa: But resident above sixty years in the United States of America, Related by himself.* New London: Printed by C. Holt, 1798.

Social Reform; or An Appeal in Behalf of the Association Based Upon the Principles of a Pure Christianity. Northampton: Press of John Metcalf, 1844.

Sterling, Dorothy, ed. *Speak Out in Thunder Tones: Letters and Other Writings by Black Northerners, 1787–1865.* Garden City, N.Y.: Doubleday, 1973.

Steward, Austin. *Twenty-two Years a Slave. Forty Years a Freeman.* Edited with an introduction by Graham Russell Hodges. Syracuse: Syracuse University Press, 2001.

[Stewart, Maria]. *Productions of Mrs. Maria W. Stewart, presented to the First African Baptist Church & Society, of the City of Boston.* Boston: Published by Friends of Freedom and Virtue, 1835.

Still, William. *The Underground Rail Road. A Record of Facts, Authentic Narratives, Letters. &c Narrating the Hardships Hair-breadth Escapes and Freedom Struggles of the Slaves in their Efforts for Freedom as Related by Themselves and Others, or Witnessed by the Author Together with Sketches of Some of the Largest Stockholders. and Most Liberal Aiders and Advisers of the Road.* Philadelphia: Porter & Coates, 1872.

Tappan, Lewis. *The Life of Arthur Tappan.* 2 vols. New York: Published by Hurd and Houghton, 1871.

[Thompson, John]. *The Life of John Thompson, A Fugitive Slave; Containing His History of 25 Years in Bondage, and His Providential Escape Written by Himself.* Worcester, Mass.: Published by John Thompson, 1866.

Trall, R. T. *The Hydropathic Encyclopedia: A System of Hydropathy and Hygiene in Eight Parts Designed as a Guide to Families and Students and a Text-book for Physicians*. New York: Fowlers and Well, 1853.

Trial of Amos Broad and His Wife, on Three Indictments for Assaulting and Beating, Bett, A Slave, and Her Little Female Child Sarah, Aged Three Years . . . New York: Printed by Henry C. Southwick, 1809.

[Truth, Sojourner]. *Narrative of Sojourner Truth, a Bondswoman of Olden Time Emancipated from Bodily Servitude by the State of New York, in 1828 with a History of the Labors and Correspondence drawn from the "Book of Life."* Boston: Published for the Author, 1875.

———. *Narrative of Sojourner Truth a Northern Slave Emancipated from Bodily Servitude by the State of New York, in 1828*. Boston: Printed for the Author, 1850.

Vital Records of Norwich, Connecticut, 1659–1848. 2 vols. Hartford: Society of Colonial Wars in the State of Connecticut, 1913.

Walker, David. *Walker's Appeal, in Four Articles; Together with a Preamble to the Colored Citizens of the World, but in Particular, and Very Expressly to Those of the United States of America. Written in Boston, in the State of Massachusetts, Sept. 28, 1829*. 3rd and last edition. Boston: D. Walker, 1830.

Ward, Samuel Ringgold. *Autobiography of a Fugitive Negro: His Anti-Slavery Labours in the United States, Canada, & England*. London: John Snow, 35 Paternoster Row, 1855.

The Water-Cure in America Over Three Hundred Cases of Various Diseases Treated With Water, by Dr. Wesselhoeft, Shew, Bedortha, Shieferdecker, Trall, Nichols, and Others with Cases of Domestic Practice; Designed for Popular as well as Professional Reading. Edited by a Water Patient. New York: Fowlers and Wells, Publishers, 1852.

Wesley, Dorothy Porter, and Constance Porter Uzelac, eds. *William Cooper Nell: Selected Writings, 1832–1874*. Baltimore: Black Classic Press, 2002.

Williams, Reverend Geo W. *Centennial of the American Negro from 1776–1876. Oration Delivered July 4, 1876 at Avondale, Ohio*. Cincinnati: Robert Clarke & Co., 1876.

Wilson, Henry. *Rise and Fall of the Slave Power in America*. 3 vols. Boston: James R. Osgood and Company, 1874–77.

Wilson, James Grant, and John Fiske. *Appleton's Cyclopedia of American Biography*. 6 vols. New York: D. Appleton and Co., 1889–1900.

[Winslow, Harriet Wadsworth]. *A Memoir of Mrs. Harriet Wadsworth Winslow Combining A Sketch of the Ceylon Mission by Miron Winslow, One of the Missionaries*. New York: Published by Leavitt, Lord & Co., 1835.

Woodson, Carter G., ed. *The Mind of the Negro as Reflected in Letters Written During the Crisis, 1800–1860*. Washington, D.C.: The Association for the Study of Negro Life and History, 1926.

Wright, Elizur, ed. *Quarterly Anti-Slavery Magazine*. New York: American Anti-Slavery Society, 1835–37.

BROADSIDES

Eastern New York Anti-Slavery Society. Albany, N.Y.: n.p., 1843.

Proceedings of the Session of Broadway Tabernacle against Lewis Tappan, with the Actions of the Third Presbytery of New York and General Assembly. New York: n.p., 1839.

DIRECTORIES

Longworth's American Almanac, New York Register and City Directory . . . New York: Published by Thomas Longworth, 1827–41.

The Norwich City Directory Containing the Names of the Inhabitants of Norwich, Norwich Town, Bean Hill, Yantic, Greenville and Part of Preston. A Business Directory State and City Record with an Appendix of Much Useful Information. Comp. William H. Boyd. Norwich: John Stedman, Printer, 1857–.

MAGAZINES

American Anti-Slavery Almanac for 1839 (Boston)

Boston: Anti-Slavery Fair, 1844–58

Mirror of Liberty (New York), 1838–41

Trumpet and Universalist Magazine (Boston)

NEWSPAPERS

Abolitionist (Boston)

Advocate of Freedom (Brunswick, Me.)

African Repository and Colonial Journal (New York)

American Masonic Register and Literary Companion (Albany, N.Y.)

Amsterdam News (New York)

Anti-Slavery Record (New York)

Anti-Slavery Reporter (New York)

Atlanta Daily World

Baltimore Gazette and Daily Advertiser

Barre Weekly Gazette (Barre, Vt.)

Boston Daily Courier

Boston Evening Gazette

Boston Times

Christian Reflector (Worcester, Mass.)

Colored American (New York)

Connecticut Courant (Hartford)

Courier (Norwich, Conn.)

Daily Atlas (Boston)

Daily Missouri Republican (St. Louis)

Daily Picayune (New Orleans)

Eastern Argus (Portland, Me.)

Easton Gazette (Easton, Md.)

Elevator (Cincinnati)

Emancipator (New York)

Evening Star (New York)

Farmer's Cabinet (Amherst, N.H.)

Frederick Douglass Newspaper (Rochester, N.Y.)

Floridian (Tallahassee)

Free American (Boston)

Freedom's Journal (New York)

Friend: A Religious and Literary Journal (Philadelphia)

Friend of Man (Utica, N.Y.)

Friend's Intelligencer (Philadelphia)

Genius of Universal Emancipation (Baltimore and Philadelphia)

Green Mountain Spring (Brattleboro, Vt.)

Hampshire Gazette (Northampton, Mass.)

Herald of Freedom (New York)

Hudson River Chronicle (Ossining, N.Y.)

Jamestown Journal (Jamestown, N.Y.)

Liberator (Boston)

National Anti-Slavery Standard (New York)

National Courier

National Enquirer and Constitutional Advocate of Universal Liberty (Philadelphia)

National Era (Washington, D.C.)

National Reformer (Philadelphia)

New Bedford Daily Captain (New Bedford, Mass.)

New Bedford Mercury (New Bedford, Mass.)

New-Hampshire Patriot (Concord, N.H.)

Newport Mercury (Newport, R.I.)

New York Courier

New York Daily Express

New-Yorker

New York Evangelist

New York Evening Post

New York Journal of Commerce

New York Spectator

New York Star

New York Sun

New York Times

North Star (Rochester, N.Y.)

Northampton Democrat (Northampton, Mass.)

Northern Christian Advocate (Auburn, N.Y.)

Northern Journal (Lowville, N.Y.)

Pennsylvania Freeman (Philadelphia)

Philadelphia Inquirer

Philanthropist (Mount Pleasant, Ohio)

Pittsfield Sun (Pittsfield, Mass.)

Religious Messenger (Norwich, Conn.)

Rhode Island Republican (Newport, R.I.)

Rights of All (New York)

Rochester Daily Democrat (Rochester, N.Y.)

Union Herald (Cazenovia, N.Y.)

Water-Cure Journal and Teacher (New York)

Weekly Advocate (New York)

Western Advocate (Lyons, N.Y.)

Western Argus (Lyons, N.Y.)

Wisconsin Free Democrat (Milwaukee)

Working Man's Advocate (New York)

Zion's Watchman (New York)

SECONDARY SOURCES

Abzug, Robert H. *Cosmos Crumbling: American Reform and the Religious Imagination.* New York: Oxford University Press, 1994.

Alexander, Leslie. *African or American: Black Identity and Political Activism in New York City, 1784–1861.* Urbana: University of Illinois Press, 2008.

Andrews, Dee. *The Methodists and Revolutionary America: The Shaping of Evangelical Culture.* Princeton: Princeton University Press, 2000.

Bacon, Jacqueline. *Freedom's Journal: The First African American Newspaper.* Lanham: Lexington Books, 2007.

Bacon, Margaret Hope. *But One Race: The Life of Robert Purvis.* Albany: State University of New York Press, 2007.

Bay, Mia. *The White Image in the Black Mind: African-American Ideas about White People, 1830–1925.* New York: Oxford University Press, 2000.

Berlin, Ira, and Leslie M. Harris, eds. *Slavery in New York.* New York: New Press with the New-York Historical Society, 2005.

Bernard, Fred V. "The Question of Race in Moby Dick." *Massachusetts Review* 45, no. 3 (Autumn 2002): 384–404.

Beveridge, Laura. "The Water-Cure Days Coping with Cultural Change at Wesselhoeft's Hydropathic Establishment in Brattleboro, Vermont." M.A. thesis, University of Vermont, 1994.

Blackett, R. M. J. *Beating against the Barriers: The Lives of Six Nineteenth-Century Afro-Americans.* Baton Rouge: Louisiana State University Press, 1986.

———. *Building an Antislavery Wall: Black Americans in the Atlantic Abolitionist Movement, 1830–1860.* Baton Rouge: Louisiana State University Press, 1983.

Blackmar, Elizabeth. *Manhattan for Rent, 1785–1850.* Ithaca, N.Y.: Cornell University Press, 1989.

Blanchard, Michael D. "The Politics of Abolition in Northampton." *Historical Journal of Massachusetts* 19, no. 2 (Summer 1991): 175–96.

Blight, David W., ed. *Passages to Freedom: The Underground Railroad in History and Memory.* Washington, D.C.: Smithsonian Books in association with the National Underground Railroad Freedom Center, Cincinnati, Ohio, 2004.

Bolster, W. Jeffrey. *Black Jacks: African American Seamen in the Age of Sail.* Cambridge, Mass.: Harvard University Press, 1997.

Bordewich, Fergus M. *Bound for Canaan: The Underground Railroad and the War for the Soul of America.* New York: Amistad/HarperCollins, 2005.

Boylan, Anne. *The Origins of Women's Activism: New York and Boston, 1797–1840.* Chapel Hill: University of North Carolina Press, 2002.

———. *Sunday School: The Formation of an American Institution, 1790–1880.* New Haven, Conn.: Yale University Press, 1988.

Brink, Carol. *Harps in the Wind: The Story of the Singing Hutchinsons.* New York: Macmillan, 1947.

Brown, Barbara W., and James M. Rose, comp. *Black Roots in Southeastern Connecticut, 1650–1900.* Detroit, Mich.: Gale Research Company, 1980.

Bruce, Dickson D., Jr. *The Origins of African American Literature, 1680–1865.* Charlottesville: University of Virginia Press, 2001.

Budney, Stephen P. *William Jay: Abolitionist and Anticolonialist.* Westport, Conn.: Praeger, 2005.

Bullock, Penelope. *The Afro-American Periodical Press, 1838–1909.* Baton Rouge: Louisiana State University Press, 1981.

Burin, Eric. *Slavery and the Peculiar Institution: A History of the American Colonization Society.* Gainesville: University Press of Florida, 2005.

Burrows, Edwin G., and Mike Wallace. *Gotham: A History of New York City to 1898.* New York: Oxford University Press, 1999.

Calarco, Tom. *The Underground Railroad in the Adirondack Region.* Jefferson, N.C.: McFarland, 2004.

Campbell, Stanley W. *The Slave Catchers: Enforcement of the Fugitive Slave Law, 1850–1860.* Chapel Hill: University of North Carolina Press, 1970.

Carter, Ralph D. "Black American or African: The Response of New York City Blacks to African Colonization, 1817–1841." Ph.D. diss., Clark University, 1974.

Cayleff, Susan E. *Wash and Be Healed: The Water-Cure Movement and Women's Health.* Philadelphia: Temple University Press, 1987.

Cecelski, David S. *The Waterman's Song: Slavery and Freedom in Maritime North Carolina.* Chapel Hill: University of North Carolina Press, 2001.

Chudacoff, Howard P. *The Age of the Batchelor: Creating an American Subculture.* Princeton: Princeton University Press, 1999.

Clark, Charles E. *The Public Prints: The Newspaper in Anglo-American Culture, 1665–1740.* New York: Oxford University Press, 1994.

Clark, Christopher. *The Communitarian Moment: The Radical Challenge of the Northampton Association.* Ithaca, N.Y.: Cornell University Press, 1995.

———. *The Roots of Rural Capitalism: Western Massachusetts, 1780–1860.* Ithaca, N.Y.: Cornell University Press, 1990.

Clifford, Deborah Pickman. *Crusader for Freedom: A Life of Lydia Maria Child.* Boston: Beacon Press, 1992.

Conforti, Joseph A. *Samuel Hopkins and the New Divinity Movement.* Washington, D.C.: Christian College Consortium, 1981.

Crowley, John W. "Slaves to the Bottle: Gough's Autobiography and Douglass'

Narrative." In David S. Reynolds and Debra J. Rosenthal, eds., *The Serpent in the Cup: Temperance in American Literature*, 115–36. Amherst: University of Massachusetts Press, 1996.

Curry, Leonard. *The Free Black in Urban America, 1800–1850*. Chicago: University of Chicago Press, 1981.

Dabel, Jane. *A Respectable Woman: The Public Roles of African American Women in 19th Century New York*. New York: New York University Press, 2008.

Dain, Bruce. *A Hideous Monster of the Mind: American Race Theory in the Early Republic*. Cambridge, Mass.: Harvard University Press, 2002.

Davis, Hugh. *Joshua Leavitt: Evangelical Abolitionist*. Baton Rouge: Louisiana State University Press, 1990.

DeLombard, Jeannine Marie. *Slavery on Trial: Law, Abolitionism, and Print Culture*. Chapel Hill: University of North Carolina Press, 2007.

Dick, Robert C. *Black Protest: Issues and Tactics*. Westport, Conn.: Greenwood Press, 1974.

Donegan, Jane B. *"Hydropathic Highway to Health": Women and Water-Cure in Antebellum America*. Westport, Conn.: Greenwood Press, 1986.

Dorsey, Bruce. *Reforming Men and Women: Gender in the Antebellum City*. Ithaca, N.Y.: Cornell University Press, 2002.

Duffy, John. *A History of Public Health in New York City, 1625–1866*. New York: Russell Sage Foundation, 1968.

Earle, Jonathan. *Jacksonian Antislavery and the Politics of Free Soil, 1824–1854*. Chapel Hill: University of North Carolina Press, 2004.

Ernest, John. *Liberation Historiography: African American Writers and the Challenge of History, 1794–1861*. Chapel Hill: University of North Carolina Press, 2004.

Finkelman, Paul. *An Imperfect Union: Slavery, Federalism, and Comity*. Chapel Hill: University of North Carolina Press, 1981.

———. "The Protection of Black Rights in Seward's New York." *Civil War History* 36, no. 3 (1988): 211–34.

Finseth, Ian Frederick. *Shades of Green: Visions of Nature in the Literature of American Slavery, 1770–1860*. Athens: University of Georgia Press, 2009.

Foner, Philip. *Business and Slavery: The New York Merchants and the Irrepressible Conflict*. Chapel Hill: University of North Carolina Press, 1941.

Forman, Shepard, ed. *Diagnosing America: Anthropology and Public Engagement*. Ann Arbor: University of Michigan Press, 1994.

Franklin, John Hope. *A Southern Odyssey: Travelers in the Antebellum North*. Baton Rouge: Louisiana State University Press, 1976.

Franklin, John Hope, and Loren Schweninger. *Runaway Slaves: Rebels on the Plantation*. New York: Oxford University Press, 1999.

Friedman, Lawrence. *Gregarious Saints: Self and Community in American Abolitionism, 1830–1870*. New York: Cambridge University Press, 1982.

Frothingham, Octavius Brooks. *Gerrit Smith, a Biography*. New York: G. P. Putnam's Sons, 1878.

Gaffney, Paul. "Coloring Utopia: the African American Presence in the Northampton Association of Education and Industry." In Christopher Clark and Kerry W. Buckley, eds., *Letters from an American Utopia*, 301–53. Amherst: University of Massachusetts Press, 2004.

Gara, Larry. *The Liberty Line: The Legend of the Underground Railroad*. Lexington: University Press of Kentucky, 1961.

Gellman, David N. *Emancipating New York: The Politics of Slavery and Freedom, 1777–1827*. Baton Rouge: Louisiana State University Press, 2006.

Gilfoyle, Timothy. *City of Eros: New York City, Prostitution, and the Commercialization of Sex, 1790–1920*. New York: W. W. Norton, 1992.

Gilje, Paul. *The Road to Mobocracy: Popular Disorder in New York City, 1763–1834*. Chapel Hill: University of North Carolina Press for the Institute of Early American History and Culture, 1987.

Gillis, John R. *Youth and History: Tradition and Change in European Age Relations, 1770–Present*. New York: Academic Press, 1981.

Goodheart, Lawrence B. *Abolitionist, Actuary, Atheist: Elizur Wright and the Reform Impulse*. Kent, Ohio: Kent State University Press, 1990.

———. "The Chronicles of Kidnapping in New York: Resistance to the Fugitive Slave Law, 1834–1835." *Afro-Americans in New York Life and History* 8, no. 1 (January 1984): 7–17.

Goodman, Paul. *Of One Blood: Abolitionism and the Origins of Racial Equality*. Berkeley: University of California Press, 1998.

Greene, Lorenzo Johnston. *The Negro in Colonial New England*. New York: Columbia University Press, 1942.

Grimsted, David. *American Mobbing, 1828–1861: Toward Civil War*. New York: Oxford University Press, 1998.

Grover, Kathryn. *The Fugitive's Gibraltar: Escaping Slaves and Abolitionism in New Bedford, Massachusetts*. Amherst: University of Massachusetts Press, 2001.

Hahn, Steven. *The Political Worlds of Slavery and Freedom*. Cambridge, Mass.: Harvard University Press, 2009.

Halttunen, Karen, and Lewis Perry, eds. *Moral Problems in American Life: New Perspectives in Cultural History*. Ithaca, N.Y.: Cornell University Press, 1998.

Hansen, Debra Gold. *Strained Sisterhood: Gender and Class in the Boston Female Anti-Slavery Society*. Amherst: University of Massachusetts Press, 1993.

Hardman, Keith J. *Charles Grandison Finney, 1792–1875: Revivalist and Reformer*. Syracuse: Syracuse University Press, 1987.

Harris, Leslie M. *In the Shadow of Slavery: African Americans in New York City, 1626–1863*. Chicago: University of Chicago Press, 2003.

Harrold, Stanley. *The Abolitionists and the South, 1831–1861*. Lexington: University Press of Kentucky, 1995.

———. "On the Borders of Slavery and Race: Charles T. Torrey and the Underground Railroad." *Journal of the Early Republic* 20, no. 2 (Summer 2000): 273–92.

Headley, Russell. *The History of Orange County, New York*. Middletown, N.Y.: Van Dusen and Elms, 1908.

Henderson, Alice Hatcher. "The History of the New York State Anti-Slavery Society." Ph.D. diss., University of Michigan, 1963.

Hinks, Peter P. *To Awake My Afflicted Brethren: David Walker and the Problem of Antebellum Slave Resistance*. University Park: Pennsylvania State University Press, 1997.

Bibliography

Hodges, Graham Russell. *Root and Branch: African Americans in New York and East Jersey, 1613–1863*. Chapel Hill: University of North Carolina Press, 1999.

———. *Slavery and Freedom in the Rural North: African Americans in Monmouth County, New Jersey, 1660–1865*. Madison: Madison House Publishers, 1997.

———. *Slavery, Freedom and Culture among Early American Workers*. Armonk, N.Y.: M. E. Sharpe, 1998.

Horton, James Oliver. *Free People of Color: Inside the African American Community*. Washington, D.C.: Smithsonian Institution Press, 1993.

Horton, James Oliver, and Lois E. Horton. *Black Bostonians: Family Life and Community Struggle in the Antebellum North*. New York: Holmes & Meier, 1979.

———. *In Hope of Liberty: Culture, Community and Protest among Northern Free Blacks, 1700–1860*. New York: Oxford University Press, 1997.

Howard, Warren S. *American Slavers and the Federal Law, 1837–1862*. Berkeley: University of California Press, 1963.

Howe, Daniel Walker. *What Hath God Wrought: The Transformation of America, 1815–1848*. New York: Oxford University Press, 2007.

Huttner, Sidney F., and Elizabeth Stege, comp. *A Register of Artists Engravers, Booksellers Bookbinders, Printers and Publishers in New York City, 1821–42*. New York: Bibliographic Society of America, 1993.

Hyde, Burrell W. "Reminiscences of Bean Hill, Norwich." *Connecticut Quarterly* 3 (1897): 300.

Jacobs, Donald M., ed. *Courage and Conscience: Black and White Abolitionists in Boston*. Bloomington: Indiana University Press for the Boston Athenaeum, 1993.

Jacobs, Donald M., et al., eds. *Antebellum Black Newspapers*. Westport, Conn.: Greenwood Press, 1976.

Jeffrey, Julie Roy. *Abolitionists Remember: Antislavery Autobiographies and the Unfinished Work of Emancipation*. Chapel Hill: University of North Carolina Press, 2008.

———. *The Great Silent Army of Abolitionism: Ordinary Women in the Antislavery Movement*. Chapel Hill: University of North Carolina Press, 1998.

Jentz, John Barkley. "Artisans, Evangelicals, and the City: A Social History of Abolition and Labor Reform in Jacksonian New York." Ph.D. diss., City University of New York, 1977.

Johnson, Reinhard O. *The Liberty Party, 1840–1848: Antislavery Third-Party Politics in the United States*. Baton Rouge: Louisiana State University Press, 2009.

Jones, Martha S. *All Bound Up Together: The Woman Question in African American Public Culture, 1830–1900*. Chapel Hill: University of North Carolina Press, 2007.

Jordan, Ryan. *Slavery and the Meetinghouse: The Quakers and the Abolitionist Dilemma, 1820–1865*. Bloomington: Indiana University Press, 2007.

Jordan, Winthrop D. *White over Black: American Attitudes toward the Negro, 1550–1812*. Chapel Hill: University of North Carolina Press, 1968.

Kachun, Mitch. *Festivals of Freedom: Memory and Meaning in African American Emancipation Celebrations, 1808–1915*. Amherst: University of Massachusetts Press, 2003.

Kaplan, Michael. "The World of the B'hoys: Urban Violence and the Political Culture of Antebellum New York City, 1825–1860." Ph.D. diss., New York University, 1996.

Karcher, Carolyn L. *The First Woman in the Republic: A Cultural Biography of Lydia Maria Child*. Durham, N.C.: Duke University Press, 1994.

Kerr-Ritchie, J. R. *Rites of August First: Emancipation Day in the Black Atlantic World*. Baton Rouge: Louisiana State University Press, 2007.

Kilde, Jeanne Halgren. *When Church Became Theatre: The Transformation of Evangelical Architecture and Worship in Nineteenth-Century America*. New York: Oxford University Press, 2002.

Kraditor, Aileen S. *Means and Ends in American Abolitionism: Garrison and His Critics on Strategy and Tactics, 1834–1850*. New York: Pantheon, 1969.

Kramer, Lloyd. *Lafayette in Two Worlds: Public Cultures and Personal Identities in an Age of Revolutions*. Chapel Hill: University of North Carolina Press, 1996.

Kring, Walter Donald. *Liberals among the Orthodox: Unitarian Beginnings in New York City, 1819–1839*. Boston: Beacon Press, 1974.

Laurie, Bruce. *Beyond Garrison: Antislavery and Social Reform*. New York: Cambridge University Press, 2005.

Lemire, Elise. *"Miscegenation": Making Race in America*. Philadelphia: University of Pennsylvania Press, 2002.

Loggins, Vernon. *The Negro Author: His Development in America*. New York: Columbia University Press, 1931.

Luckett, Judith Ann Blodgett. "Protest, Advancement and Identity: Organizational Strategies of Northern Free Blacks, 1830–1860." Ph.D. diss., Johns Hopkins University Press, 1993.

Mabee, Carleton. *Black Education in New York State: From Colonial to Modern Times*. Syracuse: Syracuse University Press, 1979.

———. *Black Freedom: The Nonviolent Abolitionists from 1830 through the Civil War*. New York: Macmillan, 1970.

Mabee, Carleton, with Susan Mabee Newhouse. *Sojourner Truth — Slave, Prophet, Legend*. New York: New York University Press, 1993.

Magdol, Edward. "A Window on the Abolitionist Constituency: Antislavery Petitions, 1836–1839." In Alan M. Kraut, ed., *Crusaders and Compromisers: Essays on the Relationship of the Antislavery Struggle to the Antebellum Party System*, 45–70. Westport, Conn.: Greenwood Press, 1987.

Martin, Waldo, Jr. *The Mind of Frederick Douglass*. Chapel Hill: University of North Carolina Press, 1984.

Mayer, Henry. *All on Fire: William Lloyd Garrison and the Abolition of Slavery*. New York: St. Martin's Press, 1998.

McBee, Alice Eaton. *From Utopia to Florence: The Story of a Transcendentalist Community in Northampton, Mass., 1830–1852*. 2nd ed. Northampton: Smith College Studies in History, 1947.

McCarthy, Timothy Patrick, and John Stauffer, eds. *Prophets of Protest: Reconsidering the History of American Abolitionism*. New York: New Press, 2006.

McFeeley, William S. *Frederick Douglass*. New York: W. W. Norton, 1991.

McHenry, Elizabeth. *Forgotten Readers: Recovering the Lost History of African American Literary Societies*. Durham, N.C.: Duke University Press, 2002.

McKivigan, John R. *The War against Proslavery Religion: Abolitionism and the Northern Churches, 1830–1865*. Ithaca, N.Y.: Cornell University Press, 1984.

McKivigan, John R., and Stanley Harrold. *Antislavery Violence: Sectional, Racial, and Cultural Conflict in Antebellum America*. Knoxville: University of Tennessee Press, 1999.

McKivigan, John R., and Mitchell Snay, eds. *Religion and the Antebellum Debate over Slavery*. Athens: University of Georgia Press, 1998.

McManus, Edgar J. *Black Bondage in the North*. Syracuse, N.Y.: Syracuse University Press, 1973.

Melish, Joanne Pope. *Disowning Slavery: Gradual Emancipation and "Race" in New England, 1780–1860*. Ithaca, N.Y.: Cornell University Press, 1998.

Mintz, Steven, and John Stauffer, eds. *The Problem of Evil: Slavery, Freedom, and the Ambiguities of American Reform*. Amherst: University of Massachusetts Press, 2007.

Mitchell, William M. *The Under-Ground Railroad*. London: n.p., 1860.

Morris, Thomas D. *Free Men All: The Personal Liberty Laws of the North, 1780–1861*. Baltimore: Johns Hopkins University Press, 1974.

Mulderink, Earl P., III. "'The Whole Town Is Ringing with It': Slave Kidnapping Charges against Nathan Johnson of New Bedford, Massachusetts, 1839." *New England Quarterly* 61, no. 3 (September 1988): 341–57.

Muraskin, William Alan. *Middle-Class Blacks in a White Society: Prince Hall Freemasonry in America*. Berkeley: University of California Press, 1975.

Myers, John Lytle. "The Agency System of the Anti-Slavery Movement, 1832–1837, and Its Antecedents in Other Benevolent and Reform Societies." Ph.D. diss., University of Michigan, 1960.

Nash, Gary B. *Forging Freedom: The Formation of Philadelphia's Black Community, 1720–1840*. Cambridge, Mass.: Harvard University Press, 1988.

Newman, Richard S. "Faith in the Ballot: Black Shadow Politics in the Antebellum North." *Common-Place* 9, no. 1 (October 2008): unpaginated.

———. *Freedom's Prophet: Bishop Richard Allen, the AME Church, and the Black Founding Fathers*. New York: New York University Press, 2008.

———. *The Transformation of American Abolitionism: Fighting Slavery in the Early Republic*. Chapel Hill: University of North Carolina Press, 2002.

Nord, David Paul. "The Evangelical Origins of Mass Media in America, 1815–1835." *Journalism Monographs* 88 (1984). Columbia, S.C.

Nuermberger, Ruth Ketring. *The Free Produce Movement: A Quaker Protest against Slavery*. Durham, N.C.: Duke University Press, 1942.

Oakes, James. *The Radical and the Republican: Frederick Douglass, Abraham Lincoln and the Triumph of Antislavery Politics*. New York: W. W. Norton, 2007.

Obadele-Starks, Ernest. *Freebooters and Smugglers: The Foreign Slave Trade in the United States after 1808*. Fayetteville: University of Arkansas Press, 2007.

Orcutt, Samuel. *History of the Towns of New Milford and Bridgewater, Connecticut, 1703–1882*. Hartford: Press of the Case, Lockwood, and Brainard Company, 1882.

Painter, Nell Irvin. *Sojourner Truth: A Life, A Symbol*. New York: W. W. Norton, 1996.

Pasley, Jeffrey L., Andrew Robertson, and David Waldstreicher. *Beyond the Founders: New Approaches to the Political History of the Early American Republic*. Chapel Hill: University of North Carolina Press, 2004.

Pease, Jane H., and William D. Pease. "Black Power: The Debate in 1840." *Phylon* 29, no. 1 (1968): 19–26.

——. *They Who Would Be Free: Blacks' Search for Freedom*. New York: Athenaeum, 1974.

Perry, Lewis. *Radical Abolitionism: Anarchy and the Government of God in Antislavery Thought*. Ithaca, N.Y.: Cornell University Press, 1973.

Perry, Lewis, and Michael Fellman, eds. *Antislavery Reconsidered: New Perspectives on the Abolitionists*. Baton Rouge: Louisiana State University Press, 1979.

Pessen, Edward. *Riches, Class, and Power before the Civil War*. Lexington: D. C. Heath, 1973.

Peterson, Carla L. *"Doers of the Word": African-American Women Speakers and Writers in the North (1830–1880)*. New York: Oxford University Press, 1995.

Piersen, William D. *Black Yankees: The Development of an Afro-American Subculture in Eighteenth-Century New England*. Amherst: University of Massachusetts Press, 1988.

Porter, Dorothy B. "David Ruggles, an Apostle of Human Rights." *Journal of Negro History* 23 (1943): 23–51.

——. "David Ruggles, 1810–1849, Hydropathic Practitioner." *Journal of the National Medical Association* 49, no. 1 (January 1957): 67–73; 49, no. 2 (March 1957): 130–34.

——. "The Organized Educational Activities of Negro Literary Societies, 1828–1846." *Journal of Negro Education* 5, no. 4 (October 1936): 555–76.

Porter, Dorothy, and Edwin C. Rozwenc. "The Water Cures." In Lawrence E. Wikander, ed., *The Northampton Book: Chapters from 300 Years in the Life of a New England Town, 1654–1954*, 121–27. Northampton, Mass.: The Tercentenary Committee, 1954.

Quarles, Benjamin. "Antebellum Free Blacks and the 'Spirit of '76.'" *Journal of Negro History* 61, no. 3 (July 1976): 229–42.

——. *Black Abolitionists*. New York: Oxford University Press, 1969.

——. *Frederick Douglass*. Washington, D.C.: Associated Publishers, 1948.

——. *The Negro in the American Revolution*. Chapel Hill: University of North Carolina Press, 1961.

Rael, Patrick. *Black Identity and Black Protest in the Antebellum North*. Chapel Hill: University of North Carolina Press, 2002.

——, ed. *African-American Activism before the Civil War*. New York: Routledge, 2008.

Ratner, Lorman. *Powder Keg: Northern Opposition to the Antislavery Movement, 1831–1840*. New York: Basic Books, 1968.

Rhodes, Jane. *Mary Shad Cary: The Black Press and Protest in the Nineteenth Century*. Bloomington: Indiana University Press, 1998.

Richards, Leonard L. *"Gentlemen of Property and Standing": Anti-Abolition Mobs in Jacksonian America*. New York: Oxford University Press, 1970.

——. *The Slave Power: The Free North and Southern Domination, 1780–1860*. Baton Rouge: Louisiana State University Press, 2000.

Richardson, Marilyn, ed. *Maria W. Stewart, America's First Black Woman Political Writer: Essays and Speeches*. Bloomington: Indiana University Press, 1987.

Roberts, Brian. "'Slavery Would Have Died of That Music': The Hutchinson Family Singers and the Rise of Popular-Culture Abolitionism in Early Antebellum-Era America, 1842–1850." *Proceedings of the American Antiquarian Society* 114 (2006): 301–68.

Robinson, Donald L. *Slavery in the Structure of American Politics, 1765–1820*. New York: Harcourt, Brace Jovanovich, 1971.

Ruchames, Louis. "Jim Crow Railroads in Massachusetts." *American Quarterly* 8, no. 1
(Spring 1956): 61–75.
Rucker, Walter C. *The River Flows On: Black Resistance, Culture, and Identity Formation in
Early America*. Baton Rouge: Louisiana State University Press, 2006.
Rumonds, Richard-Gabriel. *Printing on the Iron Handpress*. London: Oak Knoll Press &
the British Library, 1998.
Ryan, Mary P. *Civic Wars: Democracy and Public Life in the American City during the
Nineteenth Century*. Berkeley: University of California Press, 1997.
Saillant, John. *Black Puritan, Black Republican: The Life and Times of Lemuel Haynes, 1753–
1833*. New York: Oxford University Press, 2003.
Salerno, Beth A. *Sister Societies: Women's Antislavery Organizations in Antebellum America*.
DeKalb: Northern Illinois Press, 2005.
Salvatore, Nick. *We All Got Freedom: The Memory Books of Amos Webber*. New York:
Random House, 1996.
Scherzer, Kenneth A. *The Unbounded Community: Neighborhood Life and Social Structure in
New York City, 1830–1875*. Durham, N.C.: Duke University Press, 1993.
Scott, Donald M. *From Office to Profession: The New England Ministry, 1750–1850*.
Philadelphia: University of Pennsylvania Press, 1978.
Seifman, Eli. "A History of the New-York State Colonization Society." Ph.D. diss., New
York University, 1965.
Sernett, Milton C. *North Star Country: Upstate New York and the Crusade for African
American Freedom*. Syracuse: Syracuse University Press, 2002.
Sharts, Elizabeth. *Land o' Goshen Then and Now*. Goshen, N.Y.: Bookmill, 1960.
Sheffield, Charles A., ed. *The History of Florence, Massachusetts including a Complete Account
of the Northampton Association of Education and Industry*. Florence: Published by the
Editor, 1895.
Sherman, Joan R. *Invisible Poets: Afro-Americans of the Nineteenth Century*. 2nd ed. Urbana:
University of Illinois Press, 1989.
Siebert, Wilbur H. *The Underground Railroad from Slavery to Freedom*. New York:
Macmillan, 1899.
Smedley, R. G. *History of the Underground Railroad in Chester and Neighboring Counties of
Pennsylvania*. Lancaster: Printed at the Office of the Journal, 1883.
Sorin, Gerald. *The New York Abolitionists: A Case Study in Political Radicalism*. Westport,
Conn.: Greenwood Press, 1971.
Spann, Edward K. *Ideals and Politics: New York Intellectuals and Liberal Democracy, 1820–
1880*. Albany: State University of New York Press, 1972.
Stauffer, John. *The Black Hearts of Men: Radical Abolitionists and the Transformation of Race*.
Cambridge, Mass.: Harvard University Press, 2002.
———. *Giants: The Parallel Lives of Frederick Douglass and Abraham Lincoln*. New York:
Twelve, 2008.
Sterling, Dorothy. *Ahead of Her Time: Abby Kelley and the Politics of Antislavery*. New York:
W. W. Norton, 1991.
Stewart, James Brewer. *Abolitionist Politics and the Coming of the Civil War*. Amherst:
University of Massachusetts Press, 2008.

————. *Holy Warriors: The Abolitionists and American Slavery*. Rev. ed. New York: Hill and Wang, 1996.

————. "Reconsidering the Abolitionists in an Age of Fundamentalist Politics." *Journal of the Early Republic* 26 (Spring 2006): 1–23.

————, ed. *William Lloyd Garrison at Two Hundred: History, Legacy, Memory*. New Haven: Yale University Press, 2008.

Still, Bayrd. *Mirror for Gotham: New York as Seen by Contemporaries from Dutch Days to the Present*. New York: New York University Press, 1956.

Stott, Richard B. *Workers in the Metropolis: Class, Ethnicity, and Youth in Antebellum New York City*. Ithaca, N.Y: Cornell University Press, 1990.

Strong, Douglas M. *Perfectionist Politics: Abolitionism and the Religious Tensions of American Democracy*. Syracuse: Syracuse University Press, 1999.

Strother, Horatio. *The Underground Railroad in Connecticut*. Middletown, Conn.: Wesleyan University Press, 1962.

Sweet, John Wood. *Bodies Politic: Negotiating Race in the American North, 1730–1830*. Baltimore: Johns Hopkins University Press, 2003.

Swift, David E. *Black Prophets of Justice: Activist Clergy before the Civil War*. Baton Rouge: Louisiana State University Press, 1989.

Taylor, Nikki M. *Frontiers of Freedom: Cincinnati's Black Community, 1802–1868*. Athens: Ohio University Press, 2005.

Terry, Esther. *Sojourner Truth: The Person Behind the Libyan Sybil, an Essay by Esther Terry with a Memoir by Frederick Douglass, What I Found at the Northampton Association*. N.p.: Printed at the Oxbow Press for the *Massachusetts Review*, 1985.

Thompson, George, Jr. *A Documentary History of the African Theater*. Evanston, Ill.: Northwestern University Press, 1998.

Thornton, Tamara Platkins. *Handwriting in America: A Cultural History*. New Haven, Conn.: Yale University Press, 1996.

Townsend, Craig D. *Faith in Their Own Color: Black Episcopalians in Antebellum New York City*. New York: Columbia University Press, 2005.

Trouillot, Michel-Rolph. *Silencing the Past: Power and the Production of History*. Boston: Beacon Press, 1995.

Walker, Peter F. *Moral Choices: Memory, Desire, and Imagination in Nineteenth-Century American Abolition*. Baton Rouge: Louisiana State University Press, 1978.

Walls, William J. *The African Methodist Episcopal Church*. Charlotte: A.M.E. Zion Publishing House, 1974.

Washington, Margaret. *Sojourner Truth's America*. Urbana: University of Illinois Press, 2009.

Weinbaum, Paul A. *Mobs and Demagogues: The New York Response to Collective Violence in the Early Nineteenth Century*. Ann Arbor: UMI Press, 1979.

Wellman, Judith. "'Born a Slave, Lived a Freeman, Died in the Lord': Discovering the Underground Railroad in New York State." Unpublished manuscript for the Underground Railroad Heritage Trail, a program of the New York State Office of Parks Recreation and Historic Preservation, 2009.

Wesley, Charles H. "The Negroes of New York in the Emancipation Movement." *Journal of Negro History* 24 (1939): 65–104.

White, David O. *Connecticut's Black Soldiers, 1775–1783*. Chester: Pequot Press, 1973.

White, Shane. *Stories of Freedom in Black New York*. Cambridge, Mass.: Harvard University Press, 2002.

White, Shane, and Graham White. *Stylin'*. Ithaca, N.Y.: Cornell University Press, 1998.

Whitman, T. Steven. *Challenging Slavery in the Chesapeake: Black and White Resistance to Human Bondage, 1775–1865*. Baltimore: Maryland Historical Society, 2007.

Wiecek, William. *The Sources of Antislavery Constitutionalism in America, 1760–1848*. Ithaca, N.Y.: Cornell University Press, 1977.

Wigger, John. *Taking Heaven by Storm: Methodism and the Rise of Popular Christianity in America*. New York: Oxford University Press, 1998.

Wilder, Craig Steven. *In the Company of Black Men: The African Influence on African American Culture in New York City*. New York: New York University Press, 2001.

Wilentz, Sean. *Chants Democratic: New York City and the Rise of the American Working Class*. New York: Oxford University Press, 1984.

———. *The Rise of American Democracy: From Jefferson to Lincoln*. New York: W. W. Norton, 2005.

Williams, George Washington. *History of the Negro Race in America from 1619–1880*. 2 vols. New York: G. P. Putnam's Sons, 1883.

Wilson, Carol. *Freedom at Risk: The Kidnapping of Free Blacks in America, 1780–1865*. Lexington: University Press of Kentucky, 1994.

Winch, Julie. *A Gentleman of Color: The Life of James Forten*. New York: Oxford University Press, 2002.

Wyatt-Brown, Bertram. "The Abolitionists' Postal Campaign of 1835." *Journal of Negro History* 50, no. 4 (October 1965): 227–38.

———. *Lewis Tappan and the Evangelical War against Slavery*. Cleveland: Press of Western Reserve University, 1969.

Yang, Guocun. "From Slavery to Emancipation: The African Americans of Connecticut, 1690s–1820s." Ph.D. diss., University of Connecticut, 1999.

Yeh, Wen-Hsin. *Shanghai Splendor: Economic Sentiments and the Making of Modern China, 1843–1949*. Berkeley: University of California Press, 2007.

Yellin, Jean Fagin, and John C. Van Horne, eds. *The Abolitionist Sisterhood: Women's Political Culture in Antebellum America*. Ithaca, N.Y.: Cornell University Press published in cooperation with the Library Company of Philadelphia, 1994.

Zaeske, Susan. *Signatures of Citizenship: Petitioning, Antislavery and Women's Political Identity*. Chapel Hill: University of North Carolina Press, 2003.

Zilversmit, Arthur. *The First Emancipation: The Abolition of Slavery in the North*. Chicago: University of Chicago Press, 1967.

ACKNOWLEDGMENTS

Many individuals and institutions enabled and pushed me to complete this book. My interest in Ruggles developed during the writing of my book, *Root and Branch: African Americans in New York and East Jersey, 1613–1883*, published by the University of North Carolina Press in 1999. I am grateful to my original editor at UNC Press, Lewis Bateman, and to his successor, Chuck Grench, and his assistant, Katy O'Brien, for their patience and trust in this project.

The American Antiquarian Society generously gave me a short-term fellowship in 1999 that allowed me to use its invaluable collection of newspapers and manuscripts. The staff at the society helped me immeasurably on that and subsequent visits. I received helpful support from the staffs at the New York Public Library, the Boston Public Library, the Massachusetts Historical Society, the New Bedford Public Library, the Boston Athenaeum, the Library of Congress, the National Archives branches in New York City and Waltham, and the Bird Library at Syracuse University. As usual, Ann Ackerson, the interlibrary loan librarian at Case Library, Colgate University, cheerfully found numerous volumes for me. I am grateful as well to the Faculty Research Council at Colgate for several years of small grants and to the stipends provided by the George Dorland Langdon, Jr. Professorship at Colgate. The Faculty Research Council provided a publication grant to help defray the production costs of this book. Kerry W. Buckley of the Historic Northampton Foundation did me a great service by sending me an advance copy of the excellent edition of the Stetson Papers that Christopher Clark and he executed, which has now been published by the University of Massachusetts Press. Chris also helped with leads about the Northampton Association. I owe an immense debt to the Northampton David Ruggles group, headed by Steve Strimer of Florence, Massachusetts. This book is far better because of Steve's help and friendship. Also of great help and encouragement were Paul Gaffney and Linda

Ziegenbein. Allow me to extend a tip of the hat to them for creating the David Ruggles Center in Northampton.

Numerous friends supplied me with leads and information. Colgate students Nancy Ng and Will Hilsman helped with research. Dale Plummer and Vic Butsch in Norwich, Connecticut, helped track down elusive documents. Scholars who helped create this manuscript include Roy Finkenbine, C. Peter Ripley, Don Wright, Shane White, Richard S. Newman, Paul Gilje, Howard Rock, Robert Breckenridge, Carl Prince, Fergus Bordewich, and Judith Wellman. At the American Antiquarian Society, I benefited from the comments and suggestions of Leslie Harris, Andy Burstein and Nancy Isenberg, and Matt Dennis and Elizabeth Ries. Peter Hinks read the manuscript with care and shared with me a number of his invigorating essays. Peter Ripley and Richard Newman, readers for the University of North Carolina Press, are to be commended for their fine criticisms. I am very grateful to Richard Brackett, Patricia Cline Cohen, David Gellman, Stanley Harrold, and Stacey Robertson for their thorough commentary on later drafts of the manuscript. Special thanks are owed to Carl Prince, the best mentor a scholar can have. Douglas Egerton has continued to be a great friend and supporter over the years, and I am particularly grateful to him for his constant support of this project. Fergus Bordewich, a good friend and Ruggles enthusiast, pushed me to finish the book. My late parents, Reverend Graham R. Hodges and Elsie Russell Hodges, are owed never-ending thanks. I miss them every day. I owe so much to my wife, Gao Yunxiang, for her loving support. Now she has given me two wonderful sons, Graham Zhen Gao-Hodges and Russell Du Gao-Hodges, and my life is truly blessed.

INDEX

Index

Index

Index

Mars, James, 24, 157

Maryland, 107, 124; fugitives from, 106–7, 124, 132, 133. *See also* Self-emancipated slaves

Massachusetts, 20, 25, 56

May, Samuel J., 55, 77, 171, 202

McClennan, Dr., 144

McDougall, Rev. John D., 81

Means, Dr. A., 193

Medical College of Georgia, 193

Memoir of William Wilberforce (Price), 67–68

Men of Mark (Simmons), 202

Merscher, Henry, 112

Methodists, 9, 17, 26, 31, 38, 109

Michaels, Mrs., 2

Michigan, 162

Middle Dutch Church (New York City), 53

Missouri Compromise, 26

Mitchell, William M., 4, 5

Mixed-race sex, 25, 65, 72, 74, 75, 79–80, 84, 109

Mobs, 36, 63, 66, 106–7, 113, 171, 185

Monroe, James, 28

Moore, Clement, 60

Moore, Ely, 76

Moral perfectionism, 48

Moral suasion, 48

Morning Courier (New York City), 63

Munde, Charles, 200–201

Myers, Stephen, 127, 180

Nantucket, 166

Napoleon, Louis, 204

Nash, Alanson, 181, 201

Nash, D. D., 95, 98, 106, 108, 119, 127

National Anti-Slavery Standard (New York City), 150, 157, 160, 162, 166, 172, 180, 181, 188, 193

National Era, 193

National Reformer, 146

Native Americans, 25

Nat Turner's Revolt, 41, 42, 89

Neagle, John, 12

Negro Cuff, 12

"Negroe's Complaint, The," 18

Negro pew, 15, 35, 169, 221 (n. 66)

Nell, William Cooper, 5, 158, 160, 161, 163–64, 167, 177, 195, 196, 202

Newark, N.J., 55, 57, 58

New Bedford, Mass., 2, 10, 29, 128, 131, 133, 135, 164, 185, 186

New Bedford Morning Register, 164

New Bedford Young Men's Anti-Slavery Society, 172

Newburyport, Mass., 127

New Divinity Movement, 22, 31

New England, 25, 27, 28, 157, 164; Underground Railroad in, 127, 135, 184

New England Anti-Slavery Society, 47, 49, 55, 122, 178. *See also* American Anti-Slavery Society

New Hartford, N.Y., 86

New Haven, Conn., 93, 104, 127, 159, 160–61

New Jersey, 21, 23, 27, 56, 66, 75, 109, 160; American Colonization Society in, 52; black soldiers in, 21; slavery in, 88, 109

New London, Conn., 19, 23, 24

New Orleans, La., 8, 45, 114, 129, 130, 143

Newport, R.I., 18, 131, 133

New Rochelle, N.Y., 168

New York (state), 21, 26; black soldiers in, 21; Convention of 1821, 113; discrimination in, 34–35, 76, 92, 113; end of slavery in, 33, 34, 50; laws of, 34, 50, 61–62, 76, 87–88, 98, 109, 113, 155, 161; schools in, 75; southerners in, 35; Underground Railroad in, 126–27, 135, 204

New York African Society for Mutual Relief, 33, 41, 69, 110

New York Association for the Political Elevation and Improvement of the People of Color, 143

New York City, 11, 15, 25; blacks in, 33–34, 41, 53, 64–66, 94; celebration of end of slavery in, 33–34; convention movement in, 160; disputes over self-emancipated slaves in, 51–52, 199; economy of, 104; kidnapping in, 35, 87, 93, 94, 104, 114, 129, 131; population of, 34; slave catchers

in, 35–36, 51–52; wards of, 63; work in, 31, 34
New York City Alms House, 37
New York City Anti-Slavery Society, 74, 79, 117
New York Committee of Vigilance, 1, 5, 89, 93, 99, 100, 103, 117, 161; aid to Ruggles, 145; annual celebrations, 126; cases, 106–9, 113, 122; cuts ties with Ruggles, 149–50, 155; fundraising and expenses, 107–8, 146, 110, 121–22, 143, 149, 170; historiography of, 89–90, 101; and kidnappers, 88, 92, 109, 111, 114; libel suit, 142–43, 145, 147; meetings, 62, 88–89, 94–97, 100, 104, 112, 120–30, 142–43, 168; methods, 90–92, 99, 107–8; as model for other cities, 156, 161–62; reports, 120–21, 130, 131; rescues, 92–94, 126, 127–28, 131, 153, 156; Ruggles resigns from, 146; and self-emancipated slaves, 134, 156, 173; and slave trade, 97. See also Kidnapping; Ruggles, David
New York Daily Express, 141
New York Enquirer, 63
New York Episcopal Diocese, 65
New-Yorker, 129
New York Evangelist, 153
New York Evening Post, 97
New York Eye Infirmary, 145
New York Manumission Society, 34, 50, 52, 87, 104, 121, 130, 141–42
New York Observer, 53
New-York Reform Society, 159
New York Spectator, 46
New York Star, 84
New York State Anti-Slavery Society, 85, 92–93
New York State Presbyterian Conference, 120
New York Sun, 97, 135, 138
New York Young Men's Antislavery Society, 62
Northampton, Mass., 48, 126, 169, 175
Northampton (Mass.) Association of Education and Industry, 169–72, 187

Northampton County, Va., 114
Northampton Democrat, 178
Northampton Silk Company, 170
North Carolina, 31
North Star, 192, 193. See also Douglass, Frederick
Norwich, Conn., 11, 20, 27, 59, 110, 121, 171; economy of, 11, 14–16, 26, 29; visit of Marquis de Lafayette to, 28–29; and Underground Railroad, 127
Norwich Antislavery Society, 68
Norwich Methodist Episcopal Church, 15
Norwich Packet, 12
Norwich Presbyterian Church, 68
Nova Scotia, 5

Oasis, The, 67. See also Child, Lydia Maria
Oberlin College, 126, 130, 169
O'Connell, Daniel, 51, 144
Ohio, 56, 56, 64, 162
Onderdonk, Benjamin, 65, 158
Oswego, N.Y., 127
Otsego, N.Y., 122

Pacifism, 48
Panic of 1837, 194, 136
Parallel Between Intemperance and the Slave Trade, A (Humphrey), 44
Paris, France, 145
Pat Lyon at His Forge (Neagle), 12
Paul, Nathaniel, 40, 91
Paul, Thomas, 40
Paulding, James, 60
Pease, Elizabeth, 191
Pennington, James W. C., 2, 5, 38, 104, 127, 133–34, 157, 160–61, 192, 200
Pennsylvania, 56, 58, 75, 146, 160, 162
Perkins, F. A., 12
Peterboro, N.Y., 85, 127
Petty urbanites, 45, 210 (n. 25)
Phelps, Amos, 55, 77
Philadelphia, Pa., 4, 8, 50, 54, 58, 66, 83, 115, 124, 129, 146, 152
Philadelphia Committee of Vigilance, 124, 152

Smith, Joshua B., 164
Smith, Venture, 24
Society of Friends (Quakers), 9, 29, 50, 66, 83, 152, 164
Souls of Black Folk (Du Bois), 202
Southampton County, Va., 51
South Carolina, 23, 24, 143
Spear, Rev. John, 165
Spring, Rev. Gardiner, 86
Springfield, Mass., 124
Stanford, David, 109
Stearns, Dr. Daniel E., 139
Stetson, Almira, 176
Stetson, Dolly Witter, 171, 176, 187
Stetson, George R., 174
Stetson, James A., 176, 187
Stetson, Sarah, 176
Steward, Austin, 91
Stewart, Alvan, 91, 120, 126
Stewart, James, 60
Stewart, Maria, 60, 61, 67, 81, 183, 203; influence on Ruggles, 81
Still, William, 4, 127, 202
Stone, William Leete, 64
Stonington Rail Road, 131
Storrs, Rev. George, 120
Stowe, Harriet Beecher, 81, 175, 195
Stuart, Charles, 71
Sullivan, George Washington, 185
Sumner, Charles, 185
Swaim, Dr., 145
Sylvia, 11
Sylvia's Lane, 12, 29
Syracuse, N.Y., 127

Tallibut, Thomas, 88
Tappan, Arthur, 48, 49, 61, 108, 121, 122, 136, 139, 141, 142, 145, 155, 156
Tappan, Lewis, 6, 48, 53, 65, 70, 85, 92, 96, 120, 126, 131, 141, 147, 160
Tappan brothers, 63, 65, 67, 70, 86, 99–100, 117, 131; support for Ruggles, 66, 72, 96, 99, 117, 145, 146
Telegraph (steamboat), 165
Teller, William, 19

Temperance, 15
Texas, 108
Third Annual Convention of the Free People of Color, 58
Third Free Presbyterian Church (New York City), 120, 121
Thomas, William, 88
Thome, James A., 108
Thompson, John, 124
Thoughts on African Colonization, 42. *See also* Garrison, William Lloyd
Torrey, Charles, 163–64, 187
Torrington, Conn., 185
Toussaint Louverture, 39
Tracy, George M., 120, 140, 145, 150
Trinity Church School, 34. *See* African Free School
Trowtrow, Boston, 27
Troy, N.Y., 168
Truth, Sojourner, 2, 39, 50, 178–79, 183; and Ruggles, 183–85
Tubman, Harriet, 2, 127
Turner, Rev. C., 149
Turnpin, William, 104

Uncle Tom's Cabin, 81. *See also* Stowe, Harriet Beecher
Underground Railroad: early examples of, 5; Free Soil Party and, 193; history of, 4–5, 151–53, 202, 204; in Midwest, 4; in New England, 127, 133, 135; in New York City, 4, 99, 135; in Ohio River Valley, 4; and Ruggles's network, 126–27, 135; in upstate New York, 5, 127, 204
Unitarians, 48
United Anti-Slavery Society of New York, 96
Utica, N.Y., 85, 126, 127
Utica Anti-Slavery Society, 85

Vale, Gilbert, 70
Van Buren, Martin, 100, 192
Van Nostrandt, Lance, 114
Van Renesellaer, Thomas, 85, 88, 92, 94
Van Wagenen, Isabel. *See* Truth, Sojourner

Vermont, 127
Vesey, Denmark, 89
Vicksburg, Miss., 109
Virginia, 36, 41, 42, 51–52, 99, 114, 140, 155, 181, 204
Vogelsang, Peter, 149

Waddy, E. R., 114
Wake, Ransom F., 149
Walker, Charity, 143–44
Walker, Dr. Charles, 196, 201
Walker, David, 9, 40, 41, 61, 72, 89, 97, 203
Wallace, John, 88
Ward, Isaiah Harper, 46
Ward, Samuel Ringgold, 5, 38, 46, 192
War of 1812, 11, 26
Warsaw, N.Y., 86
Washington, D.C., 52, 108; slavery in, 108
Washington, George, 66
Washington, John J., 88
Washington, Joseph, 53–54
Water-Cure Journal, 200
Webb, Cornelius, 64
Wedgewood, Mrs., 121
Weekly Advocate, 104. See also *Colored American*
Welch, John Robinson, 109
Weld, Theodore, 66, 86
Wells, Hiram, 171
Wesleyan Methodist Episcopal Zion Church (New York City), 167, 199
Wesselhoeft, Dr. Robert, 173–75, 196
West Florida, 10
West Indies, 5
Wheeler, Peter, 30
Whipper, William, 112, 159
Wickford, R.I., 18

Wilberforce, William, 71
Wilberforce Benevolent Society, 33
Wilberforce Colony, 58, 64, 91, 93, 99
Wilcox, William, 193
Williams, George Washington, 202
Williams, Henry, 69
Williams, Peter, Jr., 34, 40, 42, 50, 65, 66, 92, 158
Williston, John P., 145, 169, 201
Williston, Rev. Payson, 193
Williston family, 170
Wilson, Hiram, 120
Wilson, James, 185
Wilson, Capt. James Dayton, 127, 141
Windham County, Conn., 171
Winslow, Harriet Wadsworth, 17
Women's Anti-Slavery Society (Norwich, Conn.), 68. See also Norwich, Conn.
Woodson, Lewis, 160
Worcester, Mass., 159, 160
Work, 30–31; and black occupations, 37, 31
Working Man's Advocate, 75
Workingmen's Movement, 34, 75–76
Wright, Elizur, Jr., 61, 62, 121
Wright, Frances, 28
Wright, Isaac, 127
Wright, Mrs. Theodore S., 121
Wright, Rev. Theodore S., 38, 40, 42, 66, 99, 104, 112, 117, 126, 142, 147, 150, 151, 168

Yale College, 68, 172
Yantic Cemetery (Norwich, Conn.), 197
Young, Robert Alexander, 41
Young Men's Christian Association, 200

Zoological Institute of New York, 50